Praise for *Fundamentals of Metadata Management*

Fundamentals of Metadata Management by Ole Olesen-Bagneux provides a vital perspective for anyone grappling with complex IT ecosystems. Metadata management must evolve beyond data to encompass information and knowledge coordinated by a data discovery team and unified via a meta grid architecture. This book offers a practical blueprint. It acknowledges the reality of fragmented metadata repositories and proposes a coordinated approach, rather than an unachievable single source.

This strategic meta grid framework holds immense value for enhancing operational efficiency, ensuring compliance, and fostering innovation. By embracing the meta grid and empowering a data discovery team, we can move toward a more holistic and actionable understanding of our IT landscape, leading to better decision making and optimized resource use across the organization. Ole's unique perspective is in drawing our attention to and emphasizing the prominence of the often overlooked element in any enterprise: the metadata. This adds considerable value to the entire industry as it forms the basis of how we look at data management, the meta grid architecture, and overcome becoming single-view monoliths of the IT landscape.

—*Kalyan Kumar (KK), chief product officer, HCLSoftware*

Ole Olesen-Bagneux has written a book that, at first glance, addresses classical issues in the context of data in companies, and that suggests how to distill and combine the best of existing approaches. Additionally, the book recommends new, sustainable organizational practices for continuous improvement. But what Ole really does is get us thinking about what we are missing out on, due to managing our data and IT landscape in a less-than-ideal manner. Prepare to be inspired!

—*Sabrina Schiele, data professional and enthusiast*

If programs are the skeleton of the system, metadata is the brain. A sign of the maturation of the IT industry is the increasing awareness of the role and importance of metadata. I highly recommend this book as a starting point in your journey.

—*Bill Inmon*

Fundamentals of Metadata Management presents a design and a new way of treating and managing metadata for resilience and practical management of metadata systems. The meta grid is pragmatic and proposes an alternate methodology and framework for overcoming dysfunction in metadata systems architecture. The book presents ways to handle overspending with SLAs, vendor and contractor dependence, for more efficient metadata systems. Companies now have a roadmap for overcoming metadata weaknesses, as the book proposes a data discovery team to facilitate the implementation of the meta grid, and to navigate the tasks associated with the meta grid framework.

—*Jessica Talisman, senior information architect at Adobe*

Fundamentals of Metadata Management introduces the groundbreaking concept of the meta grid—a transformative architecture poised to reshape data decentralization, much like the data mesh before it. This is the missing link that will unify and elevate modern data management practices. A must-read for any data management professional.

—*Piethein Strengholt, author of* Data Management at Scale *and* Building Medallion Architectures *(O'Reilly)*

Ole is a spearhead in the quest for unifying business, information, data, and IT: platforms based on symbols, linguistics, rules, cognition, and formal logic must be understood together.

—*Thomas Frisendal, business development, data architecture, graph modeler, author, and ISO IQL graph standard contributor*

After delivering the data industry must-read *The Enterprise Data Catalog*, Ole doesn't just evolve his concepts around data discovery and metadata management in *Fundamentals of Metadata Management*—he introduces the genuinely groundbreaking acknowledgement of the meta grid. It's both a lens for seeing the "bigger picture" of metadata and a practical framework for tackling the messiest metadata management challenges we all face. Another engaging must-read for anyone brave enough to wrestle with metadata.

—*Tiankai Feng, author of* Humanizing Data Strategy *(Technics Publications)*

Fundamentals of Metadata Management is the missing piece we've been waiting for—a gift to the entire data and AI community. Ole makes it unique by delivering the foundational knowledge for handling metadata and by showing how to push the possibilities further with his forward-thinking approach. This book leads the way, explaining in detail what the third wave of decentralization looks like and what it can unlock.

—Yoann Benoit, cofounder and head of data at Hymaïa

It is inspiring to see Ole Olesen-Bagneux articulate and describe so well what we've been building for years. Combining data mesh with integrated metadata and a shared vocabulary is invaluable for any large organization. This book is essential reading for anyone seeking practical insights into building a truly data-driven organization.

—Gregor Wobbe, head of data architecture, UBS

If we just build better toasters, nothing will change. As Ole Olesen-Bagneux portrays it, the meta grid has always been there, but we've not seen it like this before, so our eyes hurt. Long live the meta grid.

—Säde Haveri, data management professional and entrepreneur

Reading this book is like switching on the lights in a dark room—you suddenly see how fragmented your metadata has been all along. And the meta grid weaves these fragments into a coherent whole for clarity and control.

—Dr. Simon Harrer, cofounder and CEO, Entropy Data

Ole Olesen-Bagneux doesn't offer yet another metadata framework built from scratch—he asks us to open our eyes to what's already there. The meta grid concept he introduces reveals a foundational truth: we all need metadata to unlock the value of our data and AI solutions, but metadata repositories already exist across a variety of tools and teams. The real challenge is not invention—it's coordination. Starting from a blank slate is never the case in real organizations. This book provides professionals with a methodology—not a standard—for making sense of fragmented metadata landscapes and transforming them into a coherent, strategic asset. A must-read for anyone serious about governing data in the real world, not just in theory.

—Nino Letteriello, award-winning data
and project entrepreneur, FIT Group

This book is a refreshingly honest and much-needed take on the real-world state of metadata in organizations. First, it expands our understanding of metadata—not just as documentation for data, but as a key enabler across IT, data, and knowledge management. Second, it highlights a crucial reason why so many technological solutions have failed: they proposed centralized architectures that ended up as unsustainable monoliths. The meta grid offers a compelling alternative—a "third wave of decentralization" that acknowledges and connects what already exists. As a lecturer and educator in the field, I see this book as a great source of methodological insight and a practical guide to follow for metadata management today.

—Michele Valentini, data management practitioner, lecturer, and educator, FIT Academy

Metadata quietly connects everything in a data-driven world. It's time we recognize it as the meta grid.

—Olga Maydanchik, data management practitioner and educator

Ole Olesen-Bagneux's *Fundamentals of Metadata Management* offers a compelling framework for streamlining metadata management, enhancing compliance, and reducing IT inefficiencies. A must-read for data governance professionals.

—Bjarte Tolleshaug, senior consultant, certified data management professional (CDMP)

The book effectively provokes thought on catalogs, data management, and, particularly, metadata management, highlighting what we have yet to uncover and what continually evolves within an organization—critical for AI initiatives. Effective metadata management is essential for building generative AI models, RAG systems, and RL frameworks. Organizing metadata throughout its lifecycle is crucial.

—Gaurav Grigo, senior director, DDIT-R&ED, Novo Nordisk

Ole Olesen-Bagneux did it again: he wrote a book to shape the industry! Metadata is more than "data about data"; it's a way to understand the reality of your organization from IT systems to data, from information to knowledge. Metadata can be the connector. At the same time, metadata management has been done differently by professionals with varying purposes in siloed repositories. This reality has been overlooked until now. Ole has given us a novel perspective on what (and where) metadata is and how we can manage it. This book is a tie-breaker: a way to change our view, accept reality, and finally be able to use metadata in organizations.

—Winfried A. Etzel, data governance professional

This is a true "fundamentals" book that will be relevant for a long time. Ole's "meta grid" is deeply original and timely, providing the architectural clarity we need to zoom out and unite the management of inherently decentralized metadata. Framed as the third wave of data decentralization, it offers an implementable approach and a way of thinking when designing systems to make data discoverable for AI and humans without causing IT landscape disruptions or unnecessary lock-ins. I also applaud the concept of the "data discovery team" as a versatile way to embed metadata management into mainstream enterprise org charts, ensuring the organization can achieve a heightened state of data management. I highly recommend this book to technical people in data and AI and to management alike.

—*Karl Ivo Sokolov, managing partner, SPG Data*

Ole Olesen-Bagneux offers a welcome and thought-provoking alternative to traditional, technical approaches that often overlook the organizational and functional divides in metadata management. He introduces the meta grid—a simple yet powerful architecture that embraces the fragmented enterprise reality and provides a tangible, scalable framework for coordinating siloed tools, functions, and practices. At the heart of this approach is the concept of a data discovery team—designed to bridge gaps, enable alignment, facilitate discovery, and offer sparring across all levels of the organization.

—*Nikolaj A. Sabinsky, principal consultant,*
data program manager

In Sufi metaphysics, the Lataif are subtle faculties of perception; layers through which hidden reality becomes discernible, not by force, but by refinement. Ole Olesen-Bagneux's meta grid belongs to this lineage of thought. It does not impose structure; it reveals it. Like a constellation only visible to the attentive, it allows metadata, architecture, and governance to cohere without centralization. This is a work of deep clarity about metadata repositories but more than that, about how we come to sense what connects them.

—*Nagim Ashufta, founder and CEO, DRIVA GmbH*

Fundamentals of Metadata Management

Uncover the Meta Grid and Unlock IT, Data, Information, and Knowledge Management

Ole Olesen-Bagneux

Foreword by Joe Reis

O'REILLY®

Fundamentals of Metadata Management

by Ole Olesen-Bagneux

Copyright © 2025 Ole Olesen-Bagneux. All rights reserved.

Published by O'Reilly Media, Inc., 141 Stony Circle, Suite 195, Santa Rosa, CA 95401.

O'Reilly books may be purchased for educational, business, or sales promotional use. Online editions are also available for most titles (*http://oreilly.com*). For more information, contact our corporate/institutional sales department: 800-998-9938 or *corporate@oreilly.com*.

Acquisitions Editor: Aaron Black	**Indexer:** Krsta Technology Solutions
Development Editor: Angela Rufino	**Interior Designer:** David Futato
Production Editor: Katherine Tozer	**Cover Designer and Illustrator:** Karen Montgomery
Copyeditor: Shannon Turlington	**Interior Illustrator:** Kate Dullea
Proofreader: Vanessa Moore	

August 2025:   First Edition

Revision History for the First Edition

2025-08-04:   First Release

See *http://oreilly.com/catalog/errata.csp?isbn=9781098162825* for release details.

978-1-098-16282-5

[LSI]

Make each program do one thing well. To do a new job, build afresh rather than complicate old programs by adding new "features."

—M. D. McIlroy, E. N. Pinson, and B. A. Tague, "UNIX Time-Sharing System: Forward," Bell System Technical Journal 57, no. 6 (1978): 1899–1904.

The truth was a mirror in the hands of God. It fell, and broke into pieces. Everybody took a piece of it, and they looked at it and thought they had the truth.

—Rumi, Fihi Ma Fihi (It Is What It Is)

Table of Contents

Foreword... xvii

Preface.. xix

1. Toward Holistic Metadata Management...................................... 1
   Metadata Management Happens in Many Places   1
   The Data Discovery Team   3
   The Meta Grid: The Third Wave of Data Decentralization   6
      Microservices   7
      Data Mesh   9
      Meta Grid   10
   Summary   13

Part I.   Metadata Repositories for IT, Data, Information, and
Knowledge Management

2. Metadata Repositories for the IT Landscape............................... 17
   What Is Metadata?   17
   Types of Metadata in IT Landscapes   20
   What Is a Metadata Repository?   21
      Driver: The Many Waves of Metadata Repositories   23
      Purpose: Core Capability   27
      Place: Metadata Repositories at Various Levels   28
      Structure: The Metamodel in Metadata Repositories   29
   Summary   32

3. **IT Management**... **35**

    Endpoint Management System   35

    Integration Repository   37

    Asset Management System   41

    Configuration Management Database   43

    IT Service Management System   46

    Enterprise Architecture Management Tool   47

    Metadata Repositories for IT Management   50

    Summary   51

4. **Data Management**.. **53**

    Data Catalog   53

    Database Model Management   55

    Other Metadata Repositories for Data Management   57

        Data Warehouse   58

        Data Lake   58

        Data Lakehouse   59

        Data Pipeline Tools   59

        Data Quality Tools   60

        Identity and Access Management   60

    Rebundling of Data Management Technologies   60

    Metadata Repositories for Data Management   61

    Summary   62

5. **Information Management**.. **63**

    Records and Information Management System   63

        Record-Retention Scenarios   64

        The Organizational Aspect of RIMS   65

        RIMS As a Metadata Repository   66

    Information Security Management System   67

        The Organizational Aspect of ISMS   68

        ISMS As a Metadata Repository   69

    Data Protection Repository   70

        The Organizational Aspect of a DPR   72

        DPR As a Metadata Repository   73

    Business Process Management System   74

    Metadata Repositories for Information Management   76

    Summary   78

6. **Knowledge Management**... **81**

    Content Management System   81

    Knowledge Management System   82

Learning Management System   84
Quality Management System   85
Collection Management System   86
Metadata Repositories for Knowledge Management   87
Summary   89

7. **Why We Have Been Doing Metadata Management Wrong.** 91
Different Practices Have Different Metamodels   92
  Dark Metadata   96
  Other Applications and Domains   97
A Possibility: The Coming Together of Teams and Technologies   98
  Money   99
  Structured Versus Unstructured   100
Summary   101

Part II.   Metadata Repositories Must Be Coordinated by a Data Discovery Team

8. **The Good, the Bad, and the Ugly.** 105
Setting the Stage   106
The Good   107
The Bad   109
The Ugly   112
Summary   113

9. **The Data Discovery Team.** 117
Our Problem: Managing Multiple Truths Across Teams   117
  Conway's Law   120
  The Metadata Monolith   121
The Solution: The Data Discovery Team   122
What Is the Data Discovery Team?   124
  On the Political and Technological Mess of Companies   126
  Embracing the Multiple Truths and Providing a Way Forward   126
How the Data Discovery Team Collaborates   127
  Collaborating with Enterprise Architects   127
  Collaborating with the Data Protection Officer   128
  Collaborating with the Chief Information Security Officer   130
  Collaborating with Records and Information Management   131
  Collaborating with Data Science Teams   132
Summary   133

Part III. Metadata Repositories Should Be Connected in a Meta Grid

10. What Is the Meta Grid?.. 137

The Meta Grid Manifesto   137
    The Meta Grid Is the Third Wave of Data Decentralization   138
    The Meta Grid Unlocks Single-View-of-the-World Monoliths   138
    The Meta Grid Is Never Finalized   138
    The Meta Grid Is Simple, Small, and Slow   139
What the Meta Grid Is and Is Not   139
Documenting the Meta Grid   141
Examples of the Meta Grid   144
    Data Types   144
    Applications   146
    Data Models   147
    Integrations   148
    Data Lineage   149
    Servers   150
    Organization   151
    Processes   153
A Real-World Meta Grid Architecture   154
    Questions   154
    Answers   154
Summary   157

11. The Meta Grid Contextualized. 159

You Don't Build the Meta Grid—You Uncover It   160
Uncovering Unconscious Meta Grid Architectures   161
    Data Driven (Ambition)   162
    FinOps   164
    Intake Funnel   165
The Meta Grid Is a Nuclear Architecture   166
    Energy   168
    Expansion   168
    Explosion   172
Microservices, Data Mesh, and Meta Grid   173
    Microservices in the Meta Grid   173
    Data Mesh in the Meta Grid   175
    Meta Grid Must Not Turn into Data Mesh or Microservices   176
Technologies That Support the Meta Grid   178
Summary   180

12. **The Benefits of the Meta Grid.** **183**

    The Meta Grid Is Not a Technology   183

        Better Overview of the IT Landscape   184

        Smoothly Implemented Metadata Repositories   184

        Empowered Owners of Metadata Repositories   185

        More Secure Data Governance for Both Risk and Privacy   187

        A Stronger Possibility of Data-Driven Innovation   187

        Reduced Cost of the IT Landscape and Consultancy Support   187

        Examples of Cost Reductions   188

        A Greener IT Landscape   189

    The Meta Grid Is a Technology   190

        Create a Knowledge Graph of Metadata Across Metadata Repositories   190

        Search the Meta Grid Conversationally with Generative AI   193

        Perform the Meta Grid Automatically with Agentic AI   199

    Summary   199

13. **The Data Discovery Team and Meta Grid As a Team Topology.** **201**

Afterword. **207**

Index. **209**

Foreword

I first met Ole several years ago, shortly after he published his book, *The Enterprise Data Catalog* (O'Reilly). Sometimes, you meet someone who has an uncommon clarity of thought and a gift for making the complex feel obvious. When I invited him onto my podcast, he struck me as a deeply thoughtful and cerebral person. We've since become good friends, and I was honored when he asked me to write this foreword.

Ole starts this book with a story that will resonate with anyone who has spent time in the trenches of enterprise technology. He recounts meeting a chemist at a large company who showed him a seemingly endless list of IT systems, the "ITSO." When asked what all these systems did, the chemist grinned and admitted that nobody knew. A significant portion were likely doing nothing, but turning them off was too risky. What if a factory shut down? The cost of the unknown was greater than the cost of maintaining the bloat.

This Kafka-meets-Dilbert anecdote is not an outlier. Sadly, it is the default state of affairs in most organizations. We are constantly grappling with foundational questions: What applications do we have? What data do they hold? How are they connected? The uncomfortable truth is that, often, no one can provide a complete and trustworthy answer. The problem isn't a lack of information but a surplus of it scattered across dozens of uncoordinated, siloed systems.

Fundamentals of Metadata Management brilliantly dissects this vicious cycle, but its actual value lies in the pragmatic path it offers us to escape. The book argues that for too long, we have been doing metadata management wrong. We've viewed it through the narrow lens of data management alone, leading to the proliferation of what Ole calls "single-view-of-the-world monoliths." Each management discipline, whether IT, data, information, or knowledge management, has independently mapped the same landscape, creating a cacophony of conflicting truths. This isn't just a technical failure but also a human one, driven by the complex sociology of employees, consultants, and vendors, each with their incentives that often perpetuate the chaos.

When the AI revolution hit a few years ago, I could see the wheels turning in Ole's mind.

The result is the meta grid. Ole positions the meta grid as the "third wave of data decentralization," a natural evolution following microservices and data mesh. Its power is not in high-speed data exchange but in logical cohesion. Ole's most critical insight here is that you don't build the meta grid—you uncover it. It already exists, unconsciously, in the fragmented relationships between your existing repositories. This book provides the methodology to make that grid conscious, transforming it from a source of chaos into a "nuclear architecture," small yet dense with the energy to power a more rational and cost-effective enterprise.

What makes this book so essential is its grounding in reality. It does not preach an idealistic future that requires ripping and replacing everything. Instead, it provides a methodology for understanding, contextualizing, and coordinating the metadata repositories you already have in place. The meta grid has been hiding in plain sight this whole time! This book serves as a guide for leaders struggling to rationalize their application portfolios, map their asset inventory, and update their architectures, particularly in the context of a rapidly evolving AI landscape.

The work detailed in these pages provides a blueprint for moving from a state of expensive ignorance to one of informed, strategic control. The benefits are tangible: reduced costs; enhanced security; and a more adaptable, greener IT landscape. But the ultimate payoff may be the most timely. By creating a robust, coordinated, and logical map of your enterprise, the meta grid provides the perfect, high-quality context needed to unlock the true potential of AI. This is very much needed today. The meta grid is the foundation upon which effective conversational and agentic AI can be built. This book gives you the tools to finally answer the fundamental questions and, perhaps, to confidently start turning off the systems that no one knows anything about.

— Joe Reis
Best-selling author and global educator
July 2025

Preface

Something crucial in how companies approach metadata management is often overlooked. This book addresses that missing piece.

Every company has a configuration management database, an endpoint management system, an information security management system, and most likely a knowledge management system, plus many more systems (don't worry—you will get to know these systems in this book if you don't already). They all depict the IT landscape and can be holders of metadata about the IT landscape—they are metadata repositories. But they are often managed in silos.

Metadata management relies heavily on repositories, each serving a distinct role in bringing companies into control of their IT landscapes. However, few companies take a holistic approach to metadata. Metadata repositories are often managed throughout various teams in organizations, leading to high costs, risks, and confusion.

During strategic initiatives, companies often encounter a recurring pattern. Whether the initiative is a merger or acquisition, a transition to cloud computing, an enhancement of data privacy, or an implementation of a durable data science project, certain questions persistently arise: What applications do we have? Who owns them? What data do we possess, and how is it utilized in our processes? Which technologies support what capabilities? Where are our servers located? How do we get access?

In most companies, management teams (and external regulatory bodies!) ask these questions and realize that no one can really answer them—or not completely. So they hire a team of external consultants or internal enterprise architects to help them create the overview of the IT landscape that they need. This snapshot is typically stored in a metadata repository, sometimes even as a simple PDF, and sporadically maintained by internal employees over time. Over the years, this process repeats itself again and again. It's not a resilient approach since the effort of the work is lost and money is spent without proper return on investment.

This book offers a way out of this vicious cycle by:

- Providing a typical (nonexhaustive) overview of metadata repositories (Part I)
- Describing a team that coordinates metadata repositories (Part II)
- Suggesting an architecture—the meta grid—that makes metadata repositories more robust (Part III)

Why I Wrote This Book

As companies grow in size and complexity, there is often a lack of understanding of the IT landscape and the data in it. Instead, some people know only certain parts of the IT landscape. This is a catastrophic reality.

My first job was in big pharma when I was 20-something years old. I remember this chemist I worked with: a brilliant guy, an industrial researcher with a PhD. He had thick glasses, a weird, evil smile, and a machine-gun kind of laugh. He used to make bombs in his spare time, just for the fun of it. One day, he showed me a long, long list of something called the "ITSO"—the IT systems overview. I just stared at the list of IT systems that went on and on. Thousands of systems. I asked him what all those systems were used for, and then he grinned at me and said that no one really knew. I remember my surprise when he told me that a large portion of the systems probably didn't do anything at all. But it was just too dangerous to turn them off, he said. Because no one knew what would happen. Maybe nothing. Maybe a factory would shut down. Nobody knew. Or at least, nobody knew if anybody knew. So instead, he continued, we keep paying the vendors of the systems. And then he laughed his machine-gun laugh.

I didn't know what to say.

As I progressed in my career and worked for several other companies, I learned that this is more or less the reality everywhere. Companies don't really know their applications, they don't know how they are integrated, they don't know what data is actually in those applications, and if they are getting what they pay for or if they are paying for the same kind of thing twice—or more!—because they buy multiple systems that are basically identical.

Over the years, I learned how to accept that reality and fight it—as a specialist, a leader, and an enterprise architect focused on data. You can only fight that reality very, very slowly, by gradually expanding your knowledge. At least I thought so.

One day, I had a simple yet powerful idea that forms the core of this book: coordination of metadata repositories. See, the big problem with not having an overview of the IT landscape is not that companies don't possess this overview. The problem is that they possess too many overviews. These are called *metadata repositories*, and they all are deeply technical, are very different in scope, and yet look at the same thing—namely, the IT landscape of a company. And the horror of it is that they never match.

But you have the power to change this—and the rewards are promising because your metadata repositories will work better!

The reason I wrote this book is to provide a pragmatic approach to gaining and maintaining a comprehensive overview of the IT landscape within a company. By understanding, grouping, aligning, and exposing all the metadata repositories of your company,[1] you can realistically achieve this goal, with returns that include:

- A smoothly running IT landscape
- Significant cost reduction
- Better use of data for innovation
- Enhanced data privacy
- Enhanced data security
- A greener IT landscape
- A company that knows its IT landscape

Understanding the basics of metadata and its management through repositories in the right way enables you to construct a more resilient and enduring overview of your IT landscape.

Metadata Management Reinterpreted

Metadata can be defined as a description that is both attached to what is described and placed somewhere else in order to make what is described discoverable and manageable.[2]

Therefore, *metadata management* can be defined as the activity of identifying or creating, storing, searching, sharing, and ultimately deleting metadata. Metadata management is performed with metadata repositories that serve as the places to discover and manage what the metadata describes.

Metadata management in many companies is seen through the lens of data management literature. But this provides an incomplete body of literature for proper guidance that has created a narrow way of performing metadata management with some

---

1 The point of this book is not to suggest a new technology or a new layer of technology but to improve your existing technologies through collaboration across existing teams.

2 This definition is not opposed to—but rather is a more detailed version of—the saying that metadata is *data about data*. The data about the data needs to be with the data as well as somewhere else to fulfill its role as metadata (this is a logical assumption in the saying, but it is not made explicit).

fatal blind spots, which will be discussed in this book. In data management literature, *metadata management* is commonly defined as the practice of managing data through a metadata layer. This interpretation is logical, given that data management is about managing…data! A notable resource advocating this perspective is the DAMA International's *DAMA-DMBOK: Data Management Body of Knowledge*, which states:

> Metadata is essential to data management as well as data usage.…All organizations produce and use a lot of data…but no individual will know everything about the data.[3]

The view that metadata management is about managing data is incorporated into this book—and the role of metadata is indeed to provide an overview that no individual alone can be expected to have and maintain.

Nevertheless, this book is different from *DAMA-DMBOK* and most other data management literature, and quite substantially so. It's about more than representing data at the metadata layer. It is also about the physical things that the IT landscape consists of as well as the nonphysical things that the IT landscape facilitates. Metadata, ultimately, is data about the "things" the enterprise manages. Laws, rules, concepts, business processes, and events are all part of this.

In light of this, this book is about contextualizing metadata repositories for IT, data, information, and knowledge *management* to one another since these management disciplines together use a plethora of metadata repositories to control the IT landscape, each with its distinct purpose. There are time and money to be saved and important accelerations of your strategic data initiatives to be won.

As mentioned, metadata management—as practiced in the discipline of data management—generally focuses on the relation between data sources and the metadata repository. Consequently, there are dense, scholarly discussions on the many ideal standards for metadata that aim to define the perfect way of representing data as metadata, as stated in the *ISKO Encyclopedia*:

> Metadata standards are commonly organized around a set of elements (such as "title," "author," "date") that manifest as computer-readable documents in one of an alphabet-soup set of formats and mark-up languages, such as MARC, XML, JSON, and YAML.[4]

---

3 DAMA International, *DAMA-DMBOK: Data Management Book of Knowledge*, 2nd ed., revised (Technics Publications, 2024), 395.

4 Matthew Mayernik, "Metadata" (*https://oreil.ly/zhm83*), in *Encyclopedia of Knowledge Organization* (ISKO, 2020) published March 16, 2020; last modified December 12, 2023.

The list of metadata standards (*https://oreil.ly/VVRDu*) is long. This book will not attempt to make a new standard for metadata. All metadata repositories build an understanding of the IT landscape into themselves at several levels: in their metamodels; in naming conventions for applications, processes, integrations, and so forth; and in the definitions of these. However, almost all metadata repositories are built in such a way that they promote a single view of the IT landscape—their own—as depicted in Figure P-1.

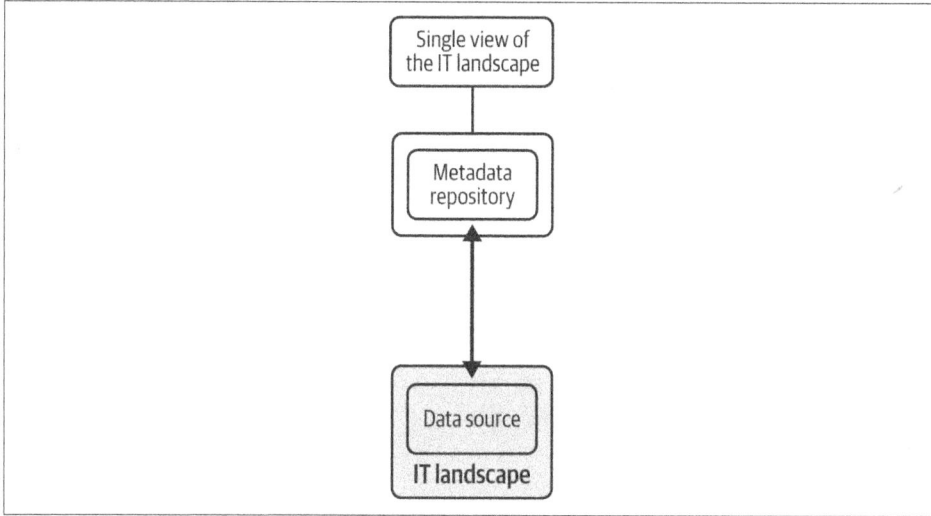

Figure P-1. Metadata repositories have single views of the IT landscape

The single view of the IT landscape creates a significant problem for metadata management because companies do not have one but rather several metadata repositories. And each metadata repository has its distinct view of the IT landscape—which most often does not match the views of other repositories. This becomes a problem because the metadata repositories manage overlapping parts of the IT landscape (Figure P-2). Because these repositories do not match, the truth about the IT landscape dissolves. No one can claim to know it. Most important, the truth dissolves at a scale so massive that verification of the actual state of it is impossible to perform.

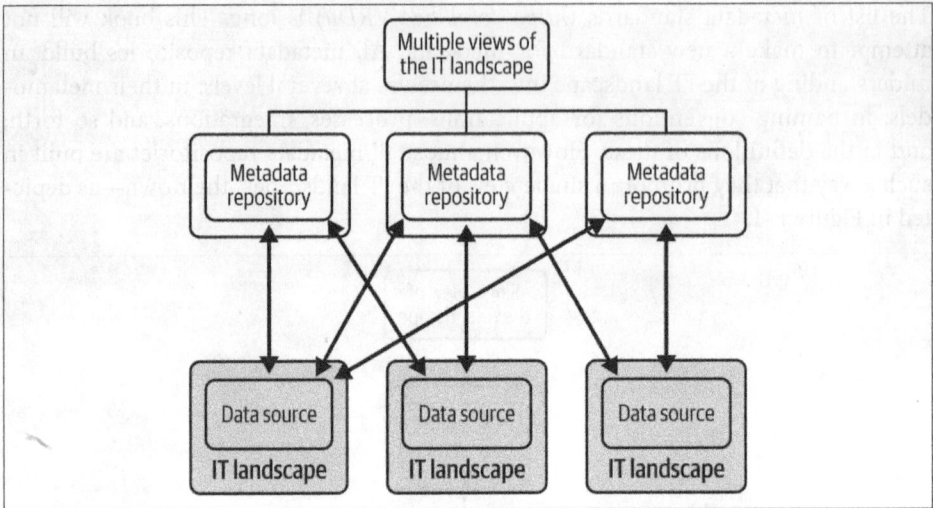

Figure P-2. This book deals with the reality of multiple metadata repositories

This reality is the reason behind the reinterpretation of metadata management put forward in this book. It's about the coordination of metadata repositories more than the representation of data in the metadata layer in one given technology, such as a graph. This is a balance because, obviously, what is discussed is—technically—still data and metadata. But as such, the "data layer" in this book consists only of metadata from metadata repositories. Lists of applications, process maps, capabilities, and project names stored in metadata repositories are used in decision-making processes of substantial innovative, operational, financial, and protective importance.

Companies at large suffer from poor implementations of these metadata repositories. Furthermore, the task of mapping the IT landscape in these repositories is repeated again and again—often in vain. Technologies are bought, implemented…and partly work. This is what *Fundamentals of Metadata Management* wants to change. Accordingly, this book discusses the actual reality in companies rather than an idealized scenario. In short, it focuses on the reality depicted in Figure P-2. Many metadata repositories overlap to a certain degree but are often uncoordinated, resulting in multiple conflicting truths about the IT landscape. This reality can be changed by understanding, contextualizing, and coordinating metadata repositories—and paving the way for a deeper, more holistic view of the IT landscape.

Accordingly, this book argues:

Metadata repositories are for IT, data, information, and knowledge management.

> This book goes beyond the typical view of metadata management as being about managing only data. Instead, metadata is about managing IT, data, information, *and* knowledge. Technically, metadata can represent data in databases connected

to applications, but metadata can also represent physical and nonphysical aspects of the IT landscape. We will discuss metadata repositories for IT, data, information, and knowledge in Part I.

Metadata repositories must be coordinated by a data discovery team.

Metadata management is not a task that can be carried out in isolation, as will be discussed in Part II and in the last chapter of the book, Chapter 13. However, that is the case today in most companies. This results in a reality with multiple uncoordinated metadata repositories that are not connected and therefore depict aspects of the same IT landscape in various and differing ways. This is not only expensive in terms of time lost to the toil of doing the same analysis of the IT landscape again and again but also produces multiple realities of the IT landscape, leading to wrong decisions and a waste of substantial amounts of money as technologies are bought, maintained, and preserved without firm knowledge of the necessity of doing so, across—and in isolation from—the domains of IT, data, information, and knowledge management. The data discovery team can change this because it will map not only the IT landscape but also the metadata repositories that map the IT landscape. In doing so, the data discovery team can coordinate the representation of the IT landscape across all metadata repositories. Furthermore, the data discovery team will allow for a hitherto unseen, powerful, enterprise-wide search—across all metadata repositories for data, information, and knowledge. We will discuss the data discovery team in Part II.

Metadata repositories should be connected in a meta grid.

This book also differs from the usual understanding of metadata management in the sense that it is not primarily focused on perfecting the metadata representation of the IT landscape in one or more metadata repositories by using standards and technologies. Instead, what is at the center of metadata management is the interplay between the many metadata repositories that exist in every company of substantial size.

This requires a brief detour to explain. *Microservices and data mesh* are IT paradigms that liberate technological capabilities from large, unmanageable solutions, which are often referred to as *monoliths*. Instead, microservices and data mesh establish the smallest possible units of operational and analytical data in order to create fast flow, flexibility, and transparency. This kind of thinking enables companies to reinvent themselves and increase their competitive advantages.

I'll argue that, just as microservices and data mesh suggest abandoning centralized monoliths of technological capabilities, so can metadata currently be considered to be managed in centralized monoliths. The silos of metadata as such opaque monoliths create, when seen as a whole, a cacophony of opposing realities about the IT landscape that is dysfunctional. I'll explain how to counter that reality and gain a deeper understanding of a company's IT landscape through a new way of performing metadata management, in a structure that, like microservices architecture and data mesh, connects small units of data—in this case, metadata—as products and metadata products. This proposed structure is what I call a *meta grid*. We will discuss the meta grid in Part III.

Now, let's look at the management disciplines that use metadata repositories to describe the IT landscape.

Who This Book Is For

You can use the insights presented in this book to gain a deeper, more holistic, and aligned overview of your company's IT landscape. This spans the many functions in your company that depict and manage dimensions of the IT landscape through metadata repositories.

I'd like to address you directly as a reader—discussing your role and the challenges you face. I want to clarify how you can benefit from reading *Fundamentals of Metadata Management*. I encourage you to review *all* the roles listed here; the reason will become clear shortly.

To the Chief Data Officer

You are the only one in the C-suite who does not know the details of your area: data. The CFO, for example, knows the exact financial status of the company. But no one, including you, has the entire overview of all the data in your company. That's a hard fact. With this book, you have the opportunity to steer away from that and get a deeper, more complete view of the data in your company by relying on coordinated metadata repositories.

I strongly encourage you to create what I call a *data discovery team*.[5] As someone with the authority to establish this team, you can significantly enhance the coordination of metadata repositories. You'll find detailed information about this team in this book. The data discovery team not only will help you adjust and execute strategies more effectively but also will enable various stakeholders to excel in their roles, many of whom are listed in this section. This team will support you in driving long-term, effective agendas—a challenging task for CDOs. As noted in the *Harvard Business Review* (*https://oreil.ly/OJnC4*), the average tenure for CDOs is only 18 months, and this needs to increase. This book is one of the building blocks to achieving that goal.

---

5 The data discovery team will perhaps not get enough attention or be empowered enough if it is created by the CDO. Ideally, it's created and backed by all C-suites—in particular, the CDO, the CIO, and the CTO.

To the Chief Information Officer

You run an IT department. If you are heading up that role in a big enterprise setting with several thousand employees and a company history that goes back a few decades or more, you know that the IT landscape is to some extent opaque. Your teams struggle with questions like: What applications integrate with one another and how? What applications are actually installed on which devices, and do we have multiple applications that deliver on the same capability? You own many metadata repositories, such as an enterprise architecture management tool and an endpoint management system, and your teams are most likely not talking enough to one another about how they depict the IT landscape in those tools—this leads them to create multiple versions of truths about the IT landscape.

Without promising you a silver bullet, I can guarantee that this book can help you. By harnessing the power of coordinated metadata repositories, you and your teams will better understand the IT landscape.

To the Chief Information Security Officer

It is your task to keep your company safe from cyberattacks, espionage, leaks that would damage the company's reputation, and so forth. You need to have an overview of all the confidential information in the company, along with a risk assessment of its possible exposure. With this book, you get the chance to create that overview in a more robust and complete way, as your asset inventory can be matched against a series of other metadata repositories, such as quality management systems and endpoint management systems, liberating time for you and your team to focus on the task at hand instead of mapping an IT landscape that has been mapped many times before.

To the Data Protection Officer

You have registered how data is processed in the company to prevent sensitive data from being used in unintended ways. Perhaps you have conducted an in-depth series of interviews with team leaders and generated a semiautomated description of data processing. But how sure are you that what you have registered is correct? With this book and the ideas I put forward, you can push data protection to the next level by exploiting the insights in all the metadata repositories in your company.

To the General Counsel

You're a legal mastermind, and this book is also for you. There may be technical aspects of the book that are not important to you. But you can use the book to get a firm grip on where to find the kind of proof you and your teams need when defining and negotiating contracts, preparing lawsuits to defend the company, performing mergers and acquisitions, and much more. You need detailed knowledge of the IT landscape in many of your activities, and I urge you not to establish that knowledge yourself from scratch—it already exists. Use this book as a key that can unlock where you can find that in the IT landscape.

To the Head of Quality Assurance

If you are heading up a quality department, you are likely in a highly regulated industry, such as the pharmaceutical industry. You are responsible for a quality management system (QMS), which is more like a stack of technologies and services than one system. In it, you are creating an overview of the IT landscape. I suggest you look to the many other metadata repositories mentioned in this book to improve the completeness of your QMS.

To the Data Teams

Data teams consist of one or more groups of data scientists, data engineers, and data operations teams.[6] If you are in one of those teams, you know it is unlikely that there is one global metadata repository covering all the data in the company. You're likely to have one or two data catalogs—maybe even more—and there may even be a corporate policy to use one of them as the enterprise data catalog. But a wealth of other metadata repositories exists that could point you to interesting data. That's the perspective you will get in this book: more metadata repositories that point to data sources that can fuel your innovative ideas!

To the Records and Information Manager

You handle the final stage of the information lifecycle, which often overlaps with what data teams call the *data lifecycle*, culminating in the archival and disposal of data, records, and documentation. You manage a records and information management system. You often lack visibility when exploring and describing the IT landscape context of the information you need to preserve, as those working with data earlier in its lifecycle don't consider long-term storage perspectives for regulatory compliance. This book provides advice on where to look and how to collaborate to improve your situation.

To the Enterprise Architect

You are most likely alone or part of a small enterprise architecture team strategically advising on the future IT landscape for your company. If so, you may rely on an enterprise architecture management tool. You are struggling with getting as complete a picture of the IT landscape as possible. This book is a guide for you—it will tell you

---

6 Jesse Anderson, *Data Teams: A Unified Management Model for Successful Data-Focused Teams* (Apress, 2020).

where you can find metadata repositories that describe the IT landscape in various parts of the business that can complete your knowledge and make your strategic advice more to the point.

I want you to consider the synergy of all of these roles—and many others—working together with a stronger, unified vision of the IT landscape. The ideas that I put forward in this book don't benefit some teams at the expense of others. Instead, the metadata management approach presented here is beneficial for *all* parts of the business—and becomes exponentially more valuable as a collective knowledge of the IT landscape is consolidated. I leave this with a question for you: what roles can you think of that I left out? Because I invite you to include them!

Who This Book Is Not For

If you expect this book to present a new universal standard for metadata, then this book is not for you. Many such standards already exist across industries, technologies, and disciplines—and assuming a global acceptance for one standardized way of expressing metadata is an illusion. Also, this book does not emphasize one metadata standard over others, claiming that this specific standard is better than others. Nor is it a detailed description of all metadata standards that exist. The book provides links to such overviews, but in itself, this book is not an encyclopedia of standards.

Rather, this book is about metadata *repositories* and how metadata *management* is performed with these metadata repositories. As such, this book puts forward a new *methodology* of metadata management (not a standard), and it proposes a decentralized architecture that your company can greatly benefit from. If this surprises you and catches your interest, I encourage you to read further. I'm confident this book will be valuable for you.

How This Book Is Organized

This book is organized into three parts. Chapter 1 precedes these three parts and describes the need for a deeper approach to metadata management in companies and explains the overall idea of the book. Part I, "Metadata Repositories for IT, Data, Information, and Knowledge Management", explores four distinct management disciplines that all have their own metadata repositories. Each management discipline is covered in its own chapter.

In Part II, "Metadata Repositories Must Be Coordinated by a Data Discovery Team", we take a look at a new kind of team: the data discovery team. This team can elevate your company's metadata management to the next level. It is easy to establish and can function effectively as a virtual organization.

Part III, "Metadata Repositories Should Be Connected in a Meta Grid", proposes a new kind of architecture for metadata management. This architecture incorporates learnings from microservices and data mesh, focusing on decentralization to break up monolithic metadata repositories and make them work together as a functional whole. But unlike other decentralized architectures, the meta grid is simple, slow, and small. It needs to be, as you will see.

Conventions Used in This Book

The following typographical conventions are used in this book:

Italic
> Indicates new terms, URLs, email addresses, filenames, and file extensions.

`Constant width`
> Used for program listings, as well as within paragraphs to refer to program elements such as variable or function names, databases, data types, environment variables, statements, and keywords.

`Constant width italic`
> Shows text that should be replaced with user-supplied values or by values determined by context.

This element signifies a tip or suggestion.

This element signifies a general note.

This element indicates a warning or caution.

O'Reilly Online Learning

O'REILLY®   For more than 40 years, *O'Reilly Media* has provided technology and business training, knowledge, and insight to help companies succeed.

Our unique network of experts and innovators share their knowledge and expertise through books, articles, and our online learning platform. O'Reilly's online learning platform gives you on-demand access to live training courses, in-depth learning paths, interactive coding environments, and a vast collection of text and video from O'Reilly and 200+ other publishers. For more information, visit *https://oreilly.com*.

How to Contact Us

Please address comments and questions concerning this book to the publisher:

> O'Reilly Media, Inc.
> 141 Stony Circle, Suite 195
> Santa Rosa, CA 95401
> 800-889-8969 (in the United States or Canada)
> 707-827-7019 (international or local)
> 707-829-0104 (fax)
> *support@oreilly.com*
> *https://oreilly.com/about/contact.html*

We have a web page for this book, where we list errata, examples, and any additional information. You can access this page at *https://oreil.ly/fundamentals-of-metadata*.

For news and information about our books and courses, visit *https://oreilly.com*.

Find us on LinkedIn: *https://linkedin.com/company/oreilly-media*.

Watch us on YouTube: *https://youtube.com/oreillymedia*.

Acknowledgments

Many of my readers all over the world expressed deep interest in this manuscript before it was published as my second book. I do not have room to thank everyone, but I do want to thank Arnaud de Chambourcy (*https://oreil.ly/bjGoE*) and Christophe Heng Rivot (*https://oreil.ly/4HY3A*), who took part in organizing the Onepoint Data & AI Summit in Paris in March 2024. Thank you for inviting me as the keynote speaker and letting me announce the book on your main stage in OnePoint's beautiful office in the center of Paris. The announcement sparked enormous interest and I was happy to see heated debate and interest in the months that followed. I'm also deeply thankful to the organizers of Helsinki Data Week in late October 2024, in particular Säde Haveri (*https://oreil.ly/cQJQQ*), but also Eevamaija Virtanen (*https://oreil.ly/GnDh3*), Antti Rask (*https://oreil.ly/2J_lE*), and Juha Korpela (*https://oreil.ly/gemWb*) for putting together such an extraordinary conference at the Apollo in Helsinki and inviting me as a keynote speaker on my book. Finally, I'm thankful to Lynn Bender (*https://oreil.ly/P2_IP*), who invited me as the opening keynote speaker at Data Day Texas in January 2025, to talk about the meta grid. For all of these events, I had the chance to talk to hundreds of people, and I have the impression they were all more intelligent than me: thank you, all of you.

Thank you to the podcasters, fellow authors, data leaders, technologists, consultants, practitioners, and academics who all believed in this project that is more about the enterprise reality than anything else.

Thank you also to the entire team of O'Reilly, Aaron Black, Angela Rufino, Katherine Tozer, Catherine Dullea, Sharon Cordesse, Marsee Henon, and Shannon Turlington.

Finally, thank you to my wife, Christina Eriksen, I love you; and Lili and Louis, my wonderful children, I love you. You know, Lev Tolstoy had it all wrong. Happy families are not alike, and I can't think of a more happy life than with the three of you.

CHAPTER 1

Toward Holistic Metadata Management

In this chapter, we will unpack the contents of the entire book. First, we'll take a brief look at the management disciplines that work with metadata in companies that use distinct metadata repositories—the topic of Part I of the book. Then, we'll discuss the concept of a *data discovery team*, which can coordinate these *metadata repositories* to improve enterprise-wide search—the topic of Part II. Finally, we'll run through the idea of the *meta grid*: a decentralized architecture for metadata and the topic of Part III.

Ready? Here we go!

Metadata Management Happens in Many Places

This book divides the domains that work with metadata management into four categories:[1]

IT management
  This domain uses metadata repositories to perform strategic planning of enterprise architecture, maintain the existing IT infrastructure, and preserve the immediate past in backup systems.

Data management
  This domain uses a set of technologies to store, extract, transform, observe, and ingest data across the IT landscape. In the late 2010s and early 2020s, this subpart of the data management toolset was called the *modern data stack*. However, this

---

[1] It must be stressed that these domains can be divided differently. The domains as laid out in this book are not canonical.

term is declining in usage and has been declared dead.[2] Several maps of data management technologies (including metadata repositories) exist. The most exhaustive and well known is the "MAD (Machine Learning, Artificial Intelligence, and Data) Landscape" (*https://oreil.ly/8aAmf*) by Matt Turck and Aman Kabeer.

Information management

This domain is a smaller discipline compared to data management. It is also closer to less technologically complex storage solutions. Besides digital data, it focuses on nondigital, physical objects, like paper and specimens, as well as concepts that are more abstract than tangible, such as business processes and capabilities. Rather than representing one big community, information management is divided into several subdisciplines. The metadata repositories for information management are, to a large extent, used for regulatory and operational purposes rather than for innovation (albeit this is changing with AI because unstructured data is highly relevant for generative and agentic AI). Information management has a vast body of theoretical literature supporting it.[3] Information management technologies are usually depicted in RegTech maps (*https://oreil.ly/T5sd9*) or as part of GovTech maps (*https://oreil.ly/EnAcA*).

Knowledge management

This is the methodology for capturing knowledge stored in human minds. As such, it is considered a subpart of human resource management by the International Organization for Standardization (ISO), with its own working group: ISO/TC 260/WG 6 (*https://oreil.ly/R6njw*). The task at hand is to capture and store more permanently the knowledge that people accumulate. To that end, knowledge management suggests storing knowledge via knowledge management technologies that use metadata repository dimensions. These knowledge management technologies can disseminate and teach the knowledge to more people. Just like for data and information, knowledge management operates with a set of technologies. The best overview is provided by EdTech Maps (*https://oreil.ly/k4_83*).

---

2 Joe Reis, "Everything Ends—My Journey with the Modern Data Stack," February 17, 2024, (*https://oreil.ly/Qa7HG*).

3 A literature review of information management can be found in Anuj Sharma, Nripendra P. Rana, and Robin Nunkoo, "Fifty Years of Information Management Research: A Conceptual Structure Analysis Using Structural Topic Modeling," *International Journal of Information Management* 58 (2021), (*https://doi.org/10.1016/j.ijinfomgt.2021.102316*).

All teams in all domains use metadata repositories. Any storage place where metadata is collected, ranging from a spreadsheet to a database or a sophisticated tool, can qualify. Metadata repositories will be defined and discussed throughout Part I.

Unlike the distinction between data and information, philosophy is relevant in the context of knowledge management. To capture knowledge, we must know what to look for, and philosophy provides answers to this. We have inherited three types of knowledge, as described by the ancient philosopher Aristotle in the *Nicomachean Ethics*:[4]

Episteme
Scientific, theoretical knowledge—knowledge that requires thinking

Techne
The knowledge of practical arts and crafts—knowledge that requires actions and has physical outcomes

Phronesis
The knowledge of ethical considerations dedicated to judging good actions

As you will see, these types of knowledge hold universal truths and are directly traceable to the knowledge management technologies implemented in companies in our era.[5]

Stephanie Barnes has put forward an avant-garde approach to knowledge management known as *radical knowledge management* (*https://oreil.ly/VbuJY*), which seeks to capture knowledge through art-based interventions—this approach is powerful since knowledge is difficult to capture.

In almost all companies, the disciplines of IT, data, information, and knowledge management operate in isolation from one another. This has severe consequences because they all depict, to a certain degree, the IT landscape upon which they rely to perform their tasks.

But there is a solution to bring them together—a new kind of team.

The Data Discovery Team

Readers of my previous book, *The Enterprise Data Catalog* (O'Reilly), and my newsletter and podcast, *Enterprise Wide Search* (*https://oreil.ly/gHvDa*), will know that I

---

4 Aristotle, *Nicomachean Ethics*, trans. by Adam Beresford (Penguin Classics, 2020).

5 For example, in the Knowledge Management System Guru (*https://oreil.ly/WUgjL*).

approach technology by suggesting new perspectives based on my academic background in library and information science (LIS). That is also true for this book.

All of Part II is dedicated to the data discovery team. This team is a facilitator of well-performing metadata repositories that are carefully aligned. The data discovery team is also a key enabler for employees in obtaining knowledge faster as answers from the data discovery team can be scaled with AI—making it an accelerator more than a bottleneck.

Accordingly, pivotal for this book is the notion of the *reference librarian*. The reference librarian is a role that helps people with their research and consolidates a topic based on many sources. This person is responsible for providing the deepest, most complete answer to any information needs that library users may have. The reference librarian will assess a variety of openly listed sources to gather an answer to even very big information needs—this discipline (*https://oreil.ly/OZ7zH*) is especially important in an education and research context. The reference librarian pushes researchers and students forward on complex endeavors with an opaque amount of data that has to be filtered to provide the most precise context. As you can see in Figure 1-1, this approach differs from the "monolithic" approach of having "one single source of truth" that can answer all questions.

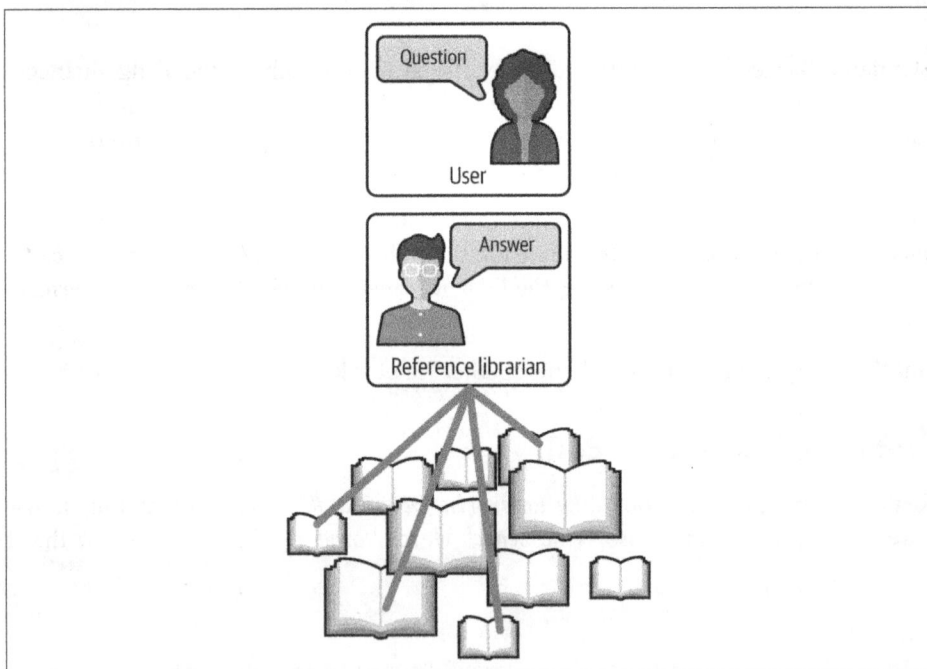

Figure 1-1. Reference librarian using many sources to create a complete answer

Asking questions and getting answers from one or many sources is also at play in metadata repositories. Let's take the example of an *application*. We could imagine a simple question like this one: what is an application, and what applications do we have in this company?

If you ask the team of enterprise architects, they have a firm answer about what defines an application. Along with the definition of *application*, they have a complete list of applications in their enterprise architecture management (EAM) tool—their metadata repository and their single source of truth about the IT landscape (they may be aware of more sources, but they don't use them in their daily work).

However, do the facts in the EAM tool match the reality of other metadata repositories? What would have happened if we had asked another team about what an application is and which applications we have—and that team then used their metadata repository to answer us? Can we expect that these metadata repositories match exactly? Or for applications to even be registered in them? Unfortunately, that is not the case because metadata repositories are built and maintained in silos by teams all over the company with little or no communication among them.

To address this challenge, you should respond like a reference librarian. You need to coordinate metadata repositories to provide solid answers, as shown in Figure 1-2.

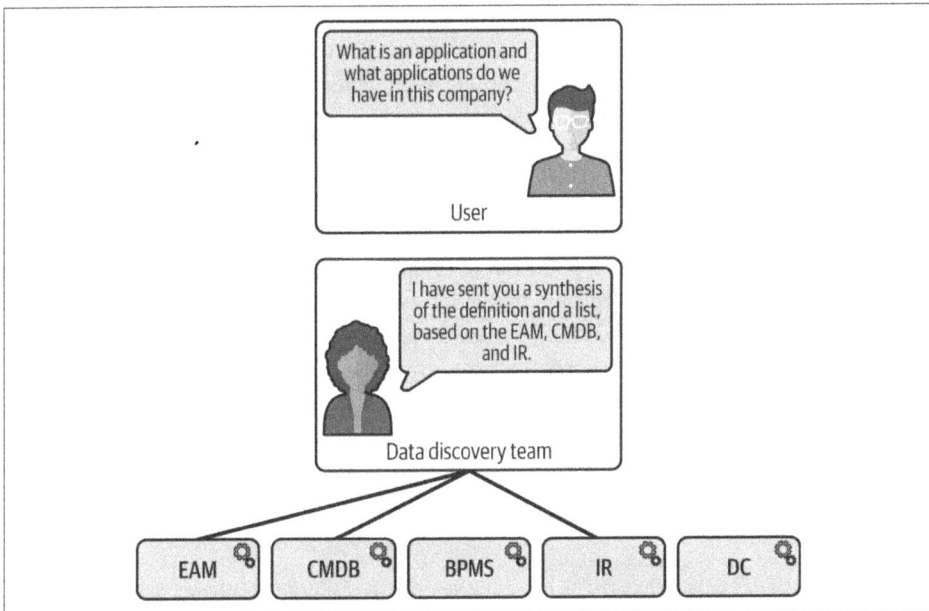

Figure 1-2. Providing a solid answer to the application question based on multiple metadata repositories

Think of these repositories as part of a grid, all connected so that they constitute a collective truth and not isolated, opposing truths. Such a reality is, in a nutshell, what this book seeks to establish for your company's IT landscape. We'll discuss this further in Chapters 3, 4, 5, and 6.

You need to understand that metadata repositories are normally managed as monoliths, so let's unfold that—and get a first glimpse of a new, decentralized architecture for metadata management.

The Meta Grid: The Third Wave of Data Decentralization

In short, the *meta grid* can be defined as an architecture of metadata to be decentralized and shared among many metadata repositories.[6]

In this way, a meta grid establishes a core set of metadata elements that is extracted from one metadata repository to be shared with multiple other metadata repositories. Let's circle back to traditional data management and see how a meta grid differs from traditional thinking.

The *DAMA Data Management Body of Knowledge (DAMA-DMBOK)* (*https://oreil.ly/Q5_t8*) provides two architecture diagrams for metadata management (Figure 1-3).

Both diagrams include a metadata portal that enables searching for metadata across the typical subset of metadata repositories discussed in data management. This can be done either through a middle layer known as an *enterprise metadata repository* or directly within the metadata repositories.

However, both architectures have problems. The centralized metadata architecture suggests pulling all metadata into a shared repository while the distributed metadata architecture suggests searching metadata directly across both sources. But neither addresses the fact that there is a potential overlap of metadata in the various repositories; for example, how are endpoints described in extract, transform, load (ETL), and business intelligence (BI) tools? This creates somewhat redundant, uncoordinated repositories. This is a technical architecture and does not take into account a crucial aspect of how metadata is managed: as if all sources simply contain unique metadata that in no way overlaps with the other sources.

---

6 I must emphasize that this decentralization is to be viewed with an enterprise perspective, with deeply heterogeneous data sources. Prior to these waves (three, counting the meta grid), similar thoughts have been formulated for the open web; e.g., *The Semantic Web: A New Form of Web Content That Is Meaningful to Computers Will Unleash a Revolution of New Possibilities* (*https://oreil.ly/fWQVH*) by Tim Berners-Lee and James Hendler, and the entire concept of Linked Data (*https://oreil.ly/CTw6S*). However, these ideas stretch substantially further back in time; e.g., to the Mundaneum vision (*https://oreil.ly/mc524*) by the Belgian documentalist Paul Otlet in the 1920s.

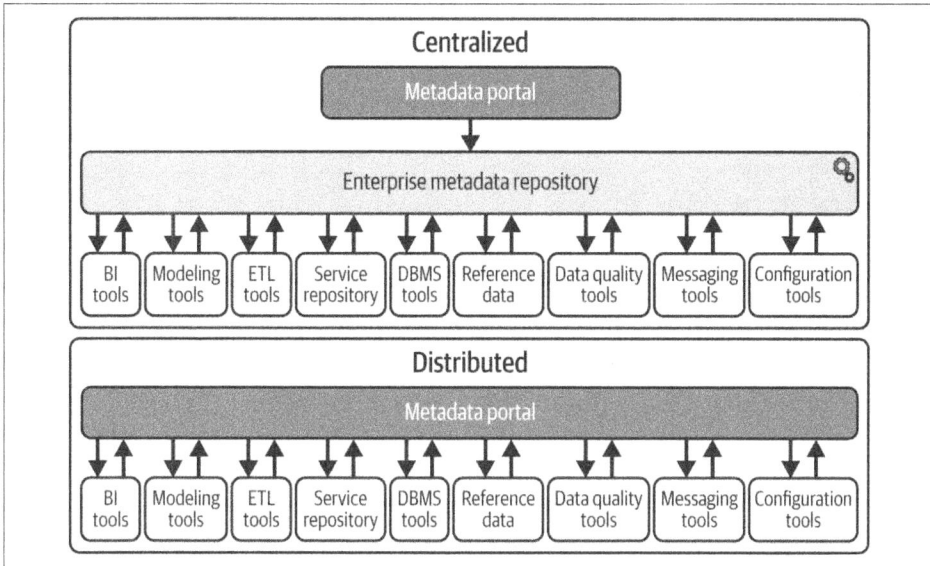

Figure 1-3. The two styles of metadata management described in DAMA International's DAMA-DMBOK[7]

As such, each metadata repository can be considered a monolith (more on this in Part II), not related to one another, and in the case of the centralized metadata repository, there is an additional monolith on top. This means that metadata shared across repositories is not considered an independent entity; it is only considered in the context of the repository in which it is represented. Instead, the same metadata is listed again and again, almost always misaligned and imperfect.

Accordingly, this book suggests decentralizing metadata into a meta grid. Unlike previous methods, the meta grid aims to think of metadata in smaller, more manageable pieces. To better understand the concept of the meta grid, let's take a brief look at two earlier waves of decentralization that successfully managed to break up gigantic data monoliths inside companies. These two waves were *microservices* and *data mesh*.

Microservices

Microservices break up the monoliths of operational data. *Operational data* describes the data that runs companies, making sure that the value chain of the company is functioning smoothly. It traditionally sits in big technology components, like enterprise resource planning (ERP) systems, customer relationship management (CRM)

---

7 *DAMA-DMBOK*, 2nd ed. (Technics Publications, 2024), 406–407.

systems, product information management (PIM) systems, and content management systems (CMS). You can see these in Figure 1-4.

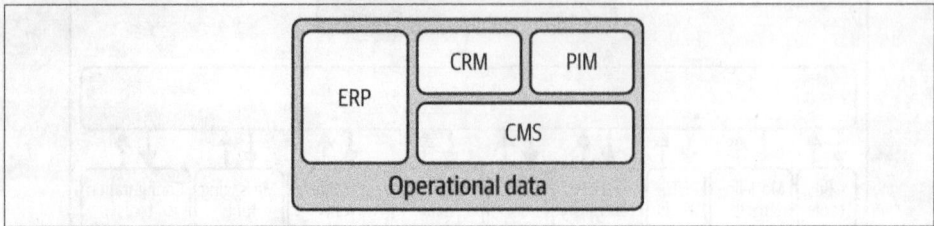

Figure 1-4. Big technology components for operational data

The architecture depicted in Figure 1-4 faced challenges from emerging software styles, notably introduced as early as 2001 in the Manifesto for Agile Software Development (*https://agilemanifesto.org*). These styles eventually evolved into what is now known as *microservices*.[8] This shift was prompted by the recognition that large technology components lacked the necessary speed and agility for companies to evolve, scale, and adapt to change effectively. This results in a "locked in" syndrome where companies become so dependent on the technologies running their value chain that they can no longer modify that very same value chain, causing a gradual loss of competitiveness as reality changes.

Microservices was successfully put forward as an alternative that breaks up these big components (monoliths) into the smallest possible services—*service* meaning a technology that is capable of performing an action. This architecture is called "hexagonal" because each service is packaged as a product and visualized as a box (Figure 1-5).

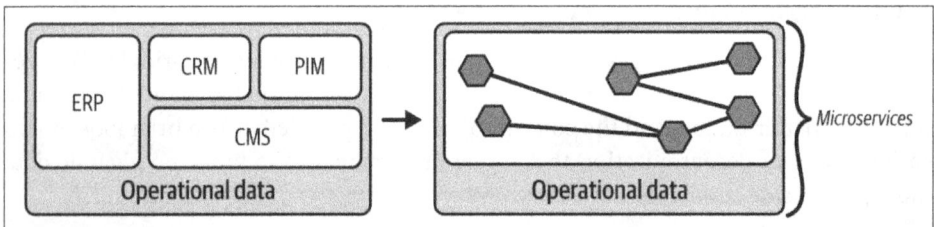

Figure 1-5. Microservices for operational data

Microservices architecture is completely flexible, with a plasticity that allows for speed, scale, and reorientation. Amazon, Netflix, and Uber run on microservices architecture (indeed, Amazon pioneered microservices, with an API-first approach).

---

8 Some essential sources on microservices are: "Microservices—A Definition of This New Architectural Term" (*https://oreil.ly/5YJOQ*) by Martin Fowler; *Building Microservices—Designing Fine-Grained Systems*, 2nd ed., by Sam Newman (O'Reilly); and *Scrum en action* by Guillaume Bodet (Pearson).

This makes it possible for these companies to adapt to customer behaviors and needs while adding new services to their platforms. Eventually, the microservices architecture inspired a new movement: data mesh.

Data Mesh

Data mesh breaks up the monoliths for analytical data. Based on lessons learned from using microservices, *data mesh* was put forward as a vision in the late 2010s.[9] Data mesh proposed an architecture of decoupled, small units of analytical data. Contrary to operational data, analytical data does not run the value chain of a company. Instead, it reflects on the company and innovates via analytical use cases driven by machine learning (ML) and AI. Analytical data has traditionally been stored, consumed, and exposed in big, rather complex data platform technologies, such as:

- Data warehouses for BI
- Data lakes for BI, ML, and AI
- A data lakehouse hybridizing the data warehouse and data lake

As the need for analytical data increased during the past 20 years, all three of these data platforms became bottlenecks due to slow speed, employees lacking subject matter knowledge, and poor data quality.

The inconveniences of the architecture shown in Figure 1-6 are manifold. First, its reality mimics the operational data in Figure 1-4, meaning that analytical data is meticulously placed in a data platform that lacks the capacity to scale and reorient itself while operating very slowly. A centralized data platform cannot keep up with increasing demand for analytical data—providers can't get their data into the platform fast enough, in good enough quality, and consumers can't use and access data accordingly.

Data mesh was proposed as an alternative that advocated for a similar architecture for analytical data as what microservices offer for operational data.[10] The centralized data platform is broken up into business domains with data products, as visualized in Figure 1-7.

---

9 Zhamak Dehghani, "How to Move Beyond a Monolithic Data Lake to a Distributed Data Mesh," May 20, 2019, (*https://oreil.ly/V_xLY*); Zhamak Dehghani, "Data Mesh Principles and Logical Architecture," December 3, 2020, (*https://oreil.ly/3ulT4*).

10 Two books were published simultaneously on this topic: *Data Mesh: Delivering Data-Driven Value at Scale* by Zhamak Dehghani (O'Reilly) and *Data Management at Scale: Modern Data Architecture with Data Mesh and Data Fabric*, 2nd ed., by Piethein Strengholt (O'Reilly).

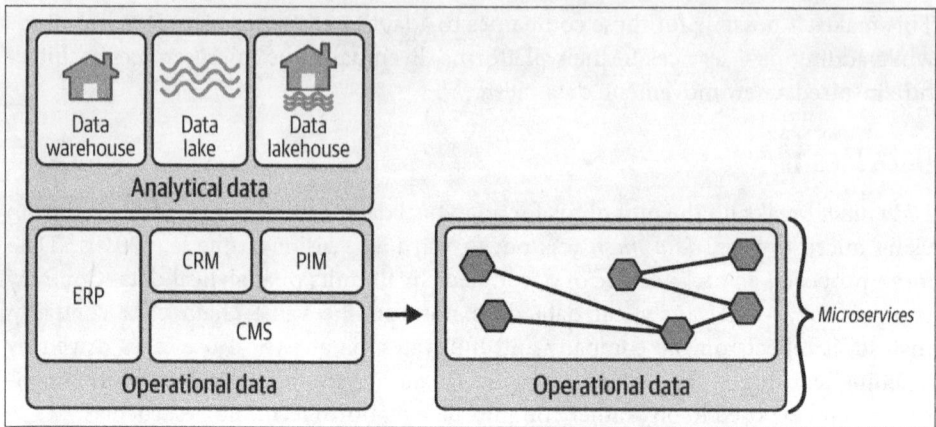

Figure 1-6. Centralized data platforms for analytical data becoming bottlenecks

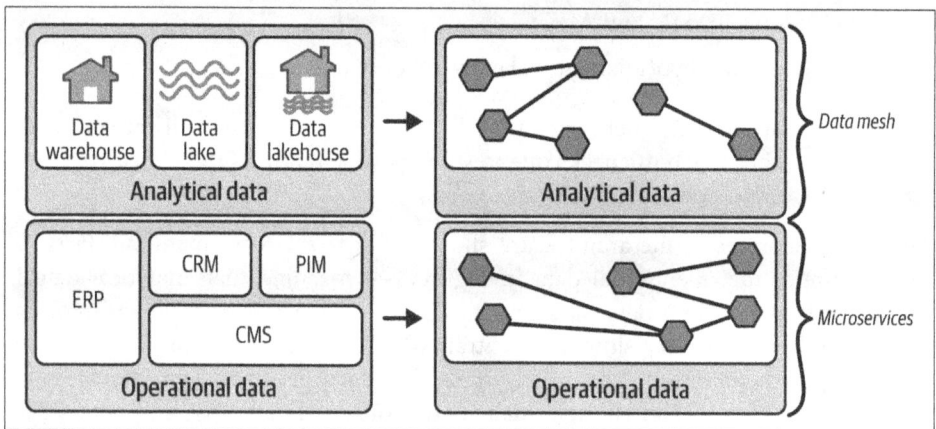

Figure 1-7. Data mesh for analytical data

A data mesh architecture will scale faster than a centralized architecture and express each domain more clearly because the lack of plurality in the centralized solution is avoided; this is due to the fact that a data mesh has multiple domain-specific models, not one central, canonical data model.

Meta Grid

The meta grid is a different decentralization than microservices and data mesh. With the meta grid, I suggest sharing metadata from various metadata repositories—as a grid—that will make metadata management more robust and subsequently let you succeed with metadata management altogether.

A *metadata repository* is a mirror of your company's IT landscape. I'll explain and discuss this in depth in Chapter 2. Metadata repositories have monolithic tendencies in the sense that they all claim that they—and they alone—represent the entire truth about the IT landscape. However, none of them do. They all represent a certain vision of the IT landscape—a single view of the world. The monolithic tendency in metadata repositories is in fact an illusion—the illusion of the total view of the IT landscape that every metadata repository is prone to impress on you. With this book, I aim to dispel that illusion and instead create a more methodological and holistic approach to metadata.

In Figure 1-8, you can see metadata repositories depicted as both centralized tools and, at the same time, silos of metadata that are not coordinated.

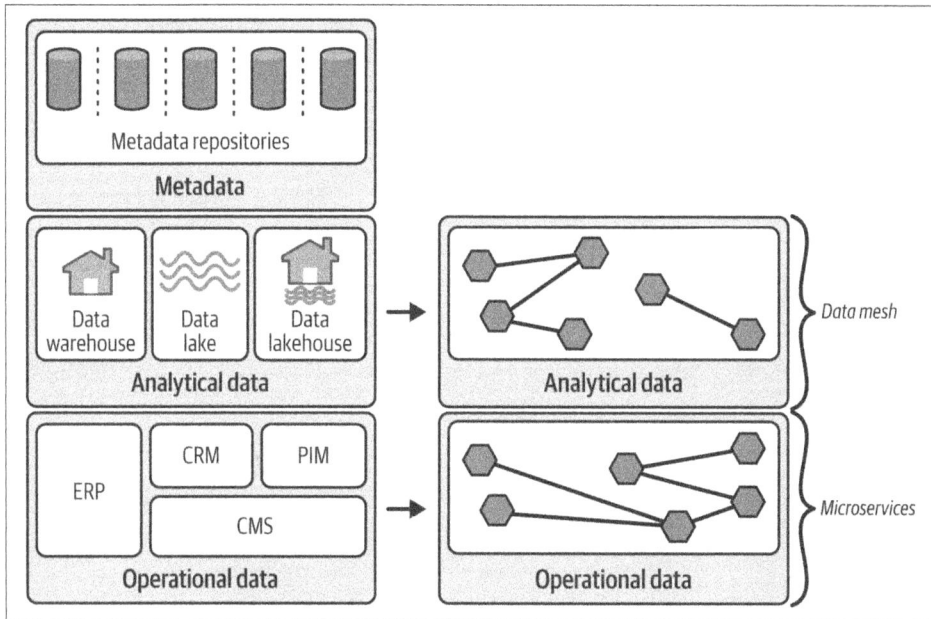

Figure 1-8. Metadata repositories for metadata

Microservices and data mesh employ comparable thinking and architectural patterns for distinct purposes: executing the value chain and creating analytical use cases. The meta grid follows a similar approach and architecture, albeit with its own distinct purpose. The meta grid is about obtaining a more robust overview of your IT land-scape through aligned metadata repositories. Creating a robust, coordinated overview of the IT landscape across all metadata repositories enables you to succeed with IT, data, information, and knowledge management. The meta grid inscribed in this context is shown in Figure 1-9.

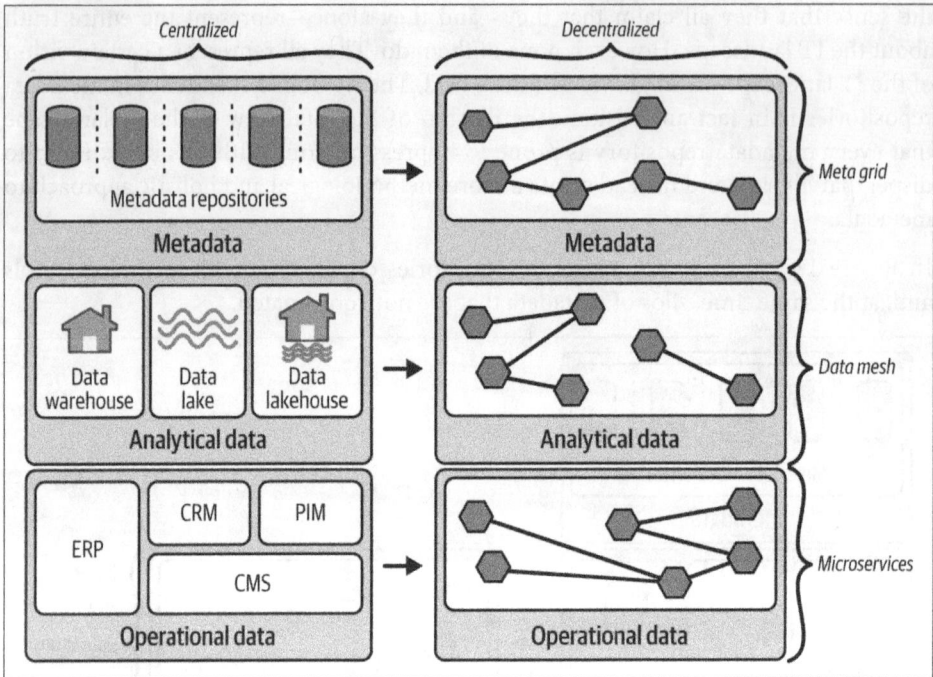

Figure 1-9. The third wave of data decentralization: the meta grid

Notice that all metadata repositories will be placed in an IT, data, information, or knowledge management domain. These four management disciplines are the only four domains in the meta grid, and they have distinct metadata repositories. The meta grid architecture will be detailed in Part III of this book.

> Figure 1-9 is the main concept and essence of the book. The meta grid is data mesh and microservices–"ish" but for metadata—and simpler, smaller, and with fewer requirements. You can see depictions of the meta grid in Chapters 10 and 11.

It's important to note that this book doesn't encompass every single metadata repository in existence. Instead, think of the meta grid as something that can expand continuously to accommodate more repositories.

Setting up microservices and data mesh architectures can be difficult, requiring deep technical exercises and theoretical discussions. In comparison, a meta grid architecture is simple and easy to improve, but the organizational change aspect may be substantial.

Summary

In this chapter, you got an overview of the contents of this book in a condensed, introductory way. The most important thing to note from this chapter is that metadata management must be understood as a way to coordinate the many existing metadata repositories in companies. Subsequently, we discussed metadata management and metadata repositories. I explained that there are metadata repositories for IT, data, information, and knowledge management, and I introduced the data discovery team that will play a key role in your company: creating a valuable overview of your IT landscape by joining forces between already existing teams in your company. Finally, I put forward the idea of a meta grid, which will address the real problem that metadata poses and allow you to get a more thorough depiction of your IT landscape.

Here are the key takeaways from this chapter:

- Metadata management must be reinterpreted to expand beyond traditional data management activities because this does not reflect the reality in companies.
- IT management holds many metadata repositories that depict the IT landscape.
- Information management and knowledge management also depict the IT landscape in various metadata repositories.
- The data discovery team is inspired by reference librarians, who make use of not one but a series of sources to provide complete answers to complex information needs.
- Likewise, the data discovery team trains in providing answers about the IT landscape from not one but many sources to give as complete answers as possible.
- The meta grid is a third wave of decentralization, following in the footsteps of microservices and data mesh.
- The meta grid is smaller and simpler than microservices and data mesh.

Metadata Repositories for IT, Data, Information, and Knowledge Management

In Part I, we'll take a look at what characterizes metadata and metadata repositories.

Chapter 2 explores metadata beyond traditional data management literature, drawing insights primarily from LIS as well as from enterprise architecture and relevant theoretical literature. This opens a more holistic perspective on metadata management, its repositories, and its potential. It also presents the data discovery team and the meta grid.

Chapters 3, 4, 5, and 6 describe metadata repositories for IT, data, information, and knowledge management, respectively. While the discussed repositories are common in these disciplines, they do not constitute an exhaustive representation of all existing metadata repositories. The purpose of metadata repositories keeps expanding with new innovations, especially in AI, as well with new regulations and operational requirements that emerge as technology evolves.

Chapter 7 explores the interplay and overlap of metadata repositories and discusses why this has not been addressed in organizations. It serves as a bridge to Part II about the data discovery team, which can solve exactly this challenge.

Flip ahead and take a look at Table 7-1. It condenses all of Part I into one big overview.

Now, let's examine what metadata and metadata repositories are.

CHAPTER 2

Metadata Repositories for the IT Landscape

In this chapter, we'll explore the concept of metadata and metadata repositories. We'll discuss how metadata repositories can depict the IT landscape within your company. Then, you'll learn about metadata repositories for the IT landscape and their four characteristics: driver, structure, place, and purpose.

You'll discover that metadata repositories can be divided into operation, regulation, and innovation drivers, although they often address multiple drivers simultaneously. You will learn that all metadata repositories have core capabilities as their primary purpose, along with peripheral capabilities that can extend into external functions. You'll understand that metadata repositories have a specific structure called a *metamodel*, which often overlaps different repositories. Finally, you'll become aware that metadata repositories can exist in various forms, ranging from simple spreadsheets to complex platforms.

As you will see, things can start to get complicated. But fear not! Once we understand metadata repositories, we can begin to control them and reap great benefits.

What Is Metadata?

When explaining what metadata *is*, most technological literature falls into the trap of focusing too much on the different types of metadata. Instead of defining what metadata actually is, the literature lists various subcategories of metadata that exist, such as operational, technical, analytical, and so on. These subcategories are important, and we will return to them, but they do not capture what metadata actually is—they only show how metadata manifests in various forms. So let's first recap the definition of metadata presented in the Preface:

> Metadata is a description that is both attached to what is described and placed somewhere else in order to make what is described discoverable and manageable.

This means that metadata is in two places at the same time and that the selection of metadata is about maximizing the discoverability of something somewhere else.

For context, let's consider the metadata of a book. I was trained in LIS, and I have BA, MA, and PhD degrees in that field. It's a field that is more technical than most people know. When I was a freshman at university, there was this exercise where each student was given a physical book, and then we were asked to describe that book. Most of us would describe the color of the book, its size, the title on the cover, and perhaps the author's name. The professor told us that we weren't wrong but pointed out an important place to look—in the first pages of the book. There, the publisher put all the important information about the book: the number of pages, the authoritative title, the International Standard Book Number (ISBN)—we learned that every book in the world has its own unique number!—as well as the authoritative name and address of the publisher, the names of the editors, and much more.

> Flip to the front of *this* book and you'll see that all the metadata is there in this book too.

The professor explained that these first pages aren't the book itself but rather information about the book: its metadata. The publisher has included this data according to standards, and it's attached to the book as well as available elsewhere. For example, if you search for this book in your favorite online bookstore, you'll find the same information as in the first pages of the book: title, author, publisher, ISBN, and so on.

That's the wonderful purpose of metadata: it helps you find things by being in two places at once. It binds the things we want to find, such as a book, with places where we can find it, such as Amazon.com. What you need to be good at is understanding what exactly will help people find things in the smoothest, fastest way—which will also put you in a position to manage whatever it is the metadata represents. That's *metadata management*.

It's no different in tech. The columns of tables in a database, the folders and titles of files in data lakes, and the documents in Microsoft SharePoint sites can all be used in the same way as the first pages in books. Tables, folders, and files are identified as metadata and are exposed in data catalogs and data lineage tools, or clustered a bit more, they become records within records and information management systems.

Figure 2-1 visualizes the definition of metadata, showing that metadata is in two places at once—in this case, metadata about the IT landscape.

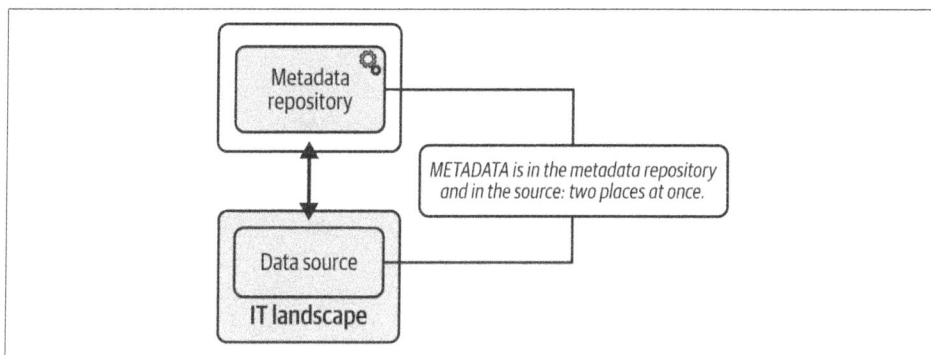

Figure 2-1. Metadata is both in the source and in the metadata repository

This book is about the metadata that describes an IT landscape within a company. It builds on concepts from LIS. To strengthen your understanding of metadata, I suggest studying some of the classics in LIS, such as *The Intellectual Foundations of Information Organization* by Elaine Svenonius (MIT Press),[1] "Machine-Readable Cataloguing (MARC) Program" (*https://oreil.ly/pjEZs*) by Henriette Avram,[2] and "What Is Documentation?" by Suzanne Briet (Scarecrow Press).[3]

---

1 In her preface, Svenonius distinguishes "between metadata that are derived and metadata that is assigned: the former provide the means to find information, and the latter provide the normalization to organize it." This distinction will become apparent later in this book, and it is *always* at play in metadata management: the constant symbiosis of searching and organizing with metadata, and refining it accordingly, is the key to success with metadata management.

2 Avram describes the laborious task of digitizing the analog cataloging practices in the United States by the use of MARC in the second half of the 20th century. Avram in particular highlights that "MARC is an *assemblage* of formats, publications, procedures, people, standards, codes, programs, systems, equipment, etc., that has evolved over the years, stimulating the development of library automation and information networks." If we consider MARC an example of metadata management, then this assemblage is key to understanding how to overcome the challenges of metadata management.

3 In this pamphlet translated from the French, "Qu'est-ce que la documentation?" (EDIT, 1951), mid-20th-century documentalist Briet argues that anything can be a document—living animals, for example. Provocative for its time, this idea may be widely accepted in our era. However, particularly for metadata management, practitioners with a traditional data management background may benefit from this perspective as it points to the fact that technological metadata is more than what is normally conceived to be so within data management.

Types of Metadata in IT Landscapes

This book focuses on metadata that describes the IT landscape through metadata repositories. These types of metadata include business, technical, operational, reference, social, hardware, asset, documents and records, company metadata, and more.

> Suppose you want to see the unique types of metadata for each metadata repository described in Chapters 3, 4, 5, and 6. In that case, you can find it by looking at the figures of the metamodels of the repositories. I'll discuss concrete examples of metamodels in "Structure: The Metamodel in Metadata Repositories" on page 29.

Let's quickly run through the various types:

Business metadata
> The human-defined type of metadata, such as business terms, definitions, lists rs, and so on.

Technical metadata
> More detailed metadata that is closely related to technology, with a focus on architecture and development (design time). Examples include schema structures in databases, file formats, identity and access management (IAM) models, and so on.

Operational metadata
> Even more detailed metadata that is very close to the running IT landscape, with a focus on operations (runtime). Examples include ETL batch job logs, schema anomalies, data backups, and retention policies, among others.

> Business, technical, and operational metadata are the traditional types of metadata most commonly discussed in technical literature, first and foremost in *DAMA-DMBOK*.

Reference metadata
> Used to tag other data. Examples include authoritative lists of company product names and geographic naming standards, such as those from ISO.

Social metadata
> Data about search traffic from specific individuals or groups as well as user behaviors, preference ratings, and more.[4]

---

4 Piethein Strengholt, *Data Management at Scale* (O'Reilly, 2023), 264.

Hardware metadata

Refers to the physical reality of the IT landscape. Examples include endpoint management information, such as lists of laptops, servers, and so on.

Asset metadata

Refers to physical items beyond just hardware that are still integrated with the IT landscape. Examples include manufacturing machinery with built-in IT, buildings with sensors, and various layers of access control.

Document and records metadata

Provides detailed information about individuals and entities that a company interacts with, including customers, competitors, high-profile employees, and more. This type of metadata is crucial for risk and privacy management activities.

Company metadata

Encompasses comprehensive knowledge about the company, including standard operating procedures, company history, and public presentation as well as research, memos, strategies, and more.

Is Metadata "Data About Data"?

Technically, yes—within a digital context (as opposed to an analog one), metadata is indeed data about data. However, this view often leads to a "data-centric" perspective on metadata that overlooks its broader implications. Metadata is more than just information about the types of data stored in data warehouses, lakes, and lakehouses. This traditional focus of data management and data catalogs represents only a part of what metadata management entails. The perspective here on metadata management is much broader because metadata also exists outside of the normal tooling of data management—namely, in IT, information, and knowledge management.

Now that we've described metadata, let's explore where we can store it: metadata repositories!

What Is a Metadata Repository?

I would like to begin this section with a passage from *Data Management at Scale* by Piethein Strengholt (O'Reilly). It's useful to keep this in mind as I define a metadata repository:

> Metadata is complicated to manage, scattered as it is across many tools, applications, platforms, and environments. Typically, a multitude of organized metadata repositories coexist in a large data architecture....Today metadata can be found everywhere; in applications, databases, data integration technologies, master data management, cloud

infrastructure, analytical services, and more. Consequently, it is also more siloed: each platform and tool may have its own database for managing metadata.[5]

This quotation illustrates that there is no easy way out of the challenge of managing metadata. There will never be *one* single technology—one metadata repository—that manages a company's metadata, and striving for that is going down the wrong track. Instead, we must accept that complex organizations will always have multiple metadata repositories and that it is their strategic coordination that will make them successful. Metadata repositories can be defined like this:

> A *metadata repository* is a list/collection of things of interest to your company. The metadata repository mirrors a certain part of your IT landscape within the list/collection to perform a selected set of actions.

A metadata repository involves deciding what to extract from a data source, exposing it at a metadata layer, and possessing the technical capability to execute these actions. Furthermore, the metadata repository will enable you to perform certain actions with data—this will become evident in upcoming chapters.

Your company can manage a particular aspect of your IT landscape by looking at it through the metadata repository. For example, a metadata repository can help you perform data management and leverage:

- Integrations between applications in your IT landscape
- Knowledge of what client applications are installed on which smartphones and laptops

Or it can help you perform information management by assisting with information security, privacy, and retention or by managing the knowledge in your company.

In Figure 2-2, you can see the four main characteristics of metadata repositories that I'll discuss in this chapter. All metadata repositories have the following:

- Driver
- Purpose
- Place
- Structure

---

5 Piethein Strengholt, *Data Management at Scale* (O'Reilly, 2023), 264–265.

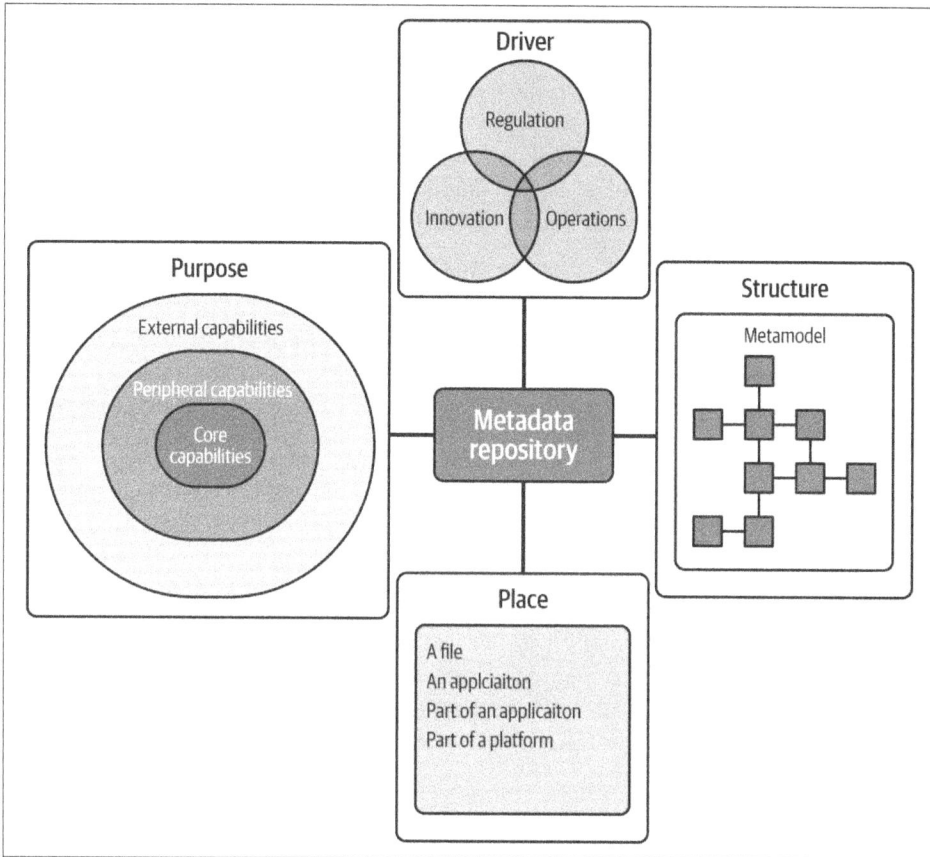

Figure 2-2. The four main characteristics of metadata repositories

All of the discussions of metadata repositories in Chapters 3, 4, and 5 include figures illustrating each metadata repository's core capability and metamodel.

Driver: The Many Waves of Metadata Repositories

Metadata repositories come in waves.

Sit tight as I take you through some flashbacks of various implementations of metadata repositories. I'll be asking you questions along the way. You might find yourself answering "yes" to some of them, but that's not crucial. You'll soon see why.

Ready? Here we go…

Do you remember the rise of information security? Back in 2005 when the ISO 27001 (*https://oreil.ly/9DzFu*) standards were published in the first edition? Or do you recall when, 10 years later, the General Data Protection Regulation (*https://gdpr-info.eu*) (GDPR) was being drafted in Europe, going into effect in 2018? Maybe you played a role in the metadata repositories that supported information security or GDPR. And maybe you are currently involved in considerations on how to perform environmental, social, and governance (ESG) reporting (*https://oreil.ly/GrfjG*).

Or perhaps you are deeply involved in operating your company's IT landscape. If that's the case, you may be implementing or managing one or more metadata repositories that operationalize IT frameworks, such as TOGAF (*https://oreil.ly/2aSFn*), ITIL (*https://oreil.ly/vmAsA*), or Scaled Agile Framework (SAFe) (*https://oreil.ly/kgZt-*). These frameworks are all dedicated to working with IT in a structured, methodologically well-planned way.

It could also be that you're working with more innovative aspects of data, making use of metadata repositories that build and document data pipelines, transporting data to new and promising technologies that analyze the potential of data in hitherto unforeseen ways.

All of these examples—and many I didn't mention—result in metadata repositories. These metadata repositories are where you map the IT landscape in your company to manage and perform actions in it. Over the course of recent decades, the number of metadata repositories has increased quite breathtakingly.

With ever-growing amounts of data, companies and society have discovered that data must be handled carefully for all sorts of agendas. That's why metadata repositories emerge and come in waves. Far too often, new waves ignore or are unaware of older waves.

Due to their wave-like nature, metadata repositories are commonly unaligned—they don't reflect the same reality. That's a big problem because it leads to one specific effect: no one knows the true reality of the IT landscape.

As you just learned, metadata repositories are introduced all the time for many purposes. A pessimistic viewpoint might suggest that a metadata repository serves as a parking space for all the well-intentioned initiatives in your company, providing a claim that some action is being taken, whether it's in terms of protecting sensitive information, managing IT costs, or signaling your company's competitiveness. A more optimistic and also pragmatic approach is the same: you are doing something about these things with the help of many different metadata repositories.

It can boost your career to manage metadata repositories effectively. If you already are where you want to be in your career, then a smooth understanding of metadata repositories can help you win important agendas. Well-maintained metadata repositories can give your company competitive advantages and ensure that your IT landscape is running smoothly in terms of cost and compliance. So I encourage you to be an optimist. You can make metadata repositories work—and work together!

Despite all the very different purposes for metadata repositories, they can be divided into three categories:

- Innovation
- IT operations
- Regulations

Let's look at these categories one by one.

Innovation

The most complex and promising metadata repositories deal with innovation. They can be placed into the context of what was known as the *modern data stack*, a term that we already established has declined in usage since 2022. These metadata repositories aim to maximize the innovative potential of your company data, including external data. They achieve this by exposing, at a metadata layer, how additional tools on the modern data stack transform, transport, and utilize data once it has been made accessible.[6]

IT operations

A more pragmatic reason to implement metadata repositories is because they are needed to operate an IT landscape. From an IT operations perspective, metadata repositories are mostly thought of as improving efficiency and saving cost. They will mimic many of the functions performed by the modern data stack, but they will go beyond that, looking deeper into economic, rational, and operative aspects of the IT landscape. Metadata repositories targeted for IT operations will typically be bigger, older, and more difficult to handle. There is less fuzz around them than those that deliver on innovation. Instead, metadata repositories for IT operations represent—there is no other way of saying it—cumbersome management tasks without the promise of exciting innovation. On the other hand, they typically contain more

---

6 For deeper insights, see "The Road to Composable Data Systems: Thoughts on the Last 15 Years and the Future" by Wes McKinney (*https://oreil.ly/klcMj*).

reliable metadata because they are crafted with careful, consistent solidity. And they operate at an enterprise scale, providing vaster overviews.

> You should never underestimate the potential of metadata repositories for IT operations. They are often considered clunky and old school, but they are likely the most reliable, well-maintained metadata repositories in your company. Respect them. They will give a lot back. Think about ways to use them as a basis for innovation.

Regulations

A third reason for implementing metadata repositories is regulations. These regulations can be focused on a particular industry, or they can be applied in general. Two examples for specific industries are:

Health Insurance Portability and Accountability Act (HIPAA) of 1996 (https://oreil.ly/ plX7e)
> HIPAA ensures that hospitals and life science industries do not treat patient data in any way that would compromise that patient—for example, selling patient data to an insurance company.

Basel Committee on Banking Supervision standard no. 239 (BCBS 239) (https://oreil.ly/ Naw0S)
> BCBS 239 ensures that banking and financial institutions can trace the flow of data to do proper reporting and minimize risk.

Documenting that regulatory processes are respected in the IT landscape has to be depicted in a human-readable format outside of the actual data-processing activities going on inside the IT landscape itself to create an understandable overview of that IT landscape. Metadata repositories are used to depict this.

The crucial point here is that, to fulfill their purpose, metadata repositories for regulations need to make an interpretation of the IT landscape. That is because they are not simply reflecting a physical reality. Instead, they reflect on the IT landscape to create a human-understandable explanation of fulfilling a specific regulatory requirement. Therefore, there is a higher degree of interpretation between the metadata repository and the IT landscape that it mirrors at the metadata level.

Metadata repositories are rarely defined purely for one purpose only, though. They will often be a blend of innovation, IT operations, and regulations, as shown in Figure 2-3.

Here, we have reached the core purpose of this book. Consider the three categories—innovation, operations, and regulations—and even the multiple repositories within each category. Every metadata repository must assess the IT landscape, each with its own specific purpose. In essence, these metadata repositories collectively represent the IT landscape.

And that is where all the complexity begins.

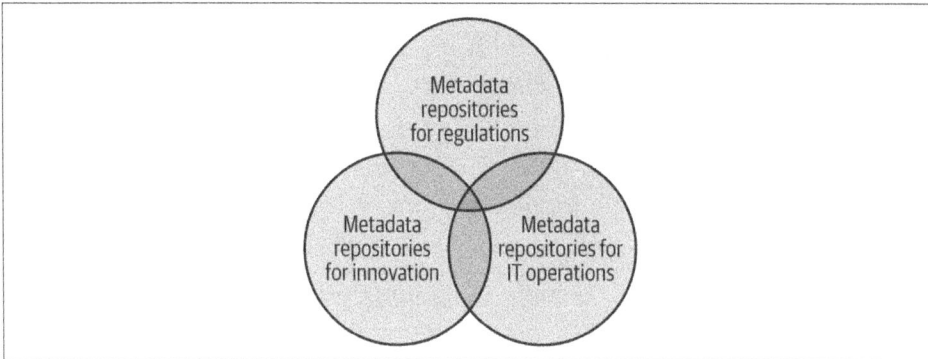

Figure 2-3. Drivers of metadata repositories are often a blend of innovation, operations, and regulations

Different parts of the organization own different metadata repositories. You should remember that these repositories come in waves, and because they come in waves, they are not coordinated. You do not have *one* metadata overview of the IT landscape in your company but *many* metadata overviews of your IT landscape. These overviews accumulated in the past and for various purposes. And that is a problem because it dissolves the possibility of knowing your IT landscape's reality. What metadata repository should you trust?

This book is your way out of that reality. A metadata repository should focus on one core capability, but it can easily expand beyond that, which we'll discuss next.

Purpose: Core Capability

At first, a metadata repository is created to deliver on a core capability. As time progresses, feedback from customers and tech trends make the software vendor of a given metadata repository expand the repository to more peripheral capabilities that were not its initial purpose. If economic success allows, the metadata repository can expand toward external capabilities that are completely outside its initial scope. This is illustrated in Figure 2-4.

The relative lack of focus on the core capability and the expansion toward peripheral and even external capabilities can lead to disoriented and uncoordinated metadata repositories. This lack of focus comes from an unchallenged belief that many tend to develop: that metadata repositories build a source of truth, not a source in a context (that they may be unaware of).

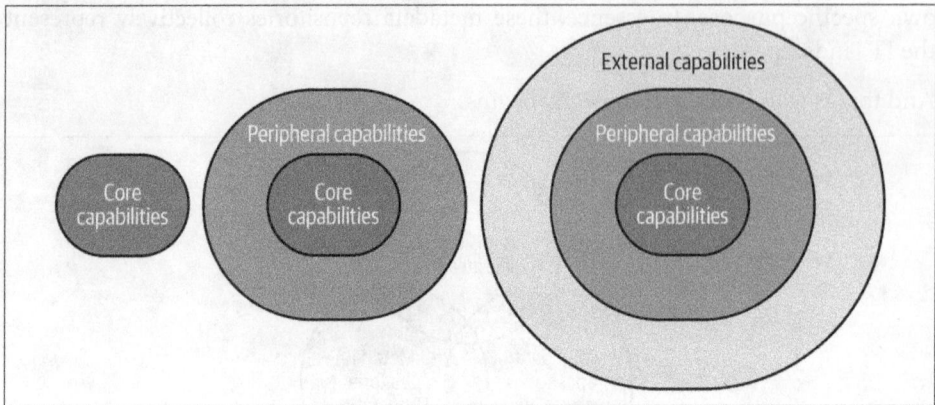

Figure 2-4. Core, peripheral, and external capabilities of metadata repositories expanding over time

> A metadata repository should focus on its core metadata domain. The data discovery team must coordinate and help the metadata domains to decide which repositories should handle the peripheral and external capabilities.

As we go through the various metadata repositories, you will see two of their pitfalls:

Not understanding or ignoring the core capability of the metadata repository
This often manifests in oddly functioning workflows and organizational conflict.

Expanding toward peripheral and external capabilities
This results in a severe lack of user adoption and buy-in. The activity of upholding capabilities by a metadata repository that is not fit for that purpose tends to die when the senior stakeholders force through such a decision.

Place: Metadata Repositories at Various Levels

Metadata repositories are easiest to imagine as standalone technology solutions. Nevertheless, that's often not the case. Metadata repositories can be:

- A file, document, or spreadsheet
- An application
- Part of an application
- Part of a system, database, or bigger platform

For example, as you'll read in Chapter 3, your organization most likely has many integration repositories (IRs). In a typical company, there are considerably more integrations than a single metadata repository alone can describe and perform. This is due to technical, organizational, and even logical reasons, as elaborated upon in Chapter 3. Therefore, integrations are typically maintained in a combination of spreadsheets and as parts of applications that build data pipelines. And that's totally fine, at least in the beginning. What your company needs to do is to gather an overview of these repositories and carefully coordinate them. That's what we'll dive into in this book.

Structure: The Metamodel in Metadata Repositories

Metadata repositories (indeed, software in general) come with a metamodel. A *metamodel* is a high-level architecture that depicts the contents of the metadata repository. Figure 2-5 is an example of a metamodel for the EAM tool that I'll discuss in Chapter 3.[7]

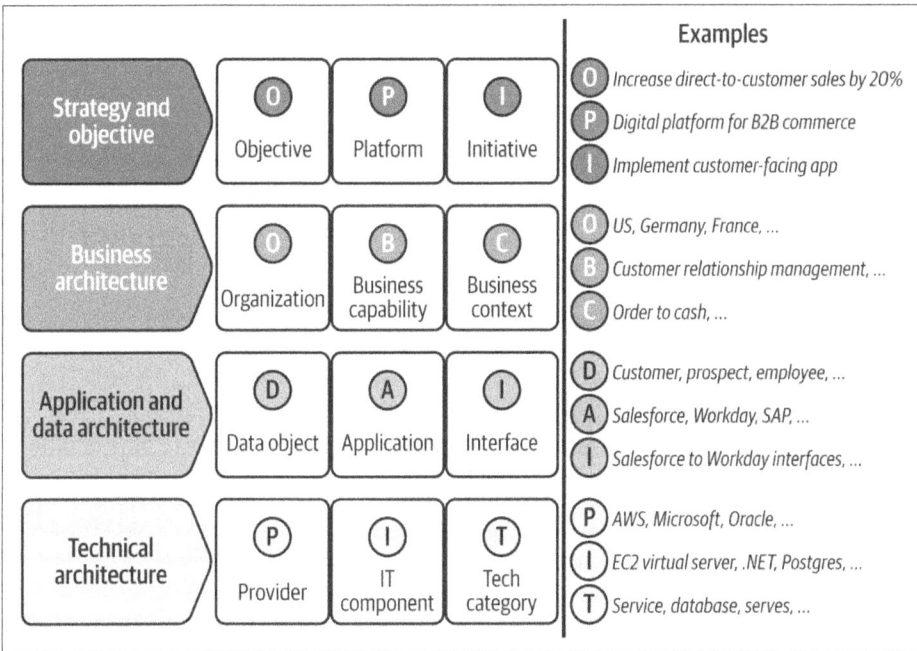

Figure 2-5. *The metamodel of an EAM tool*

As you can see, the EAM tool lists a variety of elements from the IT landscape, such as applications and capabilities. Several metadata repositories depict the same thing, and this can be discovered by carefully studying the metamodels of the metadata repositories.

---

7 The particular metamodel in Figure 2-5 is inspired by the metamodel in LeanIX (*https://oreil.ly/Cnu3f*).

For comparison, in Figure 2-6, you can see a metamodel of a CMDB that I'll also discuss in Chapter 3.[8]

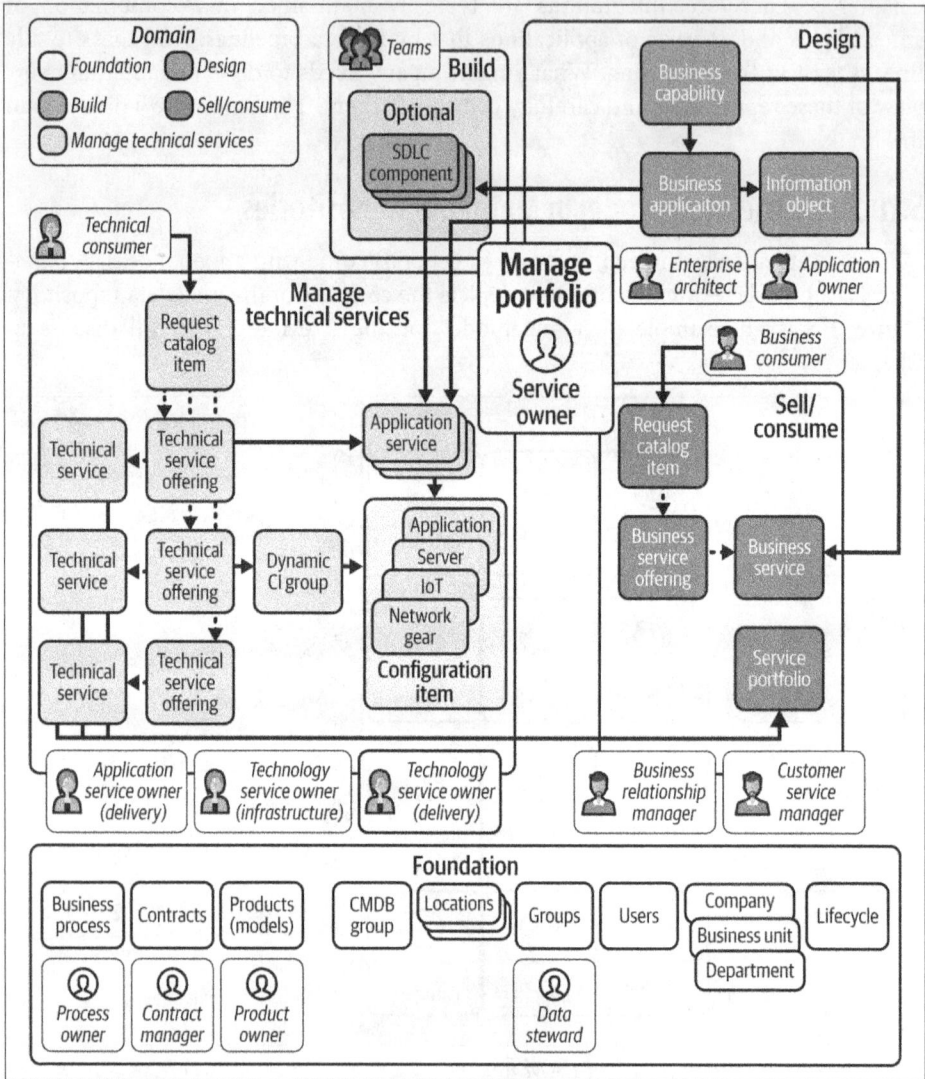

Figure 2-6. The metamodel of a CMDB tool

As you can see, the CMDB (like the EAM tool previously mentioned) lists applications and capabilities. There are even more overlaps, and some of them are subtle: is

---

8 The particular metamodel in Figure 2-6 is inspired by the metamodel in ServiceNow (*https://oreil.ly/CkCiE*) and the related ebook (*https://oreil.ly/YrClX*).

the "tech category" in the EAM tool, for example, similar to the "technical service offering" in the CMDB? Are the "data object" and "information object" likewise similar? These metadata repositories are potentially stretching their functionality out of their core capabilities and thereby touching metadata artifacts that may or may not be managed in another domain and repository. Without addressing and responding to these questions, companies create multiple truths about their IT landscapes. (I'll discuss this further in Part II.) This creates a situation where conflicting single sources of truth undermine the ability to understand a company's IT landscape.

Imagine that your company has not only an EAM tool and a CMDB but also 10 or 20 metadata repositories focused on depicting the IT landscape. Coordinating them is what this book is all about.

The following metadata types are most commonly depicted in metadata repositories:

- Application
- Integration (data lineage)
- Data
- Process

- Capability
- Person
- Organization
- Cost

You shouldn't aim to exclude these elements from being present across or in your company's various metadata repositories. They will not exist in only one repository. It would not only be counterintuitive, since these elements need to be represented in the multiple metadata repositories, but in fact, it would be impossible. This is the essence: you look at the same thing with different metadata repositories, but you look at it differently, with a distinctly unique focus for each metadata repository to carry out a specific task.

To understand the nature of this task, we need to take into account the underlying methodology at play when working with metamodels, as described in *Metamodelling for Software Engineering*:

> The subject of metamodelling is models; in other words, the input and output artifacts of a metamodelling job are "made of the same stuff", i.e. they are of the same *type*. This gives metamodelling a recursive nature that makes it much more complex than other modelling areas in which the subject being modelled is of a different nature.[9]

This means that, in the context of the EAM tool and the CMDB mentioned before, we cannot apply the *recursive* activity in isolation. Teams across the organization need

---

9 Cesar Gonzalez-Perez and Brian Henderson-Sellers, *Metamodelling for Software Engineering*, Chapter 1 (Wiley, 2008).

to have a firmly coordinated way of understanding the IT landscape. A team cannot just gather and specify a metamodel alone by declaring, "These are our company processes, these are our data types, these are our applications." No team can do that alone because this is a fundamentally *recursive* activity. It refers back to a reality that is commonly shared and practiced across the company, and specifying a metamodel in one metadata repository by one team will never alter that reality; it will only add a new layer of confusion.

Instead, to really harness the power of metadata repositories and gain a more complete understanding of your IT landscape, you need to coordinate metadata repositories, and this book teaches you how to do that.

> Certain software vendors and frameworks promote their metamodels as universal, as if they are fit for all purposes.[10] That is never the case.

Summary

In this chapter, I introduced you to metadata and metadata repositories. While this might seem straightforward at first glance, the reality is that it can be quite complex, especially for business teams managing these repositories. Often, these teams may not realize the need for alignment, leading to metadata repositories that are easily implemented but provide minimal insight into the actual IT landscape. This opening chapter of Part I has aimed to help you organize your understanding of metadata repositories, with a particular focus on learning that:

- Metadata about the IT landscape is located both in the source it describes and in a metadata repository.
- Metadata repositories have a driver, a structure, a place, and a purpose.
- The driver is either innovation, operations, or regulations, but these can overlap:
  — The waves of innovation are known as the *modern data stack*, and the metadata repositories document the movement and change of data within the modern data stack.
  — The waves of operations are focused on the various parts of the IT landscape. Look at these parts in isolation. These can be servers, laptops, and integrations.
  — The waves of regulations imply an interpretation of the IT landscape to work.

---

10 The Open Group, "Content Core Metamodel," in *The TOGAF Standard*, 10th ed. (Van Haren Publishing, 2022).

- The structure is the metamodel of the metadata repository:
  - Having multiple metadata repositories that depict the same information is not necessarily a problem.
  - This can be identified when studying the metamodels.
- The place is simply where the metadata repository is located. This can be a file, an application, a part of an application, or a platform.
- The purpose is the core capability:
  - All metadata repositories have core, peripheral, and external capabilities.
  - The core capability of a metadata repository must be understood and used.
  - Using metadata repositories only for peripheral and external capabilities will fail.

For all these reasons, metadata repositories should be considered holistically and should be coordinated.

CHAPTER 3

IT Management

In this chapter, we will run through the classical systems that an IT department uses to manage an IT landscape in a company. If you are working in data management, some of these systems may not be on your radar—but they should! As you will discover, these operational systems are really sources of gold when it comes to metadata about the IT landscape.

The chapter is structured such that we begin with the most basic, everyday metadata repositories for operations and then gradually move toward more high-level, strategic metadata repositories. The journey goes through the following repositories:

- Endpoint management system (EMS)
- Integration repository (IR)
- Asset management system (AMS)
- Configuration management database (CMDB)
- IT service management (ITSM) system
- Enterprise architecture management (EAM) tool

So lean back and explore!

Endpoint Management System

The EMS lists the servers, desktops, and mobile devices in a company. Yes, every single one—all the servers, all the desktops, all the mobile devices. It also lists all applications installed on each and every one of these devices. The purpose of the EMS is not only to list these applications but also to be able to install them on the intended device when instructed to do so.

Think of your first day at work. You're handed a laptop and a phone. On them are not only the usual applications but company-specific applications as well. These have been installed by the EMS.

> Depending on the security setup in your company, you may be able to install applications on your laptop and phone yourself. From a security point of view, this is not ideal because there have been no assessments of the applications by a centralized security team. The applications may be malware, intended to do espionage or cause damage to your company.

The EMS is a fairly simple and big metadata repository that entails a lot of practical maintenance. The point of the EMS is to have a tangible overview of:

- Technical infrastructure
- Applications on that technical infrastructure

The technical infrastructure comprises:

- Servers, including naming standards and locations
- Desktops, including names and versions
- Mobile devices, including names and versions

Applications located on the technical infrastructure include:

- All applications placed on all servers
- All applications placed on all desktops

This means that you should be able to search and retrieve every single device in your company in the EMS and see exactly what applications are installed on that specific device. You should also be able to search and retrieve every single on-premises or cloud server in your EMS.

Think of the EMS as having two categories: on premises and in the cloud. The EMS typically comes in these two versions, and they don't blend. For Microsoft Azure at the time of the writing of this book, Microsoft Endpoint Configuration Management (MECM)[1] is the on-prem solution and Intune is the cloud equivalent.

Figure 3-1 gives a bird's-eye view of the core capability of an EMS.

---

[1] An even deeper repository to supplement SCCM is the System Center Operations Manager (SCOM) (*https://oreil.ly/qXn77*).

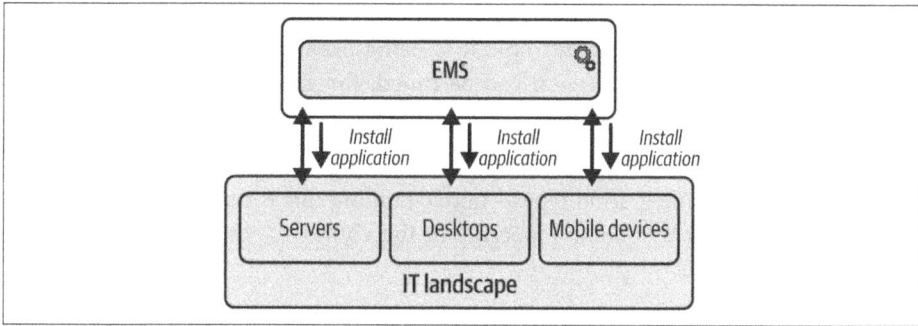

Figure 3-1. Core capability of an EMS

The EMS is mainly a tool used in the context of operations. It allows for client applications to be installed on desktops and devices once they are installed on servers (creating a layer of metadata that must be understood by the users of the EMS).

In Figure 3-2, you can see a metamodel of an EMS.[2]

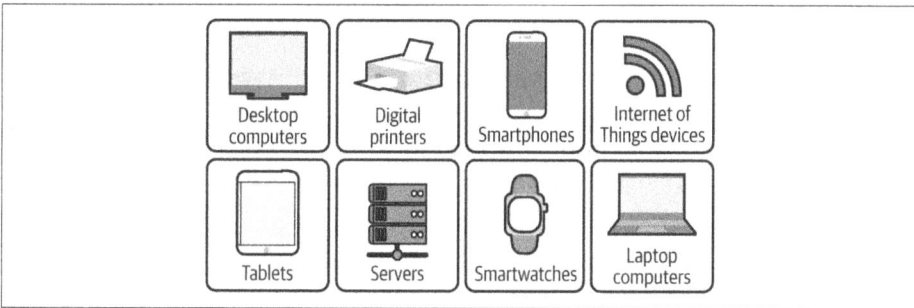

Figure 3-2. A metamodel of an EMS

Integration Repository

IRs do not focus on specific devices like the EMS does; instead, the IR lists applications and IT infrastructure and how they are integrated. But like the EMS, the IR is built to perform certain actions; it designs, tests, and executes integrations.

> Some IRs are located inside platforms dedicated to performing integrations, which are known as *integration platform as a service* (IPaaS).

---

2 This metamodel is inspired by SentinelOne (*https://sentinelone.com*)'s "What Is Endpoint Management?" (*https://oreil.ly/uEi8V*).

The IR describes the nature of the integration between two applications, in regard to what data is being exchanged and how it is being exchanged. This is described in documents stored in the IR, which can be called, for example, *data sharing agreements*, *integrations*, or *data contracts*. (For the latter, refer to the later discussion in this section.)

Let's dive a little into integration types—understanding this is crucial for grasping the overarching theme of this book, especially in the context of this chapter. There are three ways to integrate:

Batch
Batches are scheduled tasks to move large numbers of files or a lot of data from one place to another. Typically, these tasks are performed by only one team in a company, and they are overburdened because batch integration is an old integration pattern that works with on-premises technology and has been doing so for years. The advantage of batches is size: you can move a lot of data easily this way, but only when the scheduled job has gone through, meaning that you have to wait for the data to arrive.

API
API stands for *application programming interface* and is web-based communication, serving as points of exchange between applications, or a call (you can think of it as a "phone call"). Performing this requires a modern, cloud-based application. The advantage of APIs is that they can be performed faster and more easily than batches when you need data from a given source.

Stream(ing message)
This is also a modern integration pattern, but rather than exchanges as with APIs, streaming is like "leaving the mics on"—meaning that, whenever something happens, you will know instantaneously.[3] This is why streaming is also referred to as *real time*.

> Balancing the economic and technical pros and cons of batch, API, and stream is the key to data mesh and scalable data architectures—and integration architectures in general. You can read more about these topics in *Data Management at Scale*, 2nd edition, by Piethein Strengholt (O'Reilly).

At a very high level, your IRs document integrations between applications. Depending on the complexity of the integration, the repository is also the tool that executes

---

3 While this is the goal, it is not necessarily the case. Messages can get backed up in queues, consumers may fall behind, and so on.

the integration. Figure 3-3 illustrates the core capability of an IR and how IRs interact with your IT landscape.

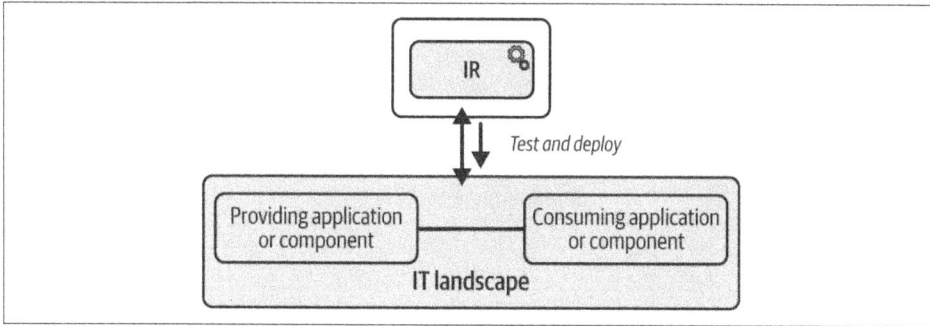

Figure 3-3. Core capability of an IR

Contrary to most other metadata repositories, it is very unlikely that you have only *one* IR. Performing integration is not the job of *one* team—the easiest scenario would be that only one data engineering team did integrations, but the reality is that's not the case.

Rather, every department in a relatively big enterprise of at least a few thousand employees has one or even multiple data engineering teams. Each of these teams will be coding data pipelines using relatively complex programming languages and specialized software, such as mathematical data warehouse services, which also serve as metadata repositories by listing the data pipelines they are performing. This reality of multiple data teams and technologies implies that there is a very large number of components in the IT landscape performing integrations and, at the same time, serving as the metadata repositories for these integrations. This creates a complexity that is, in many cases, unmanageably high.

Certain tech vendors or consultancies make it a selling point to reduce this complexity with tooling or methodological approaches. And while you can definitely reduce the complexity of integration architecture, you simply have to accept the nature of integrations as dizzying and confusing when trying to get a complete picture of them at enterprise scale.

In Parts II and III of this book, we'll see how the data discovery team will be able to reduce the complexity of the integration architecture in the enterprise.

The refining and automation of IRs has been coined *data contracts*. Although this concept is old and was used to describe integration agreements stored in IRs for decades, data contracts went through a hype cycle during the first half of the 2020s and are finding renewed, deserved relevance. A valuable source of information about data contracts is Andrew Jones's *Driving Data Quality with Data Contracts* (Packt Publishing).

Figure 3-4 illustrates the reality of integrations in most enterprises: multiple IRs orchestrate what is known as *spaghetti architecture*, meaning an opaque totality of integrations.

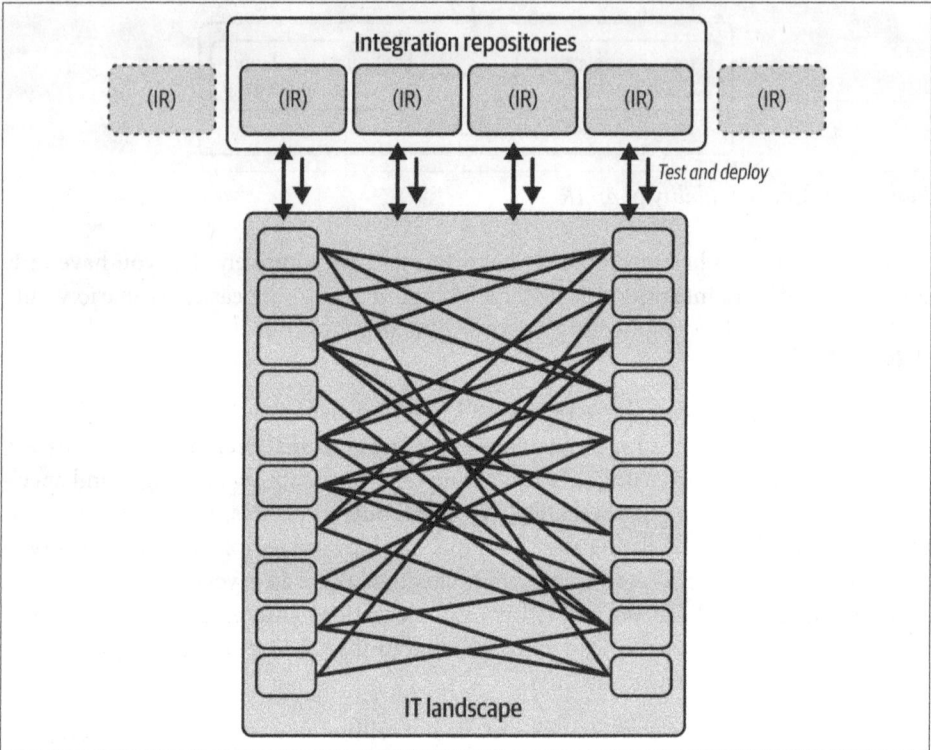

Figure 3-4. Spaghetti: the reality of integration architecture and its metadata repositories

> The IRs in Figure 3-4 do not depict an integration platform or several integration platforms.

The IR is a tool used for IT operations—it lets you understand which applications are connected. The metamodel of an IR is shown in Figure 3-5.[4]

---

4 This metamodel is inspired by SAP's integration framework, ISA-M (*https://oreil.ly/32_pJ*).

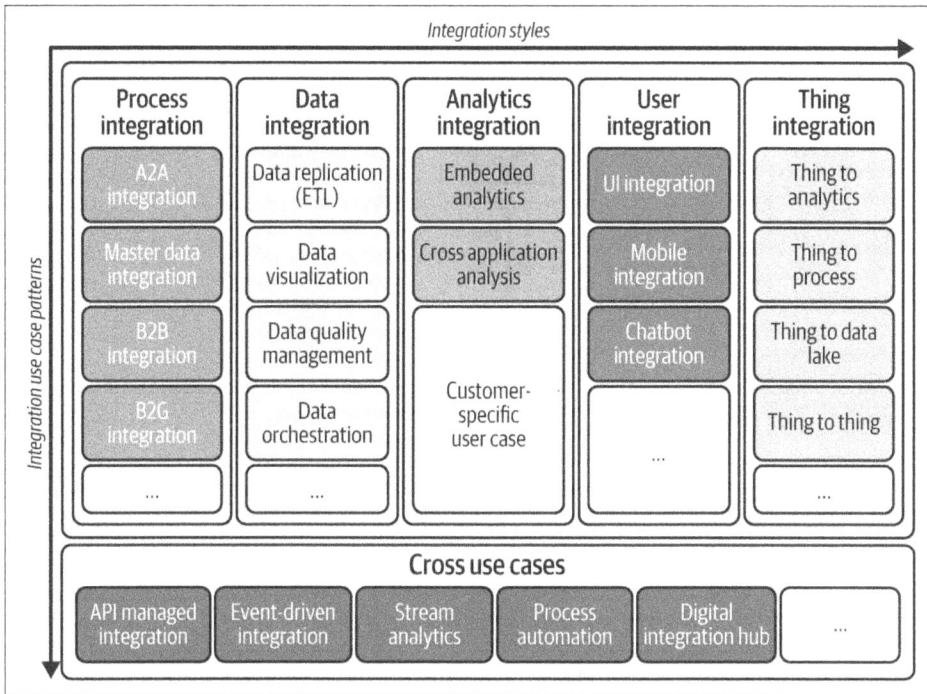

Figure 3-5. A metamodel of an IR

There are several other metadata repositories that help you improve your overview of integrations. We will discuss one of them next.

Asset Management System

An AMS is used to control the cost of an IT landscape. Typically, the AMS is also used for cost-reduction purposes. AMSs are applied reactively to understand exactly how many instances of a given software application are installed on what devices and servers and if they are actually used.

AMS resembles EMS—the main difference is that an EMS is applied proactively whereas the AMS is applied reactively. An organization is also likely to have several EMSs placed in various geographical locations or used only by distinct companies within the larger company. The EMS is also maintained manually whereas the AMS is an enormous network scan that creates a database of metadata about the IT landscape.

Furthermore, a real AMS is a more elaborate tool than an EMS. The AMS reaches out to all cloud and on-premises technology and measures the number of software licenses and the active use of those licenses, without being restrained by a focus on client applications like the EMS is. You can see an illustration of the core capability of an AMS in Figure 3-6.

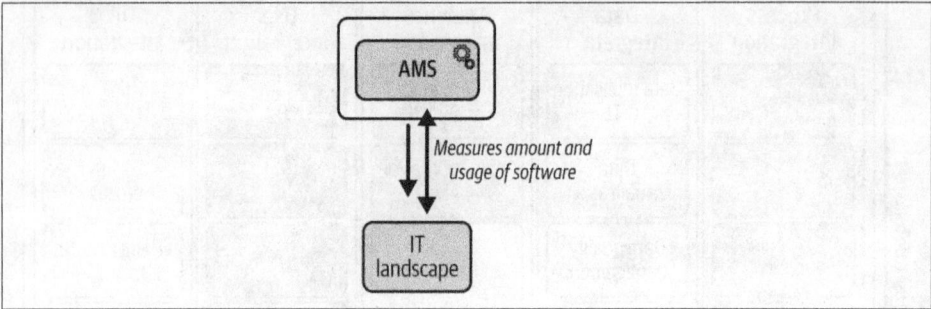

Figure 3-6. Core capability of an AMS

The AMS is used to calculate costs and as such is used for operations. Figure 3-7 shows the metamodel of an AMS.[5]

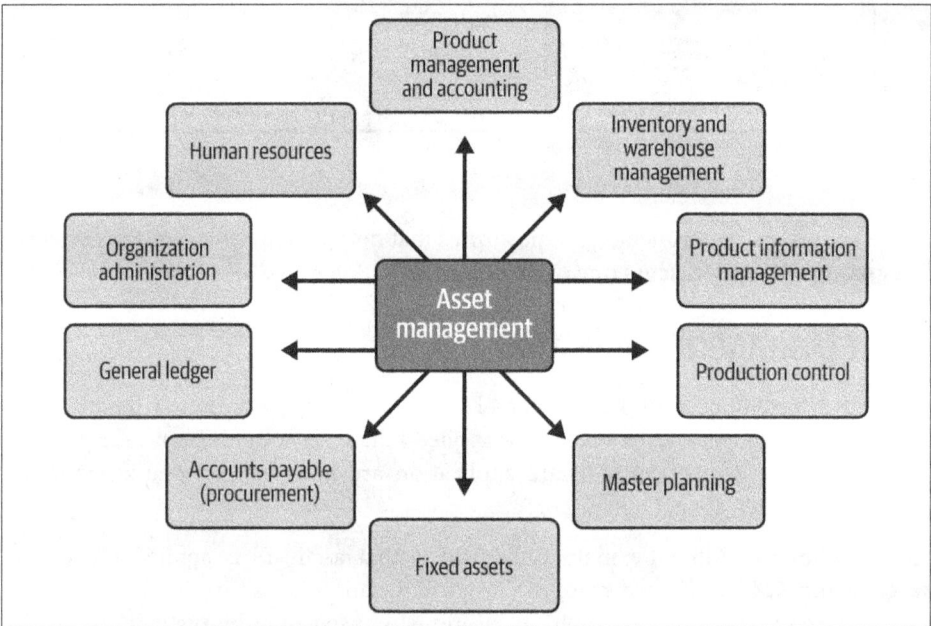

Figure 3-7. A metamodel of an AMS

---

5 This metamodel is inspired by Velosi's "The Quick Guide to Your Asset Management System" (*https://oreil.ly/3KkiT*).

Configuration Management Database

The CMDB's role is to correctly depict the past and present of your IT landscape. The CMDB depicts software and hardware at the *instance* level, meaning not only the types but also the number of each kind of software and hardware.

Software is about listing the various applications in the IT landscape along with how many instances exist of that specific application in the company. For example, Tableau is an application, and the company has four different instances of Tableau, meaning four identical applications with different owners and different content. The CMDB would furthermore list the purpose of the software, what type of data it contains, the owners of the software, how the various applications integrate with one another, and how they have been changed.

Hardware encompasses the types and amounts of your company's servers (on premises), their exact names and numbers, and other hardware devices, such as laptops and Internet of Things (IoT) devices. However, you will not find a complete list of what types of client applications are installed on which devices; that is the role of the EMS.

For each type of hardware and software (and for each instance of each software application), the current configuration is documented. Therefore, each item in the CMDB is known as a *configuration item* (CI). *Configuration* refers to how the software is set up in terms of:

- Purpose (capability)
- Owners
- Activated modules

- Integrations
- Types of data
- Level of confidentiality

Furthermore, changes of configurations are logged, so past configurations are also readable in the CMDB. As such, the CMDB is not only a picture of your present IT landscape but, ideally, also the entire past of your IT landscape.

In Figure 3-8, you can see the core capability of a CMDB.

> In highly regulated industries, the CMDB often serves as the source of truth when answering questions from the authorities about the present IT landscape.

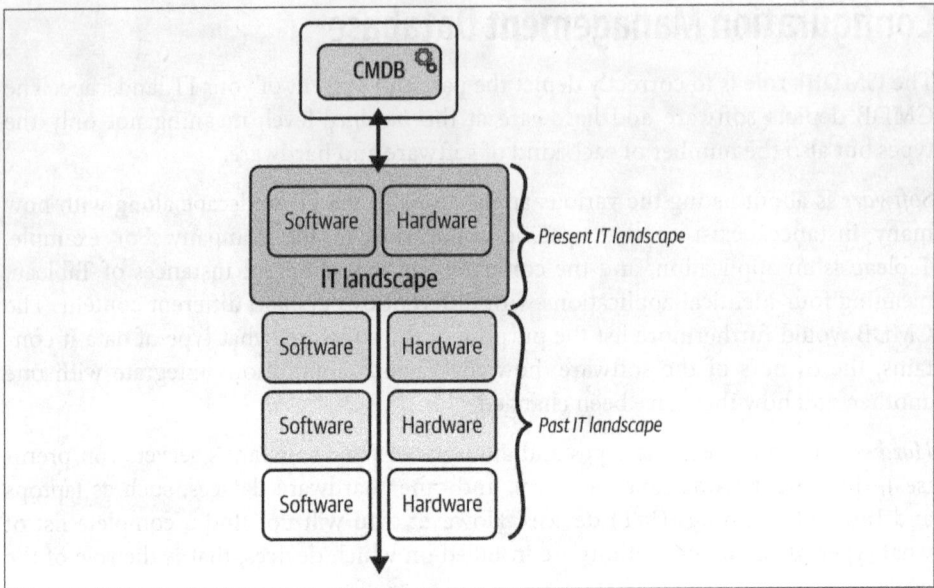

Figure 3-8. Core capability of a CMDB

CMDBs usually adhere to the Information Technology Infrastructure Library (ITIL) framework, which you should think of as a methodology for delivering IT services to the business. Accordingly, when an IT solution is introduced, changed, or taken out of service, ITIL proposes a framework to carry out the operational tasks in connection with these changes in the exact same way each time. This ensures useful, easy-to-understand IT operations and transparency regarding what has happened in the past.

> Modern software engineering is performed with the fail-fast methodology *DevOps*, which suggests frequent daily releases for end-user software as an ultra-sensible response to customer needs. DevOps follows the saying "It ain't tested before it crashes in production," thus favoring the experimental over the secure. Because DevOps is modern and fun, some software engineers despise ITIL, which is considered slow, clunky, and old. And indeed, it is from the on-premises era. But all methodologies have their place. ITIL is often used in software production with highly complicated hardware that simply can't risk a crash in production. When the Ariane 501 (*https://oreil.ly/Eqo06*) space flight exploded 37 seconds after launching on June 4, 1996, due to a single line of code, a sloppy methodology was at play. That is why rigorous methodology such as ITIL is needed. Not everything should crash in production.

The CMDB is used to maintain the existing IT landscape, and as such, it is used for operations, as shown in Figure 3-9.[6]

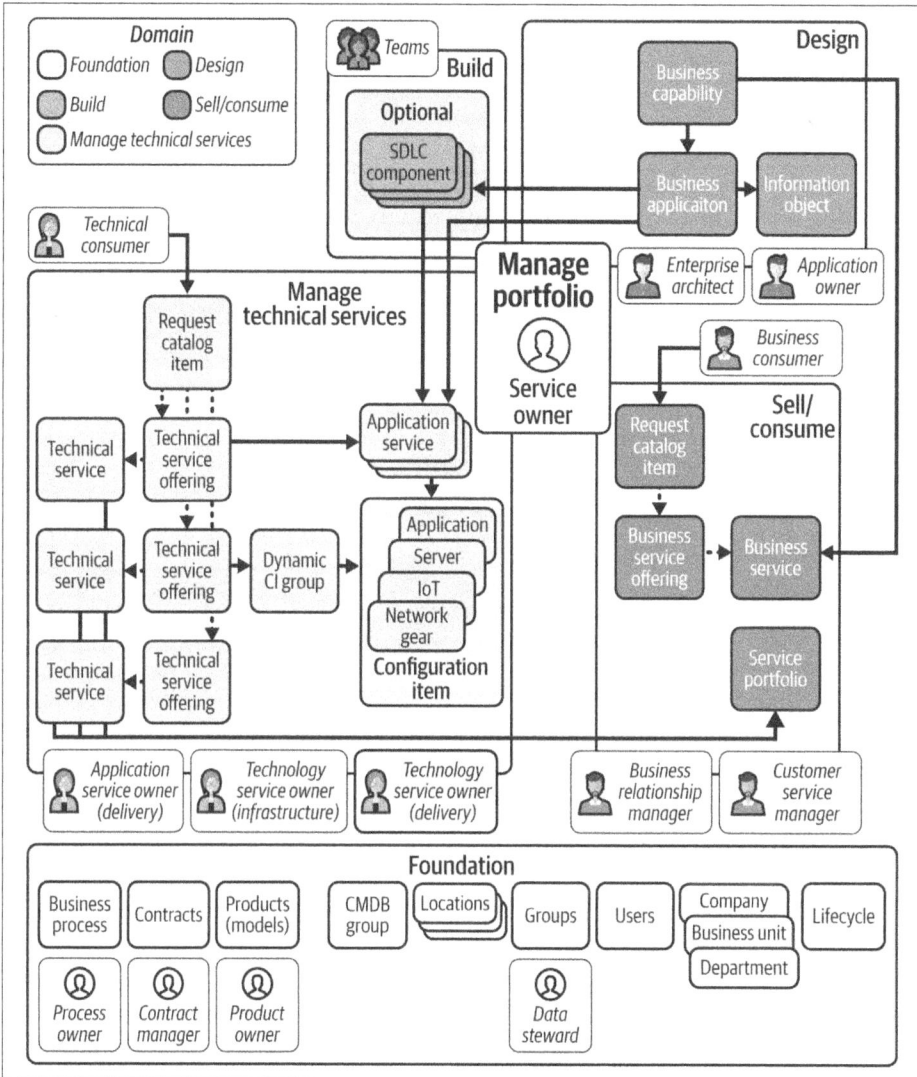

Figure 3-9. A metamodel of a CMDB

---

6 Many companies are developing applications based on CMDBs, resulting in numerous custom versions that showcase far more than what is presented here. This particular metamodel is inspired by the metamodel in ServiceNow (*https://oreil.ly/0Ynqz*) and the accompanying ebook (*https://oreil.ly/AYp2e*).

IT Service Management System

The ITSM system is a large suite of components that focuses on managing the existing IT landscape. It typically centers on a CMDB as the core component. As such, the ITSM system should be considered a CMDB metadata repository with included peripheral capabilities.

The most important feature of the ITSM system is the helpdesk. The *helpdesk* is a place where every employee in a company can ask for access to applications, report if something is malfunctioning in a given application, communicate that an application is to be taken out, and much more. All of this communication is done via a ticketing system. Therefore, the core of an ITSM system is a helpdesk application that sits on top of a CMDB to handle demands from the business, as illustrated in Figure 3-10.

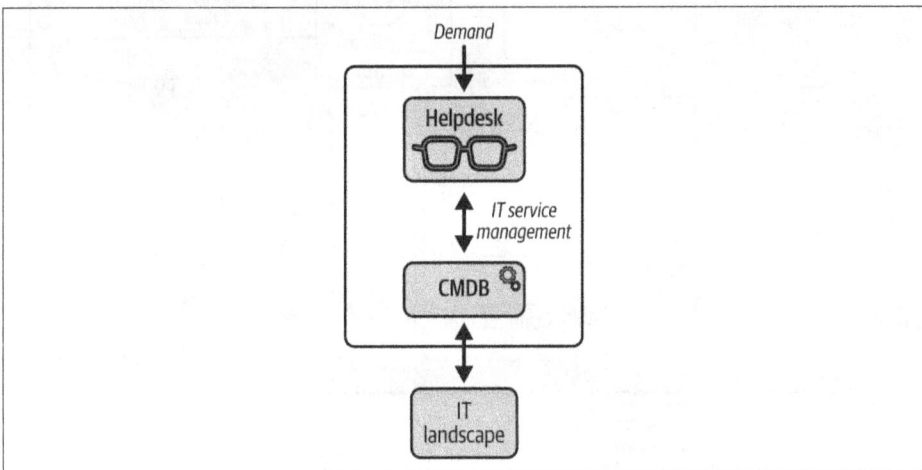

Figure 3-10. High-level view of an ITSM system

ITSM systems are typically well-established metadata repositories. They are not difficult to understand or defend, and therefore, their existence is accepted and not challenged. It's about maintaining an operational IT landscape in the present—every company should have that.

This is far from a blessing for ITSM systems, though. They are often overburdened and pushed to deliver on peripheral capabilities, such as cost, integrations, data ownership, privacy, and confidentiality. They cannot really deliver on these capabilities because they are, for the most part, manually populated and maintained, which is too slow and therefore unscalable in the case of the AMS and the IR (but not necessarily the EAM tool).

The metadata of the ITSM overlap with the repositories of information and knowledge when it comes to handling privacy, sensitivity, and enterprise knowledge.

A number of ITSM systems on the market also just sell their services as a CMDB. The ITSM system is used for IT operations, and the metamodel is identical to the CMDB's metamodel.

Now, let's take a look at the most abstract, strategic, and future-oriented tool in this chapter.

Enterprise Architecture Management Tool

The EAM tool is the most high-level and strategic tool for performing IT management. It is intended for strategic decision making about the *future state* of an IT landscape, not the *current state* of the IT landscape. Therefore, the EAM tool is your way to look into the future—and you can imagine that this requires solid, high-quality metadata.

You must keep in mind that the EAM tool should not maintain the current state of the IT landscape. It's just not intended to maintain that overview—or even to make decisions about its current configuration. Accordingly, the EAM tool relies on other metadata repositories to account for the current state of the IT landscape, typically the ITSM system, the CMDB, the information security management system (ISMS), and the privacy information management system (PIMS); we'll delve into these last two further in Chapter 5. The EAM tool must be aligned with these repositories and reflect them without containing the same level of detail that they do and without taking over their responsibilities; it looks into the future and only that. It does not and should not maintain the current IT landscape.

If you try to force the EAM tool to be the metadata repository that *maintains* the overview of your current IT landscape as well as the tool for making decisions about your current IT landscape, you push it toward external capabilities rather than its intended scope. The EAM tool will deliver poorly on those capabilities (see Table 7-1).

As its name indicates, the EAM tool is intended to perform enterprise architecture. Enterprise architecture is the IT architectural discipline that demands the most experience. Therefore, companies rarely have employed many enterprise architects since they are scarce.

Ideally, enterprise architecture is not a discipline performed only by enterprise architects but merely facilitated by them. Enterprise architecture is to be performed by everyone working with IT, from the IT operations architects to strategic leaders in the IT department all the way up to the chief information officer (CIO). The scope of stakeholders may expand outside the IT department, but it is typically limited to people with a relatively deep technical understanding.

Enterprise architecture is a discipline that ensures a fit, functional, and economically rational IT landscape. To deliver on that purpose, the heart of the EAM tool is the capability map. A *capability* consists of people, processes, and technologies that together deliver a distinct set of capabilities. Everything that a company is capable of doing is the core metadata of the EAM tool and should be listed as capabilities. EAM tools are also structured or contextualized to the many frameworks that enterprise architecture as a discipline is performed via TOGAF (The Open Group Architecture Framework).

The entire purpose of the EAM tool is to manage a company's capabilities when looking into the future and to be able to answer questions like the following:

- What will be the consequences of replacing our current CRM system with this CRM system?
- What are our on-premises dependencies, and how would they affect a cloud migration?
- Why do we have three applications delivering on the same capability, which ones could we most easily descope technically, and what would be the economic benefit?

To answer these types of questions about the future state of the IT landscape, many types of metadata are necessary, such as lists of applications, integrations, components, projects, costs, strategies, technology categories, people, roles, teams, and departments within the company. These are mirrored in the EAM tool from many other metadata repositories where the metadata is maintained.

In Figure 3-11, you can see the core capability of an EAM tool.

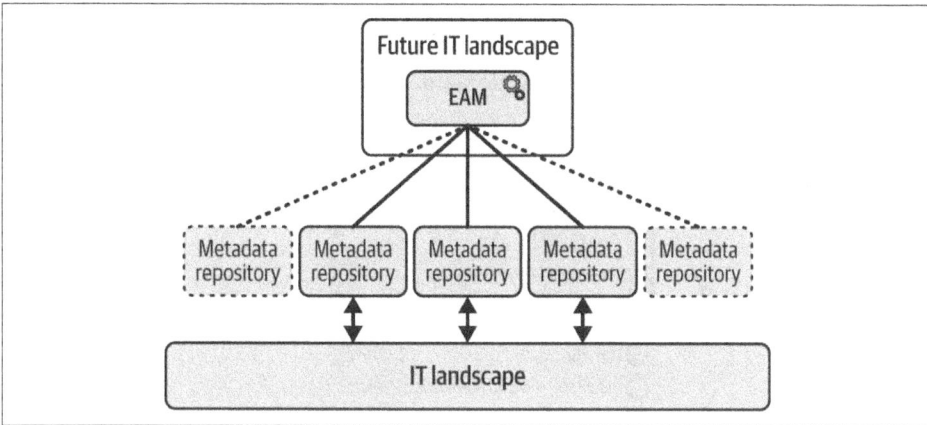

Figure 3-11. Core capability of an EAM tool

As you can see, the EAM tool is the source of truth about the future IT landscape based on knowledge about the present IT landscape, which is maintained in other metadata repositories—one of which is the CMDB. The EAM tool is used to depict the future of the IT landscape, and as such, it is a strategic tool for IT operations. Figure 3-12 shows the metamodel of an EAM tool.[7]

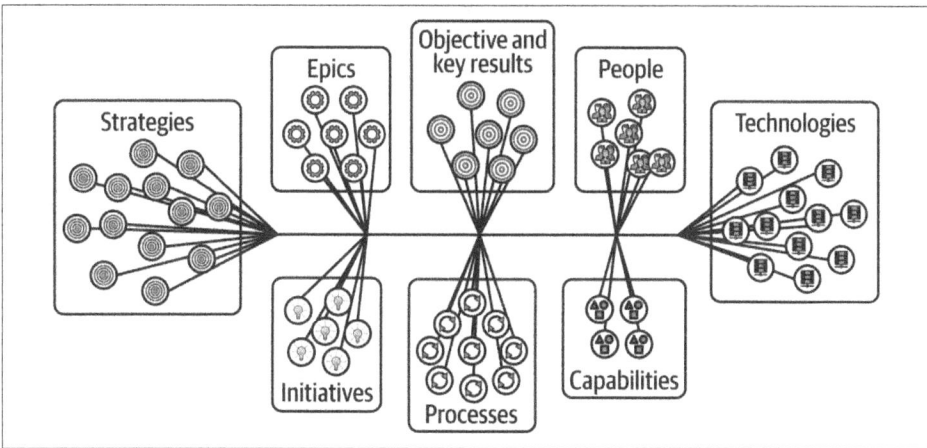

Figure 3-12. A metamodel of an EAM tool

---

7 This metamodel is inspired by the Ardoq article "Your Holistic View of People, Processes, and Technology" (*https://ardoq.com/features*).

Metadata Repositories for IT Management

You can see the entire IT management domain, complete with its core capabilities, in Figure 3-13.

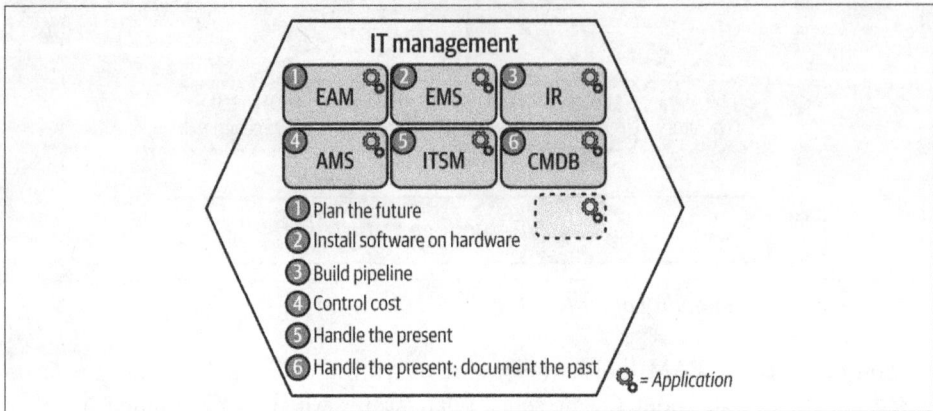

Figure 3-13. Metadata repositories for IT management

The EAM tool is designed to look into the future and show the consequences of changes to the IT landscape. In doing so, it depends on a fresh, well-maintained depiction of the current IT landscape, which it does not deliver itself—it relies on other metadata repositories to deliver that to it.

The ITSM system is a solution with the core focus of maintaining the present IT landscape documented mainly through a CMDB, combined with a helpdesk function. In doing so, it also documents the (near past) IT landscape. The ITSM system can hold an EAM tool as well as an AMS and IR.

The CMDB is focused on listing not only the hardware and software but also the amounts of all kinds of hardware, instances of software, and licenses. As such, the CMDB is an abstract, manually maintained picture of the present (and past) IT landscape.

The AMS is closer to the physical reality of the IT landscape and is applied retrospectively, after a disaster has happened. The AMS scans the reality of the IT landscape to effectively calculate usage and cost in order to reduce the cost.

The IR is not really one repository but a conglomerate of lists in tools that execute data pipelines or simpler batch jobs. However, it depicts physical reality and is able to provide guidance on how data flows through the IT landscape.

The EMS tool is used to document software installed on servers and client applications on laptops and smartphones. As such, it is closely linked to the CMDB since it enforces the statements provided by the CMDB.

Summary

In this chapter we have looked at metadata repositories for IT management data. Here are the takeaways:

- As a whole, metadata repositories for IT are to be understood as the key to managing your IT landscape.
- Used correctly, IT metadata repositories can help you plan the future of your IT landscape perfectly, mainly through the EAM tool.
- The present of the IT landscape can be managed through IT metadata repositories, mainly via the CMDB, embedded in an ITSM system.
- Likewise, the past of the IT landscape can be managed via the CMDB.
- AMSs and IRs are metadata repositories that look at costs and integrations at the physical level in the IT landscape.
- Finally, the EMS lists all software installed on all hardware—ideally!
- Ideals are great, but the reality is that most of the metadata repositories discussed in this chapter are usually poorly managed because of a lack of understanding and support by upper management.
- Metadata repositories often collide and overlap because they describe the same reality from different angles.

In the next chapter, we will take a closer look at metadata repositories for data.

CHAPTER 4

Data Management

In this chapter, we will look at the metadata repositories for data management.

As you will notice, this chapter is short. It describes data catalogs and database modeling tools as unique metadata repositories. Following these two repositories, we will look at a handful of technologies that support various aspects of data management, including data engineering and science. These are not metadata repositories as such but can still be thought of as containing crucial metadata that is relevant for the overall topic of this book. This detail is important to remember as you read the chapter.

In sum, the metadata repositories covered in this chapter are:

- Data catalogs (DCs)
- Database model management (DBM)
- Other metadata repositories for data management

Ready? Here we go!

Data Catalog

The DC is like a search engine for data in your company.[1] Some metadata repositories, such as the CMDB discussed in the previous chapter or the ISMS discussed in the next chapter, make generic and rather abstract lists of the data that is assumed to be in the IT landscape. That's not the case with the DC, which shows you the data that actually is in your IT landscape.

---

1 The *data dictionary* is a basic tool that specifies the types of data you have at a generic level, typically by listing the field name and providing a description of the kind of data the field contains. For a deeper explanation, see my book *The Enterprise Data Catalog*.

The DC depicts the data in your IT landscape at a metadata layer by either crawling or streaming metadata from the data sources in the IT landscape into the DC. It therefore has a physical connection to what it depicts, as you can see in the diagram of the core capability of a DC in Figure 4-1.

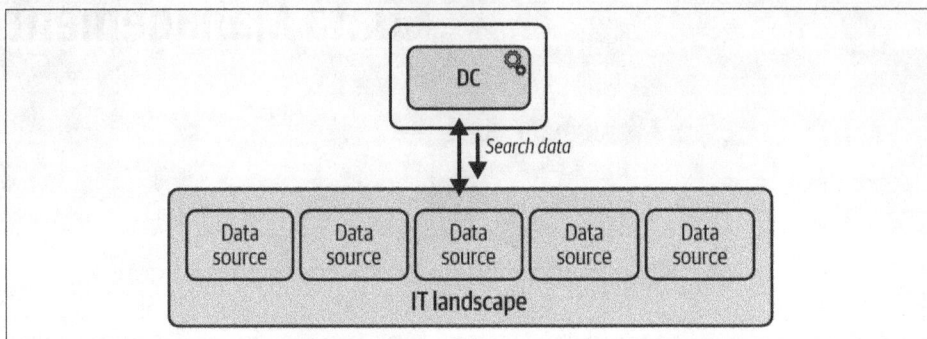

Figure 4-1. The core capability of a DC

The potential of this metadata repository is promising as it is a cornerstone to data-driven innovation. Netflix, Facebook, Amazon, LinkedIn, and many other tech giants achieved their success with the DC as a vital component. It gives the necessary overview and search capability for an IT landscape with immense amounts of data in it.

DCs are also useful for governance purposes, such as detecting and labeling sensitive data about specific individuals that is subject to GDPR. Furthermore, DCs have the benefit of depicting pipelines and other integrations at the physical level.

> If you are curious about DCs, check out my book *The Enterprise Data Catalog*, which explains how to organize all your company data so that you can search it later. DCs are really powerful, but only if you truly understand them. My book contains a secret key to unlock DCs: the learnings from LIS (I have a PhD in the field). The problem with DCs is that they are conceived by software engineers, but to really work, they need to be curated with the mindset of librarians. That's what I explain in the book, which is still being read all over the world.

DCs are tricky—implementing them often fails. Many DCs are built on a technology that is not fit for the purpose, meaning that they are too complex and not strong enough at the same time. They are difficult to organize data in, and they are not good enough at retrieving that data for you, even if you succeed with organizing it correctly. As you should think of the DC as a search engine, consider that it should also ideally be built on the same type of technology—namely, a knowledge graph. This will allow you to easily organize your data and search for it again with great power. AI is adding many capabilities to the mix: natural language search/conversational search and the usage of ontological context for agentic AI (see Part III).

The DC is mainly a tool used for innovation based on data. However, it has cross-functional potential and can be used for regulation and IT operations as well, depending on the use cases.

The metamodel of a DC should be flexible so that it can expand in all directions. Even though it is flexible, it is likely to come with a preconfigured minimalistic meta-model, like the one in Figure 4-2.[2]

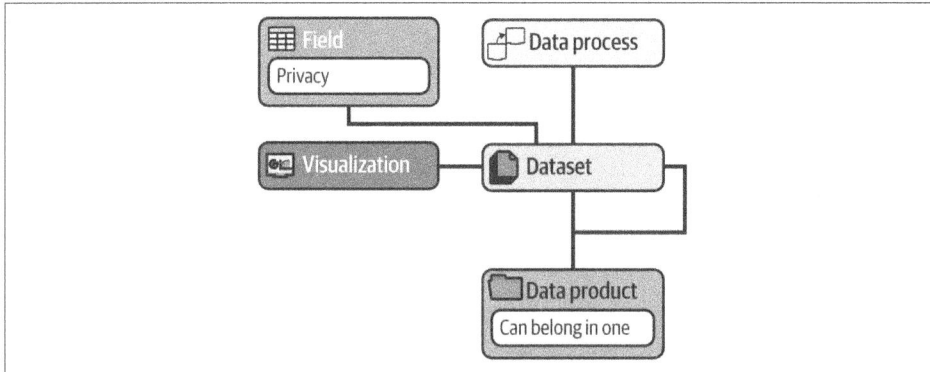

Figure 4-2. An example of a minimal, flexible metamodel for a DC

In this metamodel, *visualizations* refer to analytical reports, *fields* are sensitive data in tables, *data processes* are integrations of various sorts, and *data products* are data made consumable. Finally, the *dataset* is a table. The important thing to note here is that metamodels for DCs should not be big and complicated.

Database Model Management

Many metadata repositories have specific modules that allow you to create and store diagrams—as a drawing, for instance. However, these diagrams are not linked to a physical, technological reality. They are assumptions made by the person who created the diagrams (likely a data architect). Such diagrams are found in EAM tools and CMDBs, for example. Some EAM tools allow for *evidence-based modeling*—a function that enables models to be based on the existing metadata that is already registered. This is a nice functionality and a step away from purely assumption-based modeling. However, you can go even deeper.

---

2 This metamodel is inspired by the DC in the Actian Data Intelligence Platform (*https://oreil.ly/Gi88R*).

DBM tools offer a fact-based, empirical alternative to these modeling assumptions. DBM tools can read the structure of a database by analyzing its query language and then can create a visual data model on that basis. Furthermore, such tools can allow you to create new queries visually by modeling them as point-and-click actions instead of writing them using the keyboard in database query language. Keep in mind that a DBM tool will have a narrow scope, such as focusing on SQL only—they are not for enterprise-wide usage across all technologies. This is also why they are a key component in this book: they offer a picture of a subset of the IT landscape, which is useful knowledge for the entire company, not just for the database administrators and engineers using the DBM!

You can see the core capability of a DBM tool in Figure 4-3.

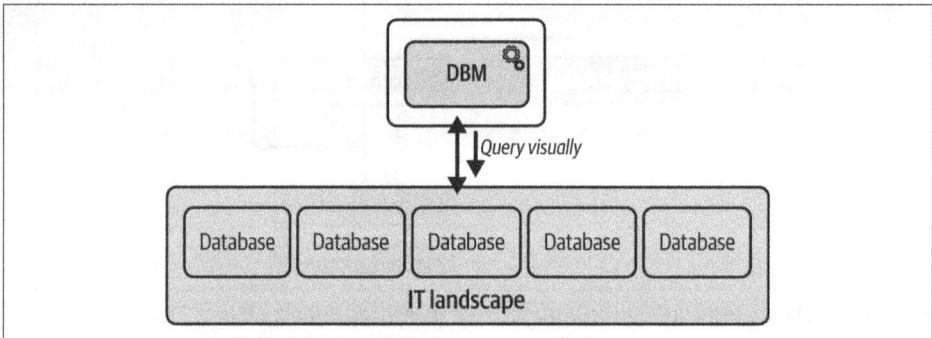

Figure 4-3. High-level view of a DBM tool

The benefit of empirical data modeling via a DBM tool is reverse engineering. In the context of data modeling, *reverse engineering* is the process of understanding database structures—in this case, visually—*after* they have been created in order to analyze them better, and from that point on, to manage them intelligently through creating functional, logical models.

The main driver for the DBM tool is IT operations. The DBM tool ensures logical modeling, whatever the purpose, and smooth management of the underlying databases. In Figure 4-4, you can see an example of a metamodel in a specific instance of a DBM tool.[3]

---

3 This very simple metamodel is inspired by a detail (explaining the physical data model) in the diagram of SAP PowerDesigner (*https://powerdesigner.biz*).

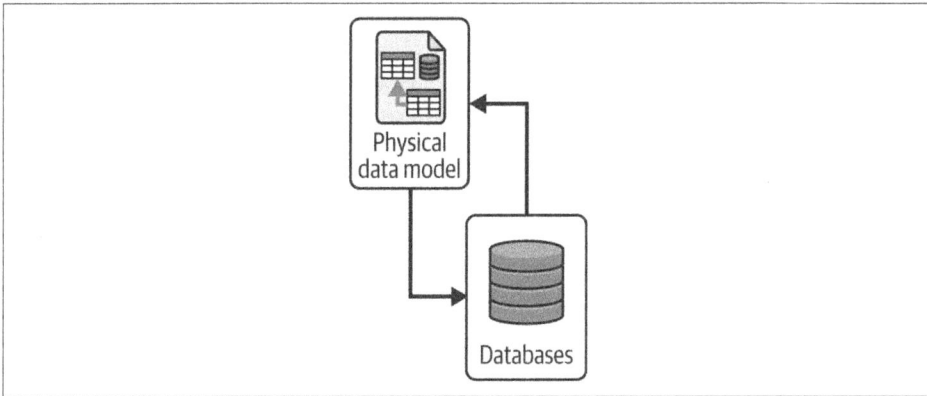

Figure 4-4. A metamodel of a DBM tool

Keep in mind that this metamodel is rather simplistic and that it refers only to the physical data model—that is, the visualization of the specific structure in the database. Above that layer are logical and conceptual data models, but these are in principle not connected to a database and can be drawn freely in Microsoft PowerPoint, Visio, and other lightweight modeling tools. This book is not about data modeling in general, but the many repositories that data models are unfortunately stored in, creating an overview problem at the metadata layer. For an introduction to data modeling, I suggest following Joe Reis's work (*https://oreil.ly/8kxy_*).

Other Metadata Repositories for Data Management

All of the tooling for data management can in fact be considered a set of metadata repositories, in the sense that these tools represent and work with data originating from somewhere else. These technologies include, for example:

- Data warehouses
- Data lakes
- Data lakehouses
- Data pipeline tools
- Data quality tools
- Identity and access management

> Each of these tools functions as a kind of DC, albeit not as general and powerful as the enterprise DC. In a sense, the role of the enterprise DC is to consolidate and improve search capabilities on these repository-specific catalogs. That's why these repositories are included in this chapter—they contain metadata.

In this section, I'll give brief descriptions of these technologies, considered as metadata repositories. However, I've deliberately kept these descriptions short because you could argue that these technologies are *not* metadata repositories but rather are simply data storage solutions with the capabilities of performing the functions needed in data management, engineering, and science. That argument is correct albeit only one—big—part of the picture because inside these tools sits vital metadata that helps structure the total sum of data in these tools: lists of applications, products, employees, and so forth that instantiate in customer orders, ETL jobs, and the like.

Data Warehouse

The *data warehouse* was a brilliant breakthrough in working with enterprise data when it was introduced by Bill Inmon in the 1980s. For the first time in data management, the data warehouse allowed us to see the operational, structured data produced by the IT systems that carried out the value chain of companies, all the way from early experiments in labs to manufacturing, sales and marketing, and finally, shipping and returns.

The big shift that the data warehouse allowed for was a shift in focus: from the hosting database technologies that ran the business toward the information/knowledge structure of the data warehouse, with all its attendant processes, including ETL, that made it possible to understand all aspects of how the business was running. Thus, the data warehouse allowed for business intelligence or, generally speaking, analytics of how the company had performed. To work, the data warehouse relies on processing data in what is known as *extract, transform, load* (ETL), as you can see in Figure 4-5.

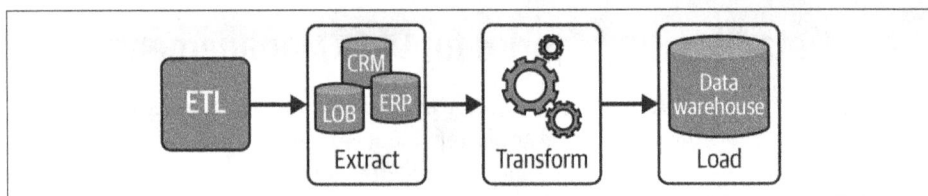

Figure 4-5. Extract, transform, load

Data Lake

The *data lake* evolved as an alternative to the data warehouse. The data lake essentially eliminates the structure of the data warehouse—even the table catalog that we get with a traditional SQL database is gone. This works well when data is large but relatively simple to characterize, but it doesn't work well when we have a great variety of data. In the 2000s and 2010s, data science was on the rise, requiring larger amounts of data than were contained in data warehouses for forward-looking use cases: predictive analytics. Unlike business intelligence, data science worked with what was coined *big data,* and the deeply mathematical programming performed on these datasets prioritized volume over quality, hence moving from data warehouse architectures toward data lake architectures. The shortest possible way to explain this change is because the use cases of (big) data science:

- Tend to prioritize correlation over causality, statistically. By identifying a connection in the total amount of data, an effective change could be made without asserting the truth of the connection.
- Perform transformations needed to solve the use case in scope (typically, smaller use cases).

Subsequently (because of the big data methodologies being statistically different from earlier BI methodologies), data lakes rely not on ETL but on ELT: extract, load, transform, as shown in Figure 4-6.

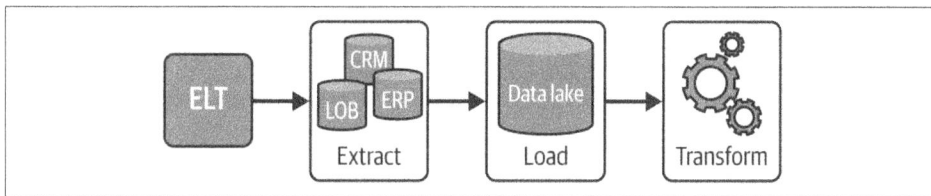

Figure 4-6. Extract, load, transform

Data Lakehouse

Data lakehouse architectures provide an effective combination of data warehouse and data lake architectures. They allow for both types of analytics performed with data warehouses and data lakes. Two things are added to the data lake to create a lakehouse: a SQL query engine and an internal overview (catalog). For an in-depth explanation, see Chapter 12 of *Deciphering Data Architectures* by James Serra (O'Reilly).

Data Pipeline Tools

Data pipeline tools are a means of transporting and transforming data to make the data ready for analytical consumption, such as in data warehouses. The transformation can be layered, meaning that it can go through various steps—typically called bronze, silver, and gold—to reach a level of pureness that makes the data perfect for analytics. The transportation part consists of integrations between various applications, going from the source system into the pipeline tool and further on, into the storage solution of the warehouse.

Data Quality Tools

Data quality tools measure the state of data to check for completeness, accuracy, and more. They are used by business owners and data analysts to execute their rules and checks of data quality.

Identity and Access Management

Identity and access management (IAM) is the vital and often ignored component that gives users access to data. Modern data architectures and platforms often make or break on exactly this feature—because getting access to data is complicated and therefore takes time. IAM is performed via one of two methods: role-based access control (RBAC) or attribute-based access control (ABAC).

RBAC is the easiest to implement and execute as it is based on roles that can easily be set up to allow people to access data. However, studies show that RBAC is the most difficult to manage over time because it fosters an explosion of roles. Managing these roles becomes complicated, prone to errors, and dangerous in terms of security.

ABAC, on the other hand, takes somewhat the opposite approach, with a point of departure not on the person wanting to access data but on the data itself. By assigning attributes to data sources, the owners of data can define up front who can access which data for what purposes. ABAC is more difficult to set up because of this up-front work, but over time, the ABAC approach is significantly easier to manage. IAM is often built into data tools, and we can combine this with cross-domain IAM services to manage data access across a large organization with many tools.

Rebundling of Data Management Technologies

The modern data stack is long gone. Instead, we are seeing a rebundling of technologies in the data management space:

> While the innovative drive of the MDS [modern data stack] ecosystem has reduced development times and analysis maintenance costs, on the other hand, it has increased operational costs in terms of developing and maintaining the underlying platform....It is likely that in the coming years, after a strongly expansive phase (unbundling), the offering will converge again toward a rationalization phase (bundling), where we may see some MDS vendors merging, others being acquired by big tech, and some potentially failing after the driving force of the collected investments diminishes.[4]

During the second half of the 2020s, data technologies offering very detailed core capabilities as standalone solutions will fade. The market has changed, and venture capital money will focus on technologies with AI as the primary use case. Such use

---

4 Andrea Gioia, *Managing Data as a Product* (Packt Publishing, 2024), 8.

cases and solutions need the support of complete, consolidated data intelligence platforms. Note that these operate at the metadata layer, so they will not contain data pipeline tools but rather data lineage tools, not data warehouses but data catalogs showing the structure and content of data warehouses, and so on.

Metadata Repositories for Data Management

At this point, we have run through the various metadata repositories for data. Now, let's put all the pieces of the puzzle together. In Figure 4-7, you will see all of the metadata repositories in a diagram.

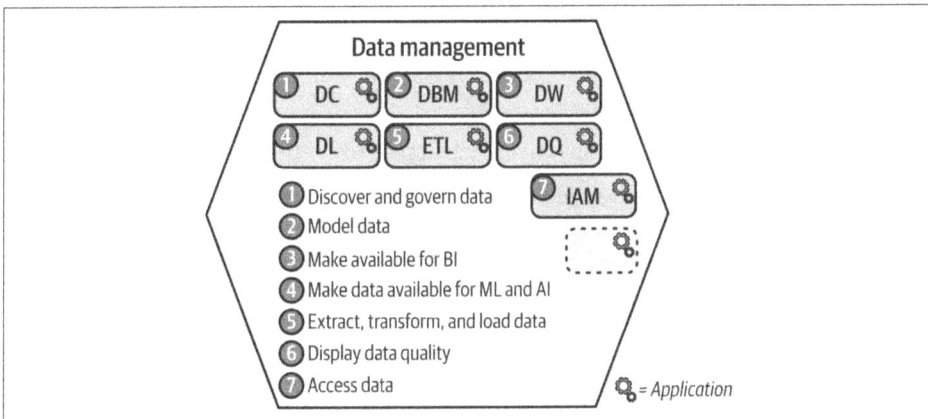

Figure 4-7. Metadata repositories for data management

Let's run through the diagram at a glance:

- The DC is close to the physical reality of the IT landscape as it also scans it to show what kinds of data exist in which sources.

- DBM tool is about getting a visual impression of a physical reality. This is rendered in empirical data models that are based on facts, not assumptions. DBM tools further allow for querying databases, thus altering the reality they visualize.

- A handful of technologies (and concepts) in data management contain metadata repositories, albeit their main focus is to make data available. These include data warehouses and data lakes for storing data, ETL/ELT tools for transforming and transporting data, data quality tools for measuring the quality of data, and IAM for providing access to data.

Summary

In this chapter, we looked at metadata repositories for data management. This chapter is short since it is not the main focus of this book to narrowly examine metadata management in a data-management context—although data management tends to think of itself as equipped with enterprise-wide authority regarding the overview of the company's IT landscape. Empirically, this is usually not the case, though, as the other chapters in the book suggest. Here are the main takeaways for this chapter:

- As a whole, metadata repositories for data management are to be understood as the key to data analytics: business intelligence and data science.

- DCs provide a holistic metadata overview of the data tooling involved in this process but can certainly also be leveraged for other purposes, spanning both operational and regulative tasks.

- DCs provide data descriptions that reach across tools and domains.

- DBM tools contain data models that emerge from an empirical process based on screening the structures of databases, such as structures of SQL databases. DBM tools are technology specific and will never describe the entire IT landscape.

- The other metadata repositories for data management discussed in this chapter and needed for data engineering—and thus for data analytics—are components that can be thought of as metadata repositories even though they deliver specific capabilities for the overall purpose of data management.

In the next chapter, we will take a closer look at metadata repositories for information management.

CHAPTER 5

Information Management

In the previous chapter, we discussed the metadata repositories for data management. In this chapter, we'll dive into the metadata repositories for information management. The difference between the two is that metadata repositories for information are richer in human interpretation, letting them serve purposes that demand a higher level of intellectual—not technical—abstraction. However, keep in mind that we will not engage in an intellectual discussion—information management exists as a discipline, complete with a set of associated technologies, ISO standards, and more.

Metadata repositories that we will cover in this chapter include:

- Records and information
- Information security
- Data protection
- Business processes

We'll mainly cover these metadata repositories for regulatory purposes, for retention of records and information throughout their lifecycles, and for information security and data protection, and we'll examine metadata repositories for business processes.

Let's dive in!

Records and Information Management System

Using a records and information management system (RIMS), your company can manage the lifecycle of the records and information it produces. A *record* is a document or set of data that serves as proof of something. This means that not every single document or dataset produced is considered a record; for example, draft documents or the temperature logs in meeting rooms are not considered records in most companies. Study reports from a research and development department, contracts with a supplier, and logs that control factors like temperature in production facilities all constitute records. The management of records is the assurance that these records will be properly handled throughout their *lifecycle* (Figure 5-1), meaning the period during which the records are to be stored within the organization.

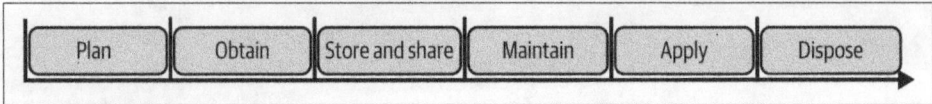

Plan	Obtain	Store and share	Maintain	Apply	Dispose

Figure 5-1. The information lifecycle

Record-Retention Scenarios

Imagine you're an employee in a pharmaceutical company. Your company must be able to defend in a court of law that its medicine was not the cause of a patient's death, despite the patient having used the medicine produced by your company. For your company lawyers to defend the case properly, they need evidence. In this case, the evidence is the clinical studies that show no reporting of side effects similar to what caused the patient to die, which led the patient's family to sue your company.

The US Food and Drug Administration (FDA) mandates that the pharmaceutical sector must retain specific types of data for the life of a product plus 35 years, aligning with the typical lifespan of a patient even after the product is no longer on the market. Consider the length of time involved—you have to store records and information for that long! That is what the RIMS does, and it requires thorough processes to uphold.

> In general, heavily regulated industries like pharmaceuticals, petrochemicals, and finance tend to have more finely structured and maintained RIMSs than more loosely regulated businesses, such as tourism and hospitality. This distinction arises from the stringent regulations imposed on these sectors, where authorities require strict compliance for what must be provable at a later time.

Records and information management is a field that is structured by international standards. Unlike the management of many other metadata repositories, there is clear guidance on how to manage a RIMS. Within ISO, Technical Committee 46 Subcommittee 11 (*https://oreil.ly/wzquG*) defines the standards of records and information management, with ISO 15489 as a central standard. Another standard is ISO 9001 as well as FDA Chapter 21, part 11 (*https://oreil.ly/Q8Uly*).

The Organizational Aspect of RIMS

Records and information management departments work in various ways to ensure that records are maintained, depending on their position within the lifecycle. As shown in Figure 5-2, all records must be mapped throughout the company by the records and information management department. These records must be under control, meaning they should be identified, assigned ownership, and undergo proper retention procedures. Furthermore, records may be managed directly by the records and information management department at the end of the records' lifecycles.

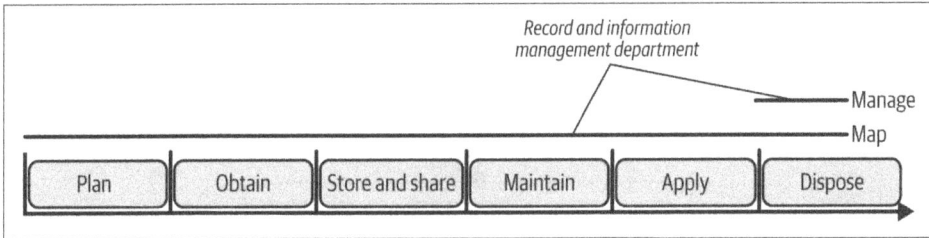

Figure 5-2. The information lifecycle, RIMS focus

You should remember that a RIMS is used to manage the lifecycle of data throughout that entire lifecycle. Consider this: would you keep an application running for the entire lifecycle of the data it contains, spanning, for instance, 65 years? In many cases, this corresponds to the product's lifespan plus an additional 35 years. Of course, that will not happen, so at a certain point, that data will be transferred from the application from where it sits to a storage solution.

If your company faces a lawsuit, the records and information management department issues a legal hold. A *legal hold* means that you identify all records relevant to the lawsuit and "freeze" them, implying that normal actions during the course of the information lifecycle are put on hold, such as sharing records between departments or deleting them according to their retention periods. The records are proof of actions, and when they are needed, they must be kept safe.

A RIMS is likely to group records in terms of their confidentiality. *Confidentiality* denotes the degree of secrecy associated with a particular record, determining the number of employees who are authorized to access it.

To provide a more in-depth understanding of the content within the RIMS, let's continue with the pharma example, illustrating the types of records it can contain. Physical or digital documents can include:

- Employee contracts
- Legal agreements
- Research studies
- Strategy documentation
- Memos

Categorized data, grouped in bigger chunks, can include:

- Clinical data
- Financial data
- Lab results
- Building monitoring

RIMS As a Metadata Repository

RIMS represents records: *physical* and *digital documents* as well as *data* grouped in larger chunks (Figure 5-3).

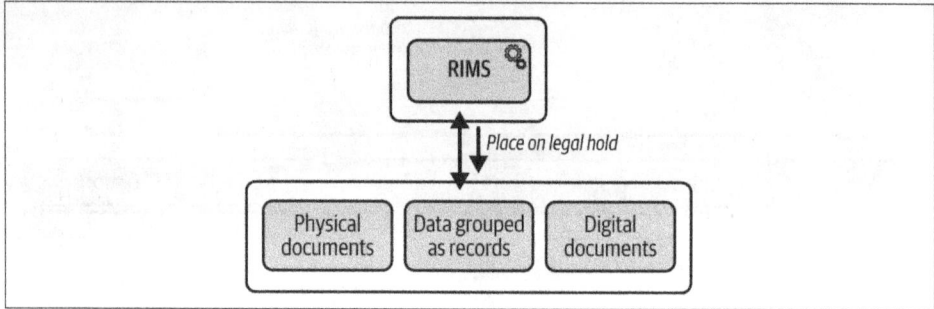

Figure 5-3. High-level view of a RIMS

Keep in mind that a RIMS doesn't depict only the IT landscape but also an analog reality of records stored in physical archives (Figure 5-4). Moreover, it encompasses dedicated long-term data storage solutions designed specifically for records and information management. This is because during the course of the information life-cycle, data grouped as records may be moved from the running IT landscape into long-term storage where access is expensive but storage is cheap—and given the fact that records are kept for regulatory compliance, the frequency of their usage is low. Records are only consulted in relation to lawsuits or during inspections. You may also have scenarios where data is printed as physical documents because long-term storage is cheapest in physical form.

RIMSs are implemented for regulatory purposes that are both industry generic and specific. The overarching purpose is retention and legal hold, with industry-specific regulations determining the duration for which data must be retained.

Some of the RIMS's role can be performed by the data protection repository (DPR), which handles retention specifically for sensitive data. Another purpose of the RIMS can be handled by the ISMS, which assesses confidentiality.

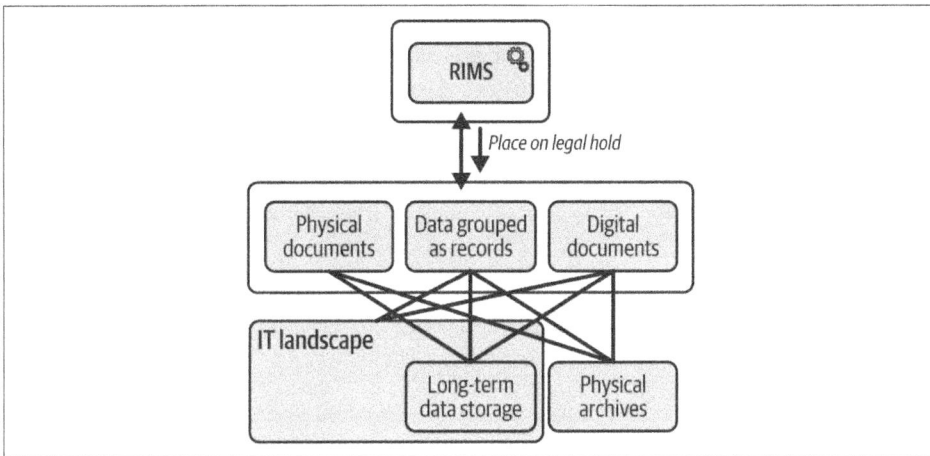

Figure 5-4. Records and information management related to the IT landscape and beyond

> Data can be categorized as "hot" and "cold" based on its frequency of use. Consider records and information management to be the overseeing process until the data reaches the point of becoming "ice cold." To learn more about this topic, check out Figure 6-9 in *Fundamentals of Data Engineering* by Joe Reis and Matt Housley (O'Reilly).

Information Security Management System

Today, the discipline of information security management is closely associated with the ISO/IEC 27001:2022 standard, which pertains to information security, cybersecurity, and privacy protection. The ISO 27001 standard—along with the connected standards, altogether known as the 27000-series—deliver a framework for information security. It's essential to recognize that information security extends beyond the confines of the IT landscape; it encompasses more than just cybersecurity. Information security focuses on three types of assets, with *assets* meaning anything of value to the company:

Intangible assets
    These assets encompass intellectual property, insider knowledge, and even rumors.[1]

---

1 Information security has to operate as an internal intelligence unit because intangible assets can be extremely powerful. Think, for example, of insider trading.

IT landscape assets
> Assets in the IT landscape encompass everything from hardware to software, including on-premises server rooms, cables, laptops, applications, and more.

Tangible assets
> Tangible assets include individuals who possess extraordinary expert knowledge or hold a special status within the company, either as high-ranking employees or public figures.

At the core of the ISO 27000-series is the creation of an ISMS. This system conducts ongoing risk assessments of identified assets based on the following criteria:

Threats
> The potential threats that a company faces toward its assets.

Vulnerabilities
> How likely these assets are to be hit by the threats.

Impact
> The order of magnitude refers to the potential size of the damage if a threat were to materialize toward an asset.

Mitigation
> The measures put in place to prevent the threat.

The Organizational Aspect of ISMS

An ISMS is overseen by a chief information security officer (CISO), who may have a team performing daily operations. Managing the information security department is an ongoing process. ISO standards—including the 27000-series—follow the Shewhart cycle, which consists of four phases:

1. Plan
2. Do
3. Check
4. Act

These steps initiate the ISMS by establishing it (plan), implementing it (do), monitoring it (check), and maintaining it (act). This cycle is then repeated annually to progressively reduce risk throughout the organization.

ISMS As a Metadata Repository

The ISMS is a repository that lists assets and the risks associated with them as well as the mitigating actions to avoid those risks. As such, the ISMS is a repository that works on the basis of classifying data in terms of its confidentiality. Essentially, the ISMS is a tool that helps companies evaluate how serious it is for the company to lose control of its various types of information.

In the context of this book, the focal point of the ISMS isn't solely the mitigation effort led by the CISO but more the awareness of the assets and the potential risks. While mitigation is the end result, the key lies in how the CISO acquires the ability to mitigate risks in the first place. This critical aspect of the ISMS is known as the *asset inventory*, and that is what I'd like you to focus on. The asset inventory is simply the list of assets collected by the CISO and their team. The asset inventory will list IT assets in the IT landscape as well as tangible and intangible assets. All the risk assessments and mitigations performed by the CISO are performed against the asset inventory. Figure 5-5 shows a high-level diagram of an ISMS.

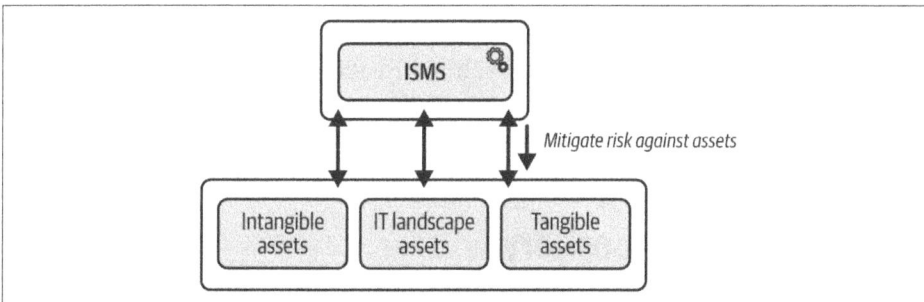

Figure 5-5. High-level view of an ISMS

One specific element inherent to the asset inventory is the concept of a *risk owner*. The risk owner is a person in the organization who has been given ownership of a certain risk. The concept of a risk owner is often challenging to manage and is, therefore, translated into a more tangible form through the identification of specific assets. Accordingly, risk owners become asset owners.

At this point, let's delve into the contents of the ISMS asset inventory, illustrated in Figure 5-5. *Intangible assets* include intellectual assets, rumors, and more. *IT landscape assets* comprise infrastructure, applications, machinery, laptops, and phones. *Tangible assets* encompass persons, objects, and buildings.

What happens if the CISO creates the asset inventory without taking into account other metadata repositories for the IT landscape? At the very least, a lot of time is wasted reproducing what should already exist. At the worst—and this is the most likely—an alternative depiction of the IT landscape has been created, resulting in uncertainty about which metadata repositories are correct.

I advise you to populate the asset inventory in the ISMS, especially when dealing with assets related to the IT landscape, by referencing other metadata repositories. You should reflect on the entries for those assets and interpret the metadata in the context of information security. This is an empirical approach to building your ISMS. We will discuss this approach more in depth in Part II.

> In most companies, the asset inventory is an information security threat in itself. This is because it relies on an imprecise, nonempirical asset inventory that does not reflect reality. It's the result of the unwillingness to take ownership from the business, resulting in too little dialogue with the CISO. But this is not the fault of the CISO or the business. And you *can* change this for the better. I'll discuss this further in Part II and give you concrete advice for how to circumvent this situation.

The ISMS is of a regulatory nature, in the sense that the ISMS is mandatory to implement and manage in order to comply with information security standards, particularly the ISO 27000-series. However, companies can choose not to follow strict information security practices, which will arguably lead to fewer business opportunities but not fines, as in the case of the RIMS discussed previously.[2]

Data Protection Repository

The GDPR (*https://gdpr-info.eu*) came into effect in 2018 and pioneered modern privacy regulations. GDPR created a European standard that serves as an inspiration for similar regulations around the world—the best known outside Europe is the California Consumer Privacy Act (CCPA) (*https://oreil.ly/lgDde*). While this law covers only the state of California, it was a pioneering law for the United States and directly affects many tech companies that operate out of the San Francisco Bay Area. Just as in the case of information security, data protection exceeds the IT landscape, in the sense that it also deals with information stored on physical media.

---

2 Standards turn into regulations. One such is NIS2 (*https://oreil.ly/Tv3oI*). To operate in consumer electronics such as telecommunications within the European Union, you need to comply with NIS2; that is a direct enforcement of the ISO 27000-series.

I will use the GDPR terminology in the following discussions. You can easily translate it to similar standards.

The heart of data protection is to protect everyone's private life—that means all of us. As technology becomes more and more ambient in our lives, it contains more precise data about us. And to prevent your data from being used against your will, your data needs to be protected. Hence the need for GDPR and all other similar regulations.

You protect data first by discovering it, then by analyzing how it is processed, and then by evaluating the impact of the risks of that processing. And you do that in a data protection impact assessment (DPIA) (*https://oreil.ly/OPfBX*). The DPIA must include a description of data that contains (among other things):

- A systematic description of the envisaged processing operations and the purposes of the processing
- An assessment of the necessity and proportionality of the processing operations in relation to the purposes

I don't want you to focus on the actual activity of data protection; that is not the purpose of this book. Instead, take a closer look at the phrasing in the first bullet: a description of the envisaged processing operations. And there you have it: to protect data, you need to map how data is processed. That map is built into every single DPIA, which makes the collection of DPIAs a metadata repository that contains a process map of your company. I call this metadata repository a *data protection repository* (DPR).

This is where the fundamentals of metadata come into play because what authority does the process map in the DPR actually have? How is it aligned with other metadata repositories—if at all? And if these repositories are not aligned, where is the truth?

You should know that the *data protection repository* is not an established concept but my concept.

A DPR stores data protection impact assessments. The DPIAs are used to answer *data subject access requests* (DSARs). The DSAR is your right to know what data a given company or organization has about you as well as to correct the data, understand how it is processed, and delete the data.

The Organizational Aspect of a DPR

Data protection in a company is performed by a data protection officer (DPO) (*https://oreil.ly/xV3uK*), who is typically a lawyer with experience working on problems of data and technology. The DPO builds the DPR by examining the data processing through the company and listing it in DPIAs. This is generally done early, when new IT projects are launched. However, when GDPR was first implemented, this assessment had to be done for the existing landscape.

When a citizen or a customer makes a DSAR to a company, it lands with the DPO, who has 28 days to answer the DSAR. The DPO has to:

- Register the DSAR
- Verify the identity of the subject performing the DSAR
- Understand the DSAR
- Match the DSAR with data processing (by consulting DPIAs in the DPR)
- Collect the data
- Inform, erase, correct, or provide the data

I want you to focus on the fact that the foundation for performing these actions may be wrong. I have personally witnessed DSARs being performed and then seen the same kind of unwanted, harmful data processing being repeated after that data's subjects had been informed that it wouldn't be repeated. This is *very* common in a big enterprise context. And it's because the DPR is not correct: it does not really reflect the IT landscape—not because the DPO has done a sloppy job but because the task is too immense and the changes to the IT landscape are so many that a manually maintained DPR cannot keep up. The typical reaction to this kind of problem is that the DPO wants to work *harder*, make more confrontational data governance, and have intrusive hard talks with business departments to improve the data quality in the DPR. And I can guarantee you that approach will not work.

Instead, the DPR needs to coordinate the other metadata repositories, contribute to them, and benefit from them. The purpose of this book is to explain to you that there is a hidden path to better, faster, improved metadata management. Read along and see how the DPO can create great results, which I will discuss in Parts II and III.

DPR As a Metadata Repository

A DPR is an inventory that lists data and the way data is processed in a company. It focuses on the *sensitivity* of data, meaning the degree to which data is personal. The DPR first performs DPIAs of the IT landscape and physical media. It is then subsequently used to answer DSARs. You can see a high-level view of a DPR in Figure 5-6.

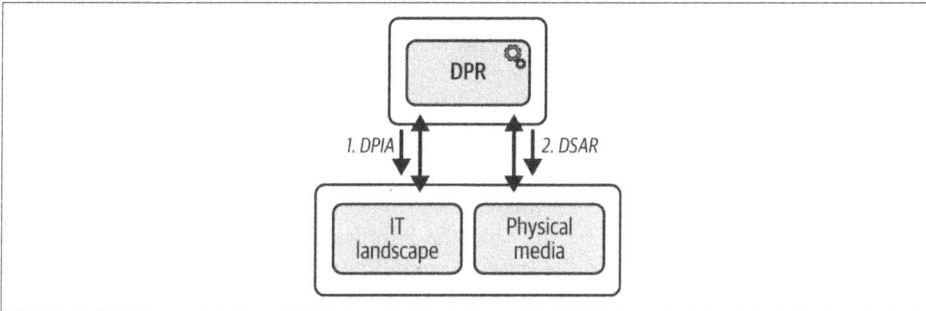

Figure 5-6. High-level view of a DPR

> An alternative to DPRs is a privacy information management system (PIMS) (*https://oreil.ly/V7JpN*) where users can determine for themselves how their data should be used. This can be a sort of DSAR as a service.

In the context of this book, neither the outcome of a DPIA or of a DSAR is important. Instead, what's important is the fact that a DPIA constructs a process landscape with data in it. That process landscape may match—or more likely, not match—other process maps in the organization. In other metadata repositories, you will find other process landscapes—subsequently, if they don't match the ones defined in the DPR, your company has multiple contrasting process landscapes at play. This will cause great confusion until you address it. I advise on this in Chapter 7 and throughout the rest of the book.

The purpose for implementing DPRs is regulation focused on data protection around the world, such as GDPR and CCPA. You will not find dedicated vendors for this section. Most ISMSs will have a data protection component that helps you manage regulations such as GDPR. However, in many organizations, this is simply done with spreadsheets and documents.

Business Process Management System

You use a BPMS to formalize business processes. *Business processes* describe how your company carries out its tasks. The BPMS lets business processes be mined, managed, and automated: *mined* in the sense that they are discovered and made understandable, *managed* in the sense that you on that premise can get them under control, and *automated* in that the BPMS allows you to automate manual tasks strategically. Together, they contribute to a smoother and faster execution of business processes.[3]

> Business processes are really important for information management because processes often need information as input, and likewise, information is often the result or outcome of a process. So business processes are linked to information objects modeled in the information architecture and the information models. This is an important part of the business architecture. Data objects in DCs translate very directly to these, and the overlap of these technologies should not be ignored in a metadata-management context.

The BPMS must visualize business processes so that it is easier to discover and understand them. Furthermore, the BPMS has no direct link to the IT landscape per se; it is only when a certain process is carried out with the help of IT that the connection exists—which is almost always the case. However, the BPMS is intended to depict processes, not the IT landscape (Figure 5-7).

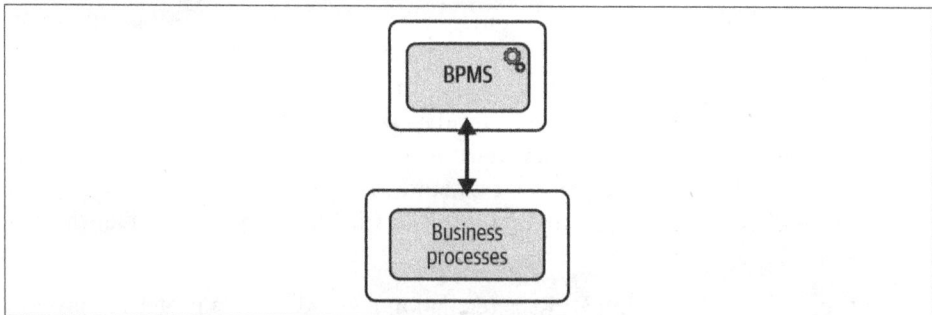

Figure 5-7. High-level view of a BPMS

In contrast to records management, data protection, and information security, business process management is not an organizationally formalized activity. However, you can set up structured team activities to perform business process management by following general guidance that can be found in ISO 9000 (*https://oreil.ly/NFDIR*).

---

3 The BPMS is placed in the information management domain because it (sometimes not explicitly) adheres to the Architecture of Integrated Information Systems (ARIS) (*https://oreil.ly/bYKJ5*).

The BPMS can also be part of a larger, more complex system. This will typically be a QMS, which is most often operated by a quality assurance department. I'll discuss the BPMS as part of a QMS in Chapter 6.

Business processes can be modeled using a standard notation, such as the Business Process Model and Notation (BPMN) (*https://omg.org/spec/BPMN/2.0*) published by the Object Management Group. Figure 5-8 shows an example of a business process model.

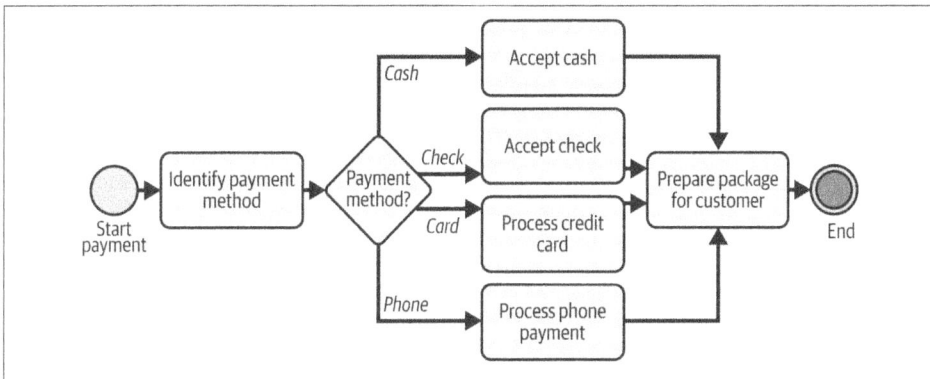

Figure 5-8. Payment business process modeled in BPMN

You should consider the level of granularity in business processes. The models that capture business processes depict very concretely the various actions that are performed. These processes are automatically or semiautomatically generated as visualizations by the BPMS. From that point on—when you have the processes mapped in your BPMS—you can use the BPMS to:

- Perform major IT transformations, such as ERP migration
- Identify weak processes and make them stronger
- Identify slow processes and make them faster
- Automate processes using AI, robotic process automation (RPA), and the like

You should not think of business processes as the value stream or value chain of your company. Value streams or value chains provide high-level overviews of a company's activities without delving into the detailed layers of actions carried out by employees, machines, or robots—a level of detail that is precisely captured by business processes. Accordingly, business processes are carried out both inside the IT landscape and as purely human processes, as shown in Figure 5-9.

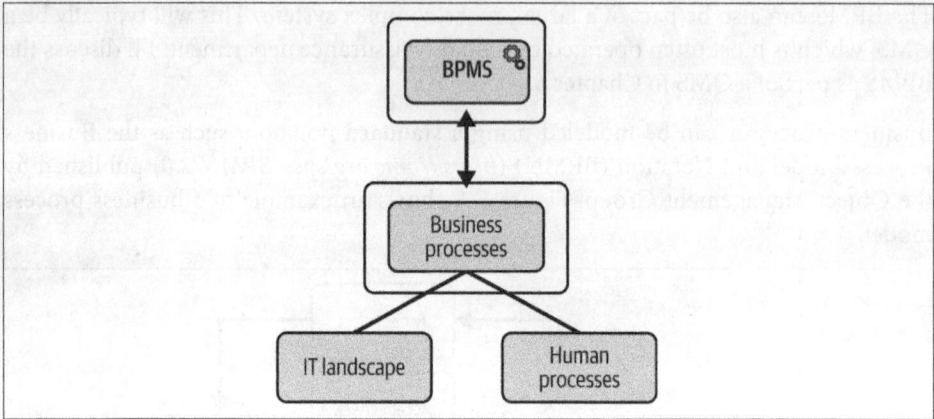

Figure 5-9. How the BPMS relates to the IT landscape and beyond

The BPMS is different in nature than the other repositories discussed in this chapter because it does not serve a regulatory purpose and should not primarily be used for such purposes. However, the BPMS depicts processes, and as such, it overlaps with the DPR.

Metadata Repositories for Information Management

In this chapter, we have explored a set of metadata repositories specifically focusing on information management. Now, let's consolidate them. Figure 5-10 illustrates all of the metadata repositories for information along with the capabilities that these repositories leverage.

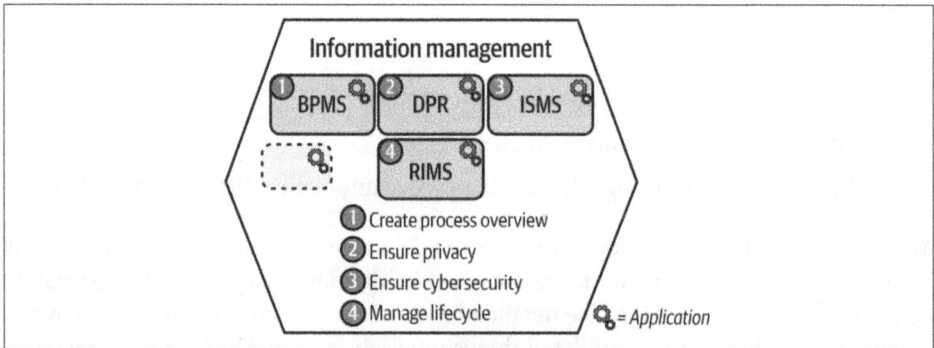

Figure 5-10. Metadata repositories for information management

Let's quickly recapitulate the repositories in the diagram:

- The BPMS depicts business processes. Business processes are thorough, detailed descriptions of the processes carried out by humans, machines, and robots in your company. The BPMS is capable of performing a rationalization of the IT landscape, transforming it and making it stronger and faster. Business processes are visualized in the BPMS.

- The DPR describes how personal data is processed. It's the repository put in place to handle regulations, such as GDPR and CCPA, that oblige companies to transparently declare how they process personal data and how they manage requests to change this processing. The DPR is managed by the DPO.

- The ISMS manages the information security of the company, both in regard to cybersecurity and the security of analog, tangible, and intangible assets. All information security risks must be listed, evaluated in terms of severity, and then mitigated. The ISMS is managed by the CISO.

- The RIMS manages the lifecycle of company records. It depicts all records, physical and digital, that a company produces, and can issue a legal hold on the records that are subject to use in a lawsuit. The RIMS is managed by a records and information management department.

> All metadata repositories for information interact less directly with the IT landscape than those for IT and data management, by adding a layer of interpretation that metadata repositories for data do not need. Also, metadata repositories for information look outside the IT landscape, such as to describe conversations (BPMS), rumors (ISMS), and physical paper documents (DPR and RIMS).

Metadata repositories for information overlap more often than not. Technologies performing information security management will, for example, offer a data protection component and vice versa, since they share a methodology for protecting data and information. Likewise, a technologically refined RIMS can push its peripheral capabilities toward information security and data protection because it handles confidentiality and sensitivity as a natural continuation of its overall purpose of assessing and managing the retention of records and information.

The BPMS is different from the other repositories discussed in this chapter as it does not serve a regulatory purpose and should not primarily be used for such purposes. However, the BPMS depicts processes, and as such, it overlaps with the DPR.

Parts of the RIMS's role can be performed by the DPR, which handles retention specifically for sensitive data. The ISMS can handle another purpose of the RIMS: assessing confidentiality. The overlapping peripheral capabilities are shown in Figure 5-11.

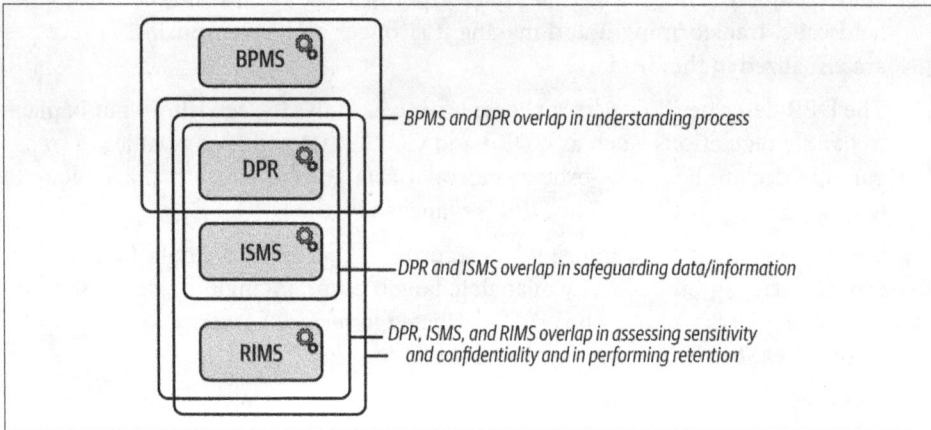

Figure 5-11. The overlapping peripheral capabilities of information metadata repositories

Summary

In this chapter, we looked at metadata repositories for information. We explored examples of metadata repositories designed for managing information—numerous other repositories exist within information management. Here are the takeaways:

- Metadata repositories for information interact less directly with your IT landscape than IT and data management by adding a layer of interpretation to it.
- Metadata repositories for information look outside the IT landscape toward physical media and abstract ideas.
- Most metadata repositories for information management are motivated by regulations such as GDPR and CCPA.
- A BPMS gives you an overview of your business processes.
- The DPR is the repository describing how personal sensitive data is processed.
- In the ISMS is an asset inventory listing all assets that are confidential.
- The RIMS manages the lifecycle of records and information.
- Legal holds can be issued by the RIMS.
- The DPR and ISMS are often found in the same technology.
- The DPR, ISMS, and RIMS overlap around processing of data.

- Like the DPR, the RIMS describes sensitivity and handles retention.
- As with the ISMS, the RIMS assigns levels of confidentiality.

Next, we will take a closer look at metadata repositories for knowledge.

CHAPTER 6

Knowledge Management

Welcome to the world of knowledge! In this chapter, we discuss metadata repositories that simply contain text, pictures, sound, and film. This chapter will also explore metadata repositories that catalog various physical objects. Altogether, these are metadata repositories focused on knowledge management.

In this chapter, we step away from the immediate IT landscape. However, as you will discover in later chapters, the metadata contained within the repositories that we'll discuss here holds significant value when taking a more holistic, strategic view of the IT landscape.

Here's what we'll explore:

- Content management system (CMS)
- Knowledge management system (KMS)
- Learning management system (LMS)
- Quality management system (QMS)
- (Historical) collection management system (CMSy)

Let's begin with the knowledge that companies want to share with the rest of the world.

Content Management System

A CMS is a system that ensures consistent and coordinated sharing of knowledge *outside* of your company. The CMS can manage websites in a user interface that is nontechnical, allowing all employees in a company to easily publish their knowledge online—in the form of a blog, for example. The CMS is the only technology that is not directly linked or integrated with operations in the internal IT infrastructure of a company. However, websites managed by the CMS can still be hosted on servers within on-premises data centers, indicating a potential connection between the CMS and the company's internal IT infrastructure through web-hosting services.

The CMS allows a subset of employees in the business to write, edit, publish, and delete content on all of your company's websites in a nontechnical, coordinated manner. The CMS contains a metadata repository that lists all the websites of the company along with their owners, what brands they promote and inform about, and so on.

A company of more than a hundred employees is likely to have multiple websites, and the bigger and more complex the company is, the more obvious it is to use a CMS to maintain an overview of them. Accordingly, the CMS becomes the metadata repository for the external knowledge of the company, displayed to the outside world on the web via the internet, as depicted in Figure 6-1.

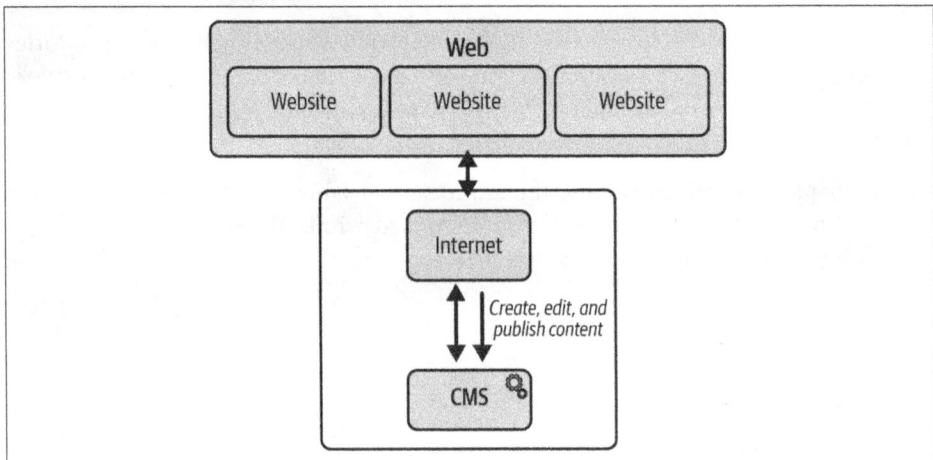

Figure 6-1. High-level view of a CMS

The main driver for a CMS is motivated by operations since the CMS facilitates external communication of knowledge from the company with the outside world.

Knowledge Management System

A KMS, also called *knowledge base software,* scans sources of knowledge, indexes those sources, and on that basis provides a portal for searching them. These sources of knowledge are text based, and the KMS does a full text crawl of them—meaning that everything in the sources is made searchable. Therefore, in the KMS you can search not only for titles of documents or threads and the names of the people who wrote them but also for everything inside those documents and threads, such as words, sentences, and references. All of the employees in the company will also be searchable, along with their certifications, educational backgrounds, technical skills, and so forth.

> The KMS isn't the only tool that you can perform knowledge management with—all of the technologies in this chapter are knowledge management technologies.

The sources that the KMS crawls and mirrors fall into three categories:

Communications platforms
Slack, Teams, Outlook, and similar communications platforms contain company knowledge in the conversations going on among the employees.

Document stores
Dropbox and SharePoint contain documents written by employees that are typically in a finalized state—and are therefore useful to expose via the KMS (draft documents are typically not useful for a KMS as it is uncertain if they contain established knowledge).

Development platforms
GitHub, Azure DevOps, and similar development platforms are used as social networks for software developers to write, store, and collaborate on code as well as to comment on and rate it.

On the basis of mirroring these three types of sources, the KMS delivers two main capabilities:

Search for knowledge
Just as the DC does for data, the KMS delivers an enterprise search functionality for knowledge. The types of questions that employees have for a KMS are defined by their needs to search for knowledge. They want to know when a new brand produced by the company is launching, the ideas behind a certain project, or why a factory owned by the company is shutting down.

Intranet
A KMS can effectively create a company intranet, which is nothing more than a subcapability of most KMSs. However, the KMS may also be a wiki with a search functionality next to an intranet.

In Figure 6-2, you can see a high-level overview of a KMS.

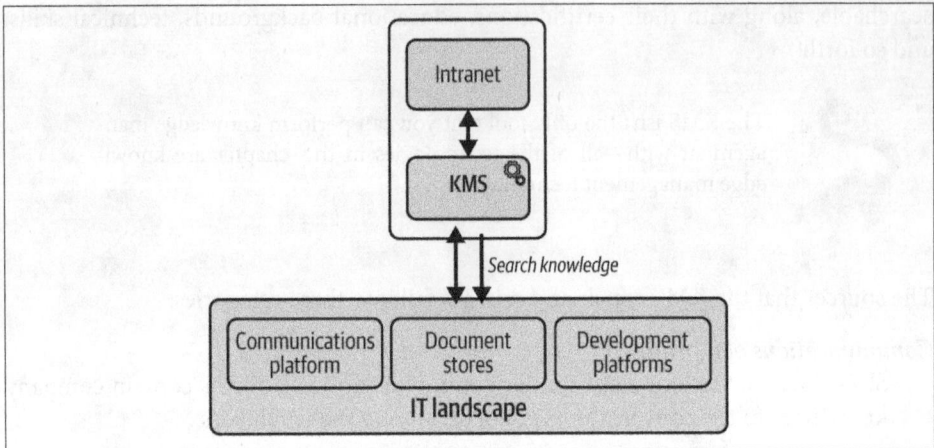

Figure 6-2. High-level view of a KMS

The main driver of the KMS is operations since it facilitates a smoothly executed value chain where the employees know what they have to do, what is happening in the company, and why it is happening.

Learning Management System

The LMS is used to train a company's employees, partners, customers, and the like. An LMS is a software application that provides the framework for handling all aspects of the learning process. It is used to administer, document, track, report, and deliver educational courses, training programs, or learning and development programs. LMSs are widely used in various educational institutions and corporate environments to enhance learning experiences.

The LMS will document that the training has been carried out according to plan, based on the type of employee. An LMS will typically contain multimedia learning materials as text, image, video, animations, and animated multiple-choice tests.

Some of the learnings that employees have to go through are stored outside the LMS, and some are stored inside it. The training taking place outside the LMS can happen in other parts of the IT landscape or in real life; for example, training in cleaning processes, mechanical processes, and the like are done in real life.

In order to function correctly, the LMS must provide an overview of the knowledge in a company that some or all of the employees have to learn. That overview will have a structure and associated business glossaries to tag the various types of learning content and make them distinguishable from other learning content. You can see a high-level view of an LMS in Figure 6-3.

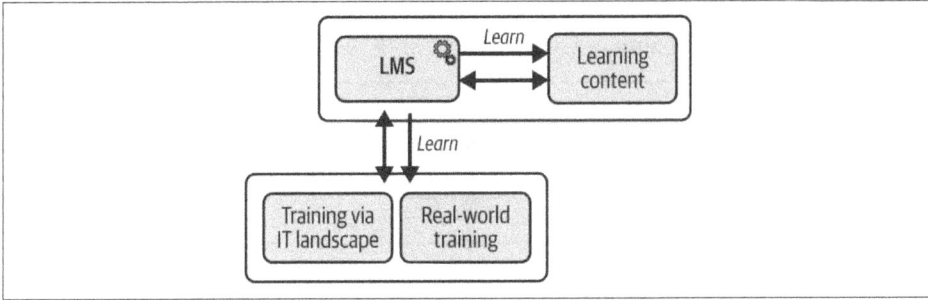

Figure 6-3. High-level view of an LMS

The LMS is intended to facilitate smooth daily operations where all employees know what they have to do. However, the LMS will typically also be used to document training needed for compliance with various regulations, such as GDPR. For more niche use cases, the LMS can be the tool used for innovation in the scenarios where technically high-skilled employees are perfecting training their programming competences, for example. That is a small use case, though.

Quality Management System

A QMS is a formalized system that documents processes, procedures, and responsibilities for achieving quality policies and objectives. Integrating the QMS with metadata repositories can significantly enhance the quality and reliability of data management within an organization.

The QMS is designed to ensure quality in especially heavily regulated industries by providing a complete overview of all processes in the company. Therefore, the QMS is a system that ensures uniformity and transparency in how industrial production takes place. The QMS is defined by ISO Technical Committee 76 in the ISO 9000 series (*https://oreil.ly/6hptU*). These standards serve as the industry-agnostic reference used at a global scale to address improved enterprise quality. The ISO 9000 series is often supplemented with industry-specific standards.

A QMS will describe a process landscape in a company and list all standard operating procedures (SOPs) that describe in detail how these processes are carried out. On that basis, the QMS serves as the heart of regulatory compliance regarding quality assurance. Inspectors from relevant authorities where the company has its activities can announce inspections in the company at any time. The inspection will always target a specific part of the company. These inspections are carried out with the assistance of the QMS, which can identify what SOPs are associated with the part of the company under inspection via the process landscape of the company. Then, inspectors can consult records and similar evidence, hopefully ascertaining that all controls have been followed and that all necessary training of personnel has been conducted. You can see the QMS's main functionality in Figure 6-4.

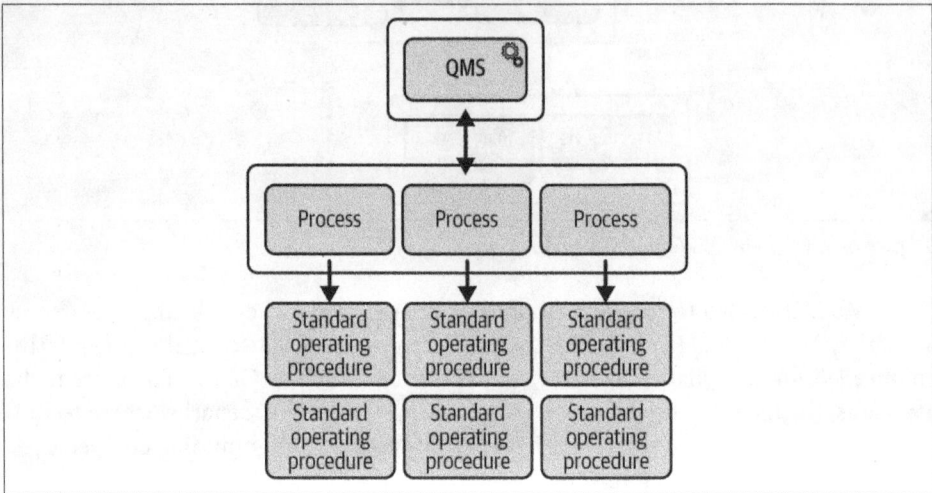

Figure 6-4. High-level view of a QMS

A QMS mostly has regulation as its driver. For heavily regulated industries, it is the most vital metadata repository for maintaining the right to be on the market. However, a well-maintained QMS standardizes processes, and it can therefore also be considered a driver for operations—as the QMS makes it crystal clear what tasks are to be carried out by whom and how.

Collection Management System

Organizations of a certain size typically have a museum explaining the history of the company. Such a museum contains:

- Art and furniture
- Artifacts, such as old products, lab equipment, and similar memorabilia
- Documents, such as letters and registries

These three elements may be digitized and made available for analytics. For example, insurance companies with decades or even centuries of data use historical data for analytics for their risk and price models.

The museum collection is described in a repository called a *collection management system* (CMSy). The CMSy is used for various purposes within the museum, including managing the collection, assigning metadata to objects, tracking current exhibitions, monitoring loans to other museums, and managing the risk of deterioration.

The management tasks of a CMSy are relatively simple in nature. However, three elements demand refined technology:

- Scans of objects, such as in formats like STL (*https://oreil.ly/BzYiC*)
- Scans of text using optical character recognition (OCR) (*https://oreil.ly/6nAqi*)
- Extremely visually compelling user interfaces

The CMSy can be contextualized to metadata management in general in two ways: its object and text content can serve analytical purposes, and its metadata structure and content can help align and smooth other metadata repositories (the latter is the case for all metadata repositories and the overall purpose of this book).

You can see a high-level view of a CMSy in Figure 6-5.

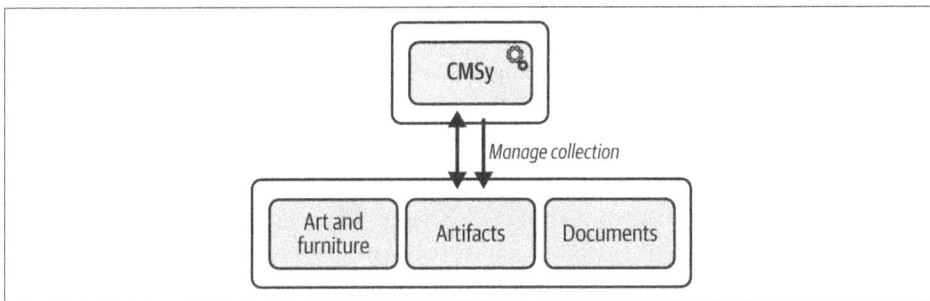

Figure 6-5. High-level view of a CMSy

The main driver for the CMSy is operations, but only indirectly. Strictly speaking, there is no need to have a company museum. Its function lies in the symbolic power of a mighty enterprise's past that can impress business partners, customers, and VIPs. Furthermore, the CMSy can direct users to sources of knowledge that can be used for innovative purposes.

Metadata Repositories for Knowledge Management

In this chapter, we explored a series of metadata repositories, this time focusing on knowledge management. Let's consolidate this information to gain a comprehensive understanding. Figure 6-6 visually presents the five repositories discussed in this chapter.

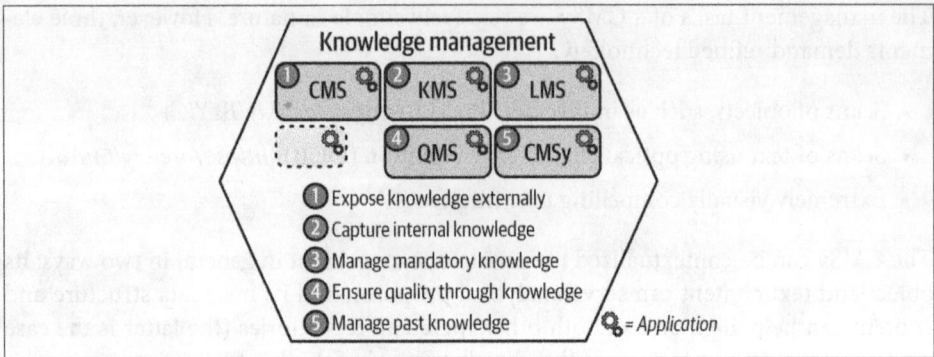

Figure 6-6. Metadata repositories for knowledge management

Let's briefly summarize the repositories:

- A CMS is your company's knowledge exposed *outside* of your company. As such, it is a source system, but it will contain an overview of the knowledge it exposes to the outside world. That overview is a metadata repository and serves as a way to coordinate all externally shared knowledge.

- A KMS is your company knowledge exposed *inside* your company. The KMS is a metadata repository that reflects knowledge from systems used to share text, speech, film, and pictures.

- The LMS is the system for learning all the relevant knowledge of all types of employees in your company. The LMS will contain a complete list of all the knowledge it is possible to learn and who has learned what kind of knowledge.

- A QMS is a dense system that depicts all processes in the company and their associated SOPs. The QMS is the metadata repository that makes it possible to run complex and highly regulated industries while guaranteeing that all processes are performed with high quality.

- Finally, a CMSy is a small metadata repository that depicts past knowledge in the company. The CMSy is uniquely used for museum and nonregulatory archiving, but its content can support daily operations.

> Metadata repositories for knowledge are the farthest apart from the IT landscape. Metadata repositories for information are a little closer, and metadata repositories for data and IT are the closest. However, metadata repositories for knowledge are very useful for understanding the complete overview of the IT landscape.

Summary

In this chapter, we looked at metadata repositories for knowledge. Here are the takeaways:

- Metadata repositories for knowledge are the farthest away from the IT landscape.
- Metadata repositories for knowledge depict knowledge that is to be communicated outside and inside the company, about the company's past and present.
- Most of the metadata repositories for knowledge are motivated by daily operations.
- The CMS communicates knowledge outside the company.
- The KMS communicates knowledge inside the company.
- The LMS ensures the learning of knowledge.
- The QMS facilitates the knowledge to run quality processes in the company.
- The CMSy displays the knowledge of the past.
- The LMS and the QMS can overlap.

CHAPTER 7

Why We Have Been Doing Metadata Management Wrong

In the previous chapters, we discussed a wealth of metadata repositories, each within a specific domain and each leveraging a specific capability—managing everything from endpoints to future states of application portfolios and data discovery, from information security to the quality of enterprise learning and knowledge. Pondering the extensive list of tooling needed to manage all these capabilities based on metadata, we can see that one thing is clear: the total sum of capabilities leveraged by metadata management tools and their subsequent repositories will never be consolidated into one technology and will never be carried out by one management practice, let alone one team.

Until now, we have not looked at most of the metadata repositories that we have discussed in their totality. However, that is what this book has set out to do: create a view of many repositories that has hitherto not been juxtaposed and compared. The purpose of this view is the following: across these many, many repositories, organizations register the same type of metadata—each time slightly differently structured—to carry out tasks in their respective teams. However, this is a substantial waste of time, and it creates inefficient, redundant, and even opposing depictions of the IT landscape.

If you are thinking, "Couldn't AI play a role in this?" then you are absolutely right. Check out Parts II and III.

Different Practices Have Different Metamodels

Enterprises cannot establish metadata management with a bottom-up approach alone. Bottom-up approaches are, for example, where data engineers meticulously depict the contents of a database in isolation from the rest of the organization. In fact, this merely creates another monolithic view of what the IT landscape consists of. To succeed with metadata management, we need to also look to other metadata repositories that already exist.

Employees tasked with metadata management derive metadata from, for example, a table, adding technical, operational, and business metadata descriptions to data. In doing so, they inadvertently create a silo. Their approach is not wrong—far from it—but it's incredibly narrow. The context surrounding what they are trying to resolve is enormous, ultimately aiming to describe the entire IT landscape.

In enterprises, the same thing therefore happens again and again: technologies are often being pushed by ambitious employees (close to or approaching the C-suite), backed by knowledgeable consultants and visionary software producers. Repeatedly, waves of metadata repositories hit organizations for regulative, operative, and innovative purposes: data protection, information security, and data-driven innovation; smaller waves, like data observability or data lineage; alongside larger, sometimes more traditional waves, such as IT service management, enterprise architecture management, quality management—and many more. Each has its own metadata repository, team, and project aimed at "mapping the IT landscape once and for all!" and working in isolation, in different parts of the organization, to handle a specific task. But all are working with a picture of the IT landscape that essentially is the same, with varying purposes and overlapping types of metadata such as:

- Applications
- Capabilities
- Processes
- Projects
- Servers

- Transit gateways
- Endpoints
- Data types, formats, and schemas
- Levels of confidentiality
- Levels of sensitivity

The problem with doing metadata management in isolation goes back to the definition of metadata: it exists in multiple places at once. Many metadata repositories can contain the same type of metadata, and evidence from the metamodels shows that the same type of metadata often appears in multiple metadata repositories.

Therefore, we must think differently about metadata management. We cannot and should not rely *only* on a bottom-up approach because when we are depicting our IT landscape, such an approach is a monolithic way of performing metadata management. Ultimately, this results in a cacophony of metadata, dissolving the truth that everyone is trying to obtain because the same types of metadata are registered again and again, in opposing ways, across many different metadata repositories. We have had decades of proof that the bottom-up approach does not work outside of a very narrow context. We cannot rely on a single tool or capability to manage metadata—it will not be effective.

Instead, we must view metadata within a holistic, horizontal context, understanding why different teams depict the IT landscape with metadata and how they do it. This is key to several things:

- We can understand the overlap of metadata between metadata repositories.
- We can make metadata more robust across domains.

But in doing this, we need to take into account that the metamodels for metadata repositories have variations. The metadata from one repository is not directly transferable to another repository—not in the sense that it is more high-level or more detailed but simply because the structure is different and untranslatable. They don't match.

Metamodels in various communities or teams do not match because the insights and actions they deliver don't exactly match, but they do overlap to some extent. For example, an application will never be expressed in the same way in an EAM tool and a CMDB, because the EAM tool is not as interested in listing instances of an application as it is focused on delivering a more generic picture that can create forecasts of the evolution of the entire IT landscape. However, listing the instances of applications is necessary in a CMDB because specific configurations may apply for a specific instance—which must be illustrated in the CMDB. Moreover, what is considered to be an application will vary: one will include software in a definition of applications, and the other will exclude it.

Table 7-1 is an overview of all of the metadata repositories discussed in this book. It also lists the core capabilities of these metadata repositories, their peripheral capabilities, some of the metadata types they typically contain, and a description of the metamodel of the repository.

Please note that this list is not exhaustive and that the metadata in these repositories can vary from what is listed in the table.

Table 7-1. Metadata repository matrix

Metadata repository	Core capability	Peripheral capabilities	Frequent metadata types	Metamodel characteristics
Asset management system (AMS)	Depict license cost per application	Application overview (EAM/ CMDB capabilities)	Applications Software Instances Users Licenses	Number of instances Number of users and licenses
Business process management system (BPMS)	Mine and examine processes to rationalize them	Data lineage (DC capabilities)	Processes Employee types	Structure and hierarchy of processes
Collection management system (CMSy)	The deep past of the company	RIMS	Products People Projects	Typically, simple objects in a list
Configuration management database (CMDB)	Manage the present and past of the IT landscape by listing hardware and software	Future planning (EAM capabilities) Integrations (IR capabilities) Deep past (RIMS capabilities)	Applications Integrations Processes Confidentiality Criticality Data owners System owners Configuration item types	A strategic, high-level dimension and deeper levels representing software and hardware at the physical level; both levels are depicted for the present and the past
Content management system (CMS)	Overview of what knowledge is shared on which websites, outside of the company	Knowledge overview (KMS capabilities)	Unstructured data Product data	Product categories Topics
Database modeler	Depending on type, either shows a logical data model or extracts a physical data model	Data model overview (DC capabilities)	Data models	Mirrors the organization of the database or databases
Data catalog (DC)	Scans data sources to make them searchable	Integrations (IR capabilities) Data models (DBM capabilities)	Data types Data lineage Physical data models	Makes data easily discoverable for the entire company
Data lake	Stores and exposes data in a way that eases ingestion by compromising quality	None	Loaded data of any type	No fixed metamodel
Data lakehouse	Combines the capabilities of the data lake and the data warehouse	None	Loaded data of any type	No fixed metamodel
Data observability	Measures the quality and state of data	Data search (DC capabilities)	Data types Data quality levels	No fixed metamodel
Data protection registry (DPR)	Depicts how sensitive data is processed in the company	Data lineage (DC capabilities) Processes (BPMS capabilities)	Sensitive data types Processes	Data types organized in levels of sensitivity

Metadata repository	Core capability	Peripheral capabilities	Frequent metadata types	Metamodel characteristics
Data warehouse	Stores and exposes data in a way that eases quality ingestion by compromising ingestion	Integration layer (antipattern)	Loaded data of any type	No fixed metamodel
Endpoint management system (EMS)	Lists all the hardware in the company and the software installed on the hardware	Application overview (CMDB capabilities)	Phones Laptops Servers Data centers	Simple set of endpoints to be completed in bulk
Enterprise architecture management (EAM) tool	Depicts the future IT landscape by calculating the consequences of changes to the IT landscape of the present	Present and past IT landscape (CMDB capabilities)	Processes Capabilities Applications Integrations	A relatively static metamodel with a high-level picture of the present and future IT landscape
Information security management system (ISMS)	Creates an overview of information security risks	Privacy	Confidential data types Enterprise applications Hardware Risks	A simple, weighted list of risks
Integration repository (IR)	Maps all integrations between applications when creating these integrations	Data lineage (DC capabilities)	Batch jobs API jobs Events	Ranging from text documents to the types of integrations
IT service management system (ITSM)	Provides an overview of small change requests to the existing IT landscape	None	Projects Applications Hardware Minor changes Employees Incident types	A simple list of requests organized after type and mirrored against the metamodel of the CMDB
Knowledge management system (KMS)	Makes (un)structured data searchable	Learning management	Knowledge types (explicit, implicit, tacit, procedural, declarative, a posteriori, a priori)	Simple folder structure, potentially combined with an ontology
Learning management system (LMS)	Depicts the IT landscape	Knowledge management	Knowledge types Learning processes Learners	Simple folder structure, potentially combined with an ontology, including learners and learning stages
Quality management system (QMS)	Ensures that overall quality policies are set, also for the entire IT landscape	Business process mapping	Policies Processes Work instructions Audit trail	Very complex metamodel spanning multiple systems and maybe not even fully documented
Records and information management system (RIMS)	Documents the deep past of the IT landscape	Past (CMDB capabilities)	Organization Data types Projects	Simple folder structure, potentially combined with an ontology

Most of the metadata repositories listed in Table 7-1 will claim that they deliver sensitivity and confidentiality capabilities. They don't. Only the DPO can assess sensitivity, and only the CISO can assess the confidentiality of data. That is done in their respective metadata repositories—not elsewhere!

There are two other elements to take into consideration:

- Dark metadata
- Other applications and domains

Dark Metadata

What Table 7-1 shows us is a comprehensive set of metadata repositories, all leveraging unique capabilities. But it also shows us that the peripheral capabilities of the metadata repositories somewhat overlap. Even more striking is that the metadata that these repositories contain clearly overlaps; managed in isolation, these repositories are endless repetitions of the same exercise to list, map, and relate the same types of metadata again and again.

Let's consider this reality in the context of dark data, applied to metadata as dark metadata. *Dark data* is data that is created or collected when executing the value chain of the company but that is not discovered and used for analytics or other purposes than its initial usage.[1]

Dark metadata is the same as dark data: (meta)data already used in one context but not harnessed in another, such as details stored in private emails that would have value in other parts of the company; configurations stored in manufacturing machines that are hand-tuned and not backed up or analyzed; and data stored inside application databases that is exposed only to application code even though it might be useful elsewhere.

It is an empirical fact that enterprises at large are full of dark metadata—this book has delivered the evidence from actual software metamodels all leveraging their own needed capabilities, all of which are used in companies all over the world yet are managed in perfect isolation from one another within these companies.

---

1 See Gartner's definition of *dark data* (*https://oreil.ly/r3zfa*) and Wikipedia (*https://oreil.ly/Huwjz*).

Think of dark metadata like this: if your data is siloed, and you only use a bottom-up approach for describing your data with metadata, then your metadata will also be siloed. What follows from the definition of *metadata*—that it is in two places at once—is that multiple silos of metadata exist because of the bottom-up approach: an endless copying of something to somewhere else without an attempt to grasp the totality. The only way to avoid dark metadata is to apply a top-down approach and analyze what metadata is already in which repositories.

It is also a matter of fact that this is a reality that can be *played*: metadata management can be performed honestly (but naively), viciously, or just as a hard, dirty job by ambitious employees, consultancy companies, and software vendors alike, something we will examine further in Chapter 9.

Other Applications and Domains

Table 7-1 lists only a selected number of the metadata repositories that depict the IT landscape—the ones discussed in this book. However, more repositories exist. The following is a list of other metadata repositories, but it is not exhaustive either:

- IT management
  - Project and portfolio management
  - DevOps tools and code repositories
  - Backup systems
  - Active directory
- Data management
  - Data lineage
  - Data observability
  - Data lakehouse
  - Master data management systems
  - Data dictionaries
  - Data products
  - ML/AI model repositories
- Information management
  - Product information management
  - Business glossary
- Knowledge management
  - Library management systems
  - Textual warehouses[2]

---

2 To explore the idea of textual warehouses, see *Turning Text into Gold: Taxonomies and Textual Analytics* by Bill Inmon (Technics Publications).

Outside of this list of concrete repositories are other domains that depict the IT land-scape, one being wisdom (AI) management. It is likely that managing AI will turn into its own distinct management domain in the future.

Other applications and domains will be discussed in depth as part of the meta grid in Part III.

A Possibility: The Coming Together of Teams and Technologies

Throughout the history of enterprise IT, various management practices and subprac-tices have emerged to manage parts of the IT landscape, both its hardware compo-nents and the software and data they contain: IT, data, information, and knowledge management, as described in the previous chapters. Quite strikingly, these practices emerged in isolation from one another. That led them to look at the IT landscape without any or little awareness of the fact—or even actively ignoring—that other practices were doing that exact same thing. Therefore, these practices identified the same types of metadata. And that led to an arabesque of metadata repositories, describing the same types of metadata in opposing ways and manifesting themselves in nonidentical metamodels. But this can be changed. These practices can come together.

Parts II and III of this book offer a collaborative approach to these practices, address-ing both organizational aspects—through a distinct team topology[3] (Part II); and technical aspects—through an architecture I call the *meta grid* (Part III).

Understanding the IT landscape is no simple task. It is vast, and the tools at our dis-posal are all limited by a certain focus, driven by a core capability they aim to lever-age. Too often, the metadata repositories claim to provide a complete description of the IT landscape. This surfaces in software sales materials in phrases such as "the sin-gle pane of glass," "enterprise-wide search," and "one entry to a single source of truth"—claims to deliver a much-desired reality.

But practical experiences over many decades show that no company, however well staffed and supported by technology and external help, will be able to obtain a solid overview of the IT landscape when multiple practices do almost the same thing with multiple technologies, all in isolation from one another.

So let's change that! The management practices described in the preceding chapters can come together, and it will make a substantial, positive difference for *your* com-pany if they do. You will be able to obtain a more consolidated overview of the IT landscape, with many benefits to follow.

---

3 Team topologies will be explained in Part II.

Here are two points you will need to take into account:

- Money
- Structured versus unstructured

Money

Money plays a crucial role in uniting the various domains that assess the IT landscape in a company. For these domains to come together, it's important to note that they have different offsets, with some being very well funded and others less so. However challenging this may be as the offset for a collective discussion, the solutions are within reach—focus on those and you will succeed.

IT management is often underfinanced, with a fiscal motivation to turn every activity into capital expenditure (CapEx). This approach can lead to long-running projects and a backlog of tasks because CapEx is typically taxed less than operating expenses (OpEx), which represent the ongoing costs of running an enterprise IT landscape. CFOs often prefer CapEx funding because it offers short-term financial relief, although this compromises long-term stability. As a result, organizations can experience poor methodologies from ever-changing external consultants, internal confusion, and a constant pressure to take on more software-as-a-service (SaaS) solutions.

In contrast, data management has seen substantial funding in recent decades as companies pursue their ambition of becoming *data driven*. This ambition has many different definitions—however, the consequences are clear and always the same: expensive data teams, with data engineers, data scientists, and a data management/ governance team, along with a "data stack" (the tooling described in Chapter 4). Compared to the typical outcomes of these teams, they have been funded disproportionately.

Information management had its heyday with the rise of the World Wide Web (1990– 2000), embodying an enterprise response to many of the challenges and possibilities that the information highway opened, such as records and information retention and information security. However, since attention has shifted from these practices focused on regulatory compliance, they now struggle with limited budgets. Despite this, the subpractices of information management survive because of their strong methodologies and deliveries that the enterprise actually needs.

Knowledge management is more split financially. Quality and learning management are demanded skills and are funded sufficiently to function while pure knowledge management systems often remain underfunded.

When bringing these domains together to create a more unified view of the IT landscape, it's important to recognize the differing levels of attention and resources they receive. We will take a deeper look at this in Part II.

Structured Versus Unstructured

Typically, technical staff from IT and data management will consider everything organized in tables as *structured* data and everything in text, image, sound, and video files as *unstructured* data (with graph technology as an expression of semistructured data). This is depicted in the scale in Figure 7-1.

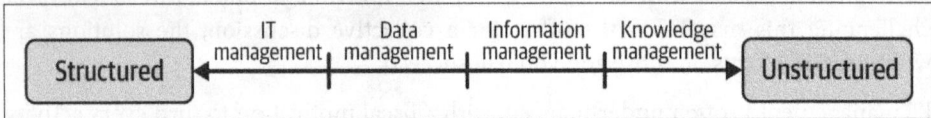

Figure 7-1. Scale of structured to unstructured data

However simple and useful this scale is, it is data centric. It has the table as the decisive element for judging whether something is structured or not. This means that uniting the management practices that look at an IT landscape will lead to misunderstandings between them. Information management and knowledge management will be trained in practices that consider language as a parameter of organization independently of storage solution (table or text). This paradox is illustrated in Figure 7-2, where a value in a field (left) is categorically thought of as structured despite the poor data quality, and the value of words in a sentence is categorically thought of as unstructured, even though the quality is complete.

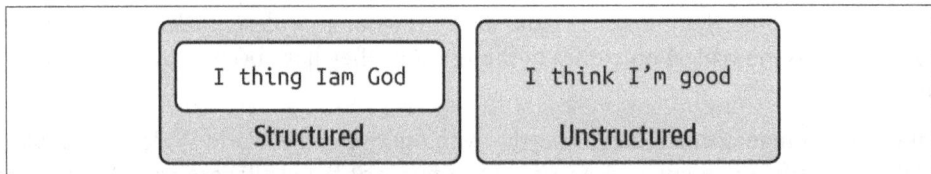

Figure 7-2. The distinction between structured and unstructured data is a paradox

Summary

In this chapter, we collected a complete view of the metadata repositories discussed throughout the book. Table 7-1 indicates that while the core capabilities of the various metadata repositories within an enterprise are unique, the peripheral capabilities more often overlap. Even more, metadata in general overlaps, even though metamodels differ. On that basis, we can see that:

- Different practices have different metamodels:
  - A metamodel depicts the types of metadata typically contained in a metadata repository.
  - All metadata repositories leverage specific capabilities, their peripheral capabilities somewhat overlap, and they contain similar metadata.
- Dark metadata is the metadata that is described in one metadata repository but unknown in other repositories, which therefore register the same type of metadata again for their own distinct purposes.
- A substantial number of practices have described the IT landscape of companies for operative, regulative, and innovative purposes. If these practices come together, they can unite forces and describe the IT landscape with substantially more solidity.

The rest of the book will describe the organizational and technical dimension of this coming together. Stay tuned!

Metadata Repositories Must Be Coordinated by a Data Discovery Team

Part II is about the organizational aspect of metadata management.

Chapter 8 describes a sociology of employees, consultants, and software vendors in a constellation of interests where each of them can play the role of the good, the bad, or the ugly. Technology implementation brings out the best and the worst in people, and in this short chapter we explore what that does to metadata.

In Chapter 9 we explore the concept of this new team and its role in structuring metadata management. The goal is to establish a team that coordinates metadata repositories to collectively enhance their quality and coverage. True to the mechanics of decentralized architecture, the data discovery team is an enabling team and a platform team, a team topology—however, this last detail will first be discussed in Part III.

Are you ready? Let's go!

The Good, the Bad, and the Ugly

Implementing technology in a company takes three types of groups:

- Employees
- Consultants
- Software vendors

Employees in companies are often tasked with finding technological answers to business problems with the help of metadata repositories. However, after having identified the desired software, companies often find themselves lacking the technological understanding and maybe even the subject matter expertise to implement the given metadata repository. The technology vendor will most likely have a *customer success team*, which—as the name indicates—will help the customer be successful after the sales team has won the client and signed a deal. But in most cases, the technology vendor will not offer dedicated implementation projects, even though the customer may be in need of those. Enter the technology consultant: companies hire consultants to help them implement technology because the companies need help with doing this and the vendors of software are focused on creating software—not implementing it.

Anyone who has been an employee, a consultant, or a software vendor in this constellation knows that it is a very special situation of high psychological intensity, time pressure, and technological challenges. This chapter provides a brief sociological analysis[1] of the interactions among the employee, the consultant, and the software vendor when assessing and implementing metadata repositories in companies.

If you hold a leadership position in an organization, read these pages carefully.

Setting the Stage

In a variety of constellations, the three groups can *all* play the part of the good, the bad, and the ugly when implementing metadata repositories in companies. Together, these groups create both great solutions and complete disasters. It depends on how they interact and what their intentions are. This is depicted in Figure 8-1.

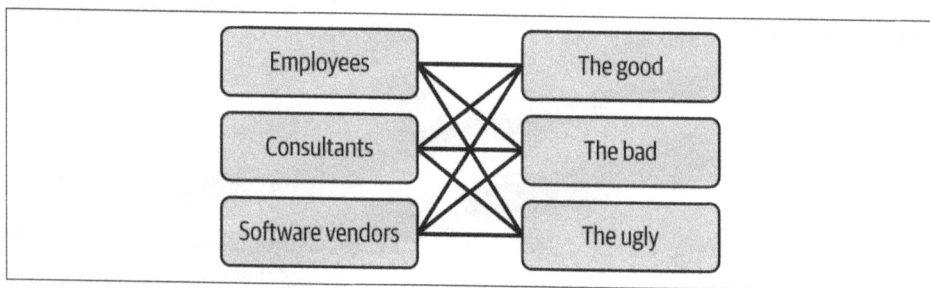

Figure 8-1. The good, the bad, and the ugly matrix

---

1 This sociology is based on practical experience—it is the reality of industrial companies globally. I have discussed this topic with countless software vendors, consultants, and company employees (and I have had all three roles myself). However, if you want to study the topic further, I suggest consulting the following: (1) Change management frameworks (*https://oreil.ly/Y2lM2*) such as Lewin's change model, the ADKAR Model, and Kotter's change model can be useful, but in regard to the sociology put forward in this chapter, they are not a one-to-one match. Change management is focused on making change happen while the real interplay of employees, consultants, and software vendors raises questions about the incentives people have for acting like they do; changes occur for reasons that are not always useful and honest, and disregarding this often leads to poorly implemented metadata repositories. (2) Data governance books such as *Disrupting Data Governance: A Call to Action* by Laura B. Madsen (Technics Publications); see, for example, the passage on pages 20–21: "Because data work can be tech-heavy, and the 'tech' part of the work is easier to tangibly define, we tend to prematurely invest money in software. But without tightly tying that investment to real, long-term benefits related to our data, we lose out on the positive portion of the calculation....Larger software projects such as metadata management...round out the 'tech-heavy' aspect." Such perspectives come closer to the sociology put forward in this chapter, but, as Madsen also points out, metadata management exceeds data governance programs and the data domain as described in Chapter 4, wherein data governance programs will typically operate.

Companies are motivated to implement metadata repositories for reasons already discussed: regulative, operative, or innovative agendas push companies to create overviews of their IT landscapes with metadata repositories. But in doing so, human nature tends to unveil itself. Human desires and intentions shape the implementations of metadata repositories—as with all technologies—and accordingly, the usefulness and appropriateness of these technologies.

People may want to create a good overview of a distinct type of metadata, help a company get the most out of a technology, or support it with software that helps speed up and smooth manual, slow procedures. But some people—not all—just want a promotion if they are employees in a company. And if they work for a software vendor, some just want to sell software licenses. Those who find themselves in the consultant position just want to bill hours. Sometimes these things blend. And sometimes they *also* blend with missing funds and bad management.

Metadata management, accordingly, is shaped by that. In the following sections, we discuss how these three groups act and interact in this order:

- The good
- The bad
- The ugly

The Good

A good employee for metadata management is a rare person—a "unicorn." This is a person who understands how to methodologically shape a given type of metadata, such as business processes. Furthermore, it's a person who understands what repository would ideally be in scope for this kind of metadata, in the context of the particular capability that is to be leveraged. This takes substantial experience, strong discipline, and clear communication skills. The good employee will make the repository fly: it will serve its purpose and deliver the desired capability. The good employee can turn naive, though, and waste time and money in operational costs. Then, such an employee believes that they are on a mission to create a complete overview of the company in the metadata repository they are working in.

The good consultant is focused on assisting the customer with getting the metadata repository up and running. This typically requires the consultant to have a thorough understanding of the technology—the specific software—that the customer is implementing, not just the technology category. For example, you would expect a good consultant to not only know EAM tools but also the specific technology. Therefore, it is a good idea to examine the certifications of consultants, as most software vendors provide certificates that attest to a person's knowledge of their technology. Furthermore, the good consultant must have a thorough understanding of the company for which they contract: their vertical, their products, and their pain points. Finally, the good consultant must be able to translate all of the aforementioned knowledge into a succinct implementation roadmap for the metadata repository in question so that the likelihood of adoption is increased by the presence of and input from the consultant—and not decreased, which may be the case with consultants who have only technical subject matter expertise.

Good software vendors are honest—and they actually exist. They will loyally inform you about the core capabilities of their technology and be able to provide in-depth explanations of the technical architecture and the choices that have led to this architecture. This includes the functionality that was descoped or not prioritized in order to deliver a functional product. Also, good software vendors honestly inform their customers about the capabilities that are peripheral or external to the technology they offer. For customers who are eager to explore and use their technology, good software vendors will steer perspectives for usage away from external and peripheral capabilities and toward the core capabilities of their technology, as illustrated in Figure 8-2.

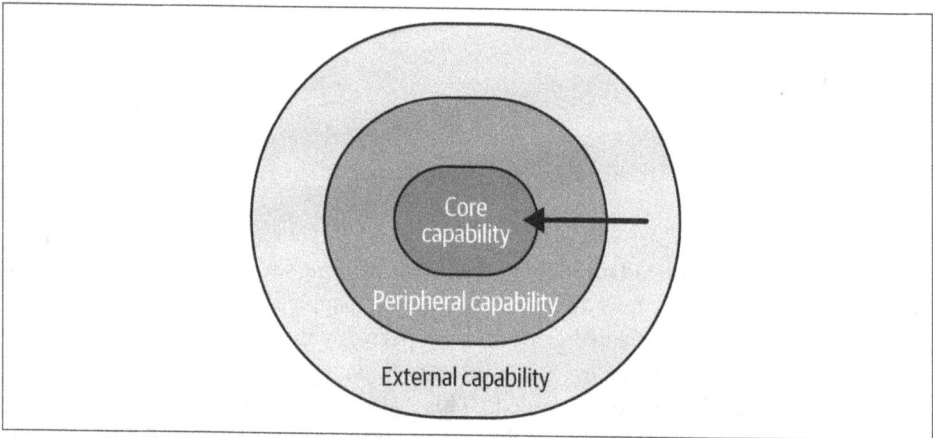

Figure 8-2. The good software vendor will focus on core capabilities

What the good do to metadata: the rest of this book is basically about how to enable the good ones to win. The good employees structure the metadata they work with by following a fit-for-purpose methodology, and what they produce is solid; the metadata is clear, it is logically phrased, and it will stand the test of time. The good consultant will ensure that the correct metadata repository is used for the core capability since the consultant knows this technology category in depth and knows the specific software vendor well. The good consultant also understands the identity of the company for which the consultant is contracting. Finally, the good software vendor will sell the software for what it is, not for what it isn't—it will serve the intended purpose for the company.

The Bad

Middle managers are rarely content with only being middle managers. They want to move up, become VP of something. One of the most used paths to promotion is implementation of technology—on time and at all costs. Metadata repositories die in the hands of managers with more ambitions for themselves than for the companies they serve. These repositories die because only the *functional requirements* are delivered: what the repository is supposed to *do*, purely technically speaking. Documenting the success of the functional requirements will typically be enough for an opportunistic middle manager to get promoted. They can say, "See for yourself, the system works. I made it happen—promote me."

The *nonfunctional requirements* however—what the system is supposed to *be*—are ignored. In those nonfunctional requirements reside the quality and completeness of the metadata in scope for the repository. The fact that it should be aligned with the other metadata repositories that leverage different capabilities but contain some of the same types of metadata is ignored. The existence of these metadata repositories is ignored. But figuring this out and confronting the middle manager is often too complex for executive management teams to grasp—they simply don't have the time and expert bandwidth to discover this. Therefore, this is the root cause of many of the poorly working metadata repositories in the world: bad employees simply want a promotion, not necessarily a fit and well-maintained metadata repository.

The bad consultant adds a layer of cynicism to the bad employee. Typically, a great selling point for a bad consultant is a big "spaghetti ball" of technical complexity (Figure 8-3). It doesn't really matter what it depicts: it can be processes, integrations, risks—as long as it looks complicated!

Because it looks extremely confusing, all the consultant needs to do is say, "My analysis shows that you are out of control; see how confusing this is? You don't know your own reality. But fear not. I can make this confusion go away. All you need to do is hire me and let me implement this technology that will allow you to get the perfect overview of your IT landscape."

However, the "analysis" that the external consultant has conducted, which has resulted in the big ball of spaghetti, has some obvious biases. It is more profitable for the consultant to pretend that:

- The company is not in control.
- The complexity is high, even though it may be low.
- Metadata repositories leveraging capabilities to handle the problem do not exist.
- The only way out is a consultancy project and more technology.

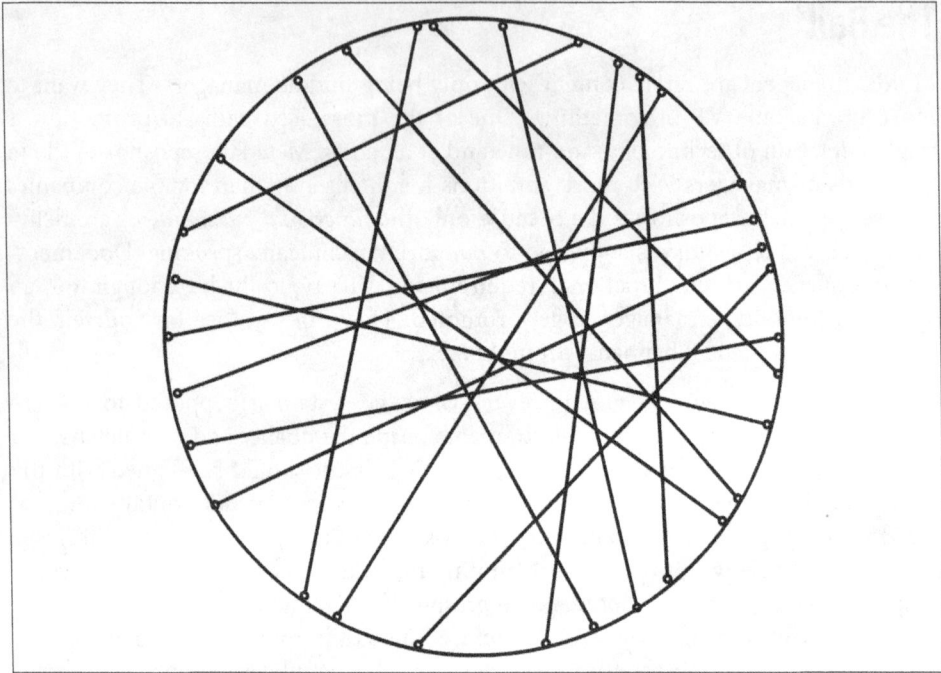

Figure 8-3. The big ball of spaghetti: the classic selling point from the bad consultant

But the bad consultant is nothing but a trickster: the analysis is not real; it's an illusion made up to make a profit. Accordingly, I suggest we call this the *confusion illusion*. Each confusion illusion will break down the solidity of your established metadata management practices, and it is highly supported by the bad employee as the vessel for promotion, together with the bad software vendor as a means to sell software licenses. Confusion illusions thrive as an opportunistic motivated concept in companies all over the world. And the consequence is that they deteriorate metadata repositories with new layers of the confusion that they were pitched to make disappear.[2]

The bad software vendor will be focused on selling licenses at all costs, even if the use case in question is not a proper fit for the technology. It boils down to what the specific core capability of the metadata repository is. The core capability of, for example, a CMDB is to manage the past and the present of an IT landscape at a detailed level, but the bad software vendor of a CMDB technology will make you believe it can do DevOps or project and portfolio management, if you say you need a solution for that. Basically, what the bad software vendor is doing is pushing the use case of their

---

2 While smoothly not pitching to solve the problems that truly hurt.

technology from the core capability toward peripheral or even external capabilities (Figure 8-4).

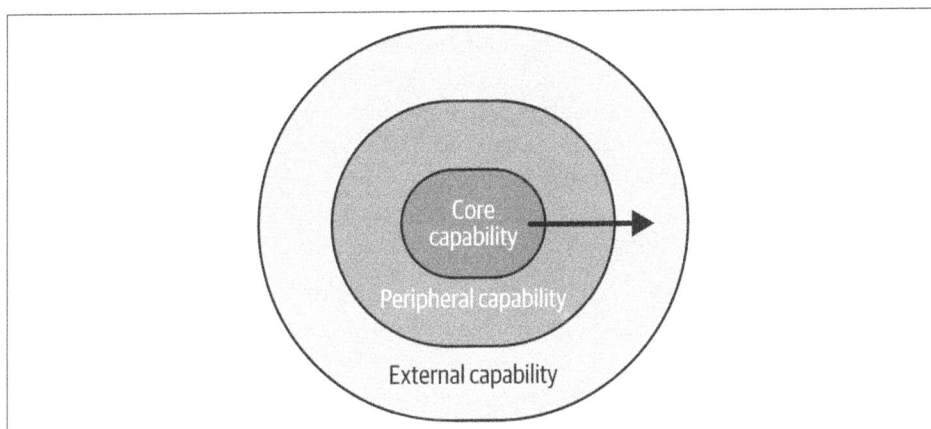

Figure 8-4. Bad software vendors push metadata repositories to external capabilities

For metadata repositories, the bad software vendor's approach entails a high churn rate. Since the specific technology will not deliver the promised capabilities, user adoption remains low, and finally, usage of the technology is descoped completely and phased out.

You may ask yourself: why would software vendors apply such an approach; what motivates some to be *bad* software vendors? There are several reasons, and they generally revolve around short-term priorities:

Sales targets

A substantial percentage of a sales employee's salary is a bonus based on how well they sell. The more licenses they sell to the more companies, the higher the bonus. That can push some software vendors to oversell their solutions because that is profitable in the short term for them. However, several mechanisms usually keep this tendency under control, aside from the ethics of the software vendor. Companies usually perform a proof of concept to really test if the technology is fit for purpose; overselling is often identified during that phase. In those cases, the objective of the proof of concept is clear, and the added value and results are measurable. Furthermore, the internal operations of the software vendors will keep the sales team focused on a reasonable use case because they have to hand the customer over to the customer success team, which is assessed based on user adoption. If they do not stand a realistic chance of making the customer successful, then their internal feedback is provided to the executive management team, which can take measures against the sales team.

Small software vendors grow as venture capitalists (VCs) invest in them. Typically, a VC will look at sales to get an indication of the potential return on investment when they are considering investing in a small software company. And that's a catch for companies that purchase software licenses as well as for metadata management: even though they are the customer, they may not be the *real* customer but merely a means to an end. Often, startups are just interested in "collecting logos"—that is, getting a company to sign up for their software even if it's free. In practice, this often means selling to a single team, creating extreme fragmentation and siloing.

What the bad do to metadata: far too often, companies find themselves in a situation where the bad ones win—the bad employees, the bad consultants, and the bad software vendors. In tech in general, and specifically for tech dedicated to metadata management, the outcome is that implementations are likely to fail. Metadata management entails an endeavor far beyond the short-term perspectives of the most basic human desires in professional life: promotion, well-paid labor, and profit. Accordingly, metadata repositories decrease in scope and quality from the get-go, not the other way around. It's the structure of the metadata in scope that will suffer; it will be haphazard and not useful.

The Ugly

The ugly employee will make a metadata repository work. Although it will be a slightly sloppy setup, it will also be pragmatic: it will work. The ugly employee knows that perfection is the enemy of the good and that metadata repositories will work best if their progress and adoption aren't stalled by long, academic discussions about how they should be implemented—which can often be the case. The ugly employee knows that the core capability isn't leveraged correctly, which may be a result of technical challenges or cultural imbalances or resistance in an organization. For example, a group or an influential person sees certain metadata substantially differently than what the metadata repository allows for and pushes that context into the repository.

The ugly consultant is the perfect delivery person for the 65% functional solution. The metadata repository will be in production on time and on budget but lacking essential features. It will most likely never get up and running, despite declarations about such intentions. The ugly consultant thrives in the delivery space that addresses the strongest pain points for the business but where value is still delivered. It is fair to assume that the ugly consultant will be closely connected to the company for which they deliver an implementation—that it is neither the last nor the first project this consultant delivers. Very good consultants are hard to find.

The ugly software vendor will attempt to make their technology work in odd cases. However, unlike the bad software vendor, the ugly software vendor is focused on making the hacks they push actually work. Ultimately, that will lead to metadata repositories being used in contexts that are not intended from the software vendor's side, but they will work to some extent.

Most enterprise realities of metadata management are *ugly*. And that's OK. It's rare to find people who master and practice metadata management capabilities at the *good* level because they will be in niche roles as praised specialist employees or in highly esteemed consultancy roles.

> If you are certified in, for example, a specific modeling discipline like Unified Modeling Language or BPMN, or you have in-depth knowledge of library classification systems like Universal Decimal Classification and Dewey Decimal Classification, claim your right to be an expert. You are well equipped to deliver solutions well beyond the typical *ugly* outcome of metadata repositories.

What the ugly do to metadata: in short, the ugly make metadata work. Really good, really clean metadata management is rarely seen in companies, and no one is to blame for that. It's a matter of too many incentives to do otherwise for all players, and the mechanics of changing this are weak. In the midst of this conundrum are the people performing ugly metadata management. They do not deliver perfectly functional solutions, but they deliver something that somehow works.

Summary

When implementing metadata repositories in companies, a delicate and difficult interplay among company employees, consultants, and software vendors unfolds. This interplay can go in many directions: it can be extraordinarily fruitful, it can be mediocre—or it can be really bad. As there are many outcomes, the summary of this chapter is placed in a table so that you can easily compare the various scenarios taking place in your company right now. Table 8-1 provides an overview of the good, the bad, and the ugly in a matrix that explains each case for the employee, consultant, and software vendor respectively.

To alter the reality of the good, the bad, and the ugly, I have one suggestion for you: the data discovery team. It will work on building a simple yet powerful approach to metadata management. The data discovery team is process oriented and in it for the long haul. If they have the power and initiative, they can evolve from an ugly state to a good state. In fact, continuous evolution is the only solution since new tools and data systems are adopted over time.

You can read all about it in the next chapter!

Table 8-1. The good, the bad, and the ugly matrix

	The good	The bad	The ugly
Employee	The good employee promotes the core capability of the metadata repository. The good employee has an extraordinary understanding of the nature of the metadata in scope for the particular metadata repository. This is both in terms of how metadata should be structured and how deep the metadata depiction should go as well as in which direction. In the context of the knowledge management domain (discussed in Chapter 6), for example, the good employee knows that a CMS is not an LMS and that the metadata in these systems is not to be shaped in the same way—even though it might describe the same reality. The good employee will have deep, context-specific knowledge of the company in which they find themselves. The good employee is closely connected to the good consultant who will support a correctly scoped contextualization.	The bad employee promotes themselves at the expense of the metadata repository. This is done with relatively functional metadata repositories, implemented just in time. The actual metadata is paying the ultimate price—its structure is not thought through. Fundamentally, the bad employee does not care about metadata management in any sense but cares only about themselves. The bad employee will be focused on short-term deliverables. That really is the only way to succeed for the bad employee—this person has to leave the metadata responsibility before any signs of poor functionality are discovered and need to be resolved. The bad employee will seek promotions as soon as possible after having implemented the metadata repository, preferably outside the company in which the repository was implemented to avoid being confronted with the poor functionality.	The ugly employee promotes both themselves and the metadata repository at the relative expense of the metadata repository but with occasional surprising usages. The ugly employee will have a reasonable targeted measure of success. The ugly employee can be motivated by the notion of a single source of truth. They might actively believe in the metadata repository's core, peripheral, and external capabilities, and therefore, in a true enterprise context, they can be naive. The ugly employee is frequently found in companies and is not necessarily bad for the metadata repository. The ugly employee takes responsibility, but not to an extent that harnesses the full potential of the metadata repository, and they may at the same time exceed the purpose of the metadata repository by pushing it toward external capabilities.

	The good	The bad	The ugly
Consultant	The good consultant focuses on the specific task at hand and the specific metadata repository in question. The good consultant will offer experience and understanding of what capability exactly is to be leveraged when implementing a metadata repository: what is in scope and what is out of scope, in terms of capability, as well as what is a peripheral capability that may be relevant in the specific case. It should be expected that the good consultant knows all relevant standards and methods for the metadata in scope. For example, in the case of the information management domain, they know ISO 27001 for information security or BPMN for business processes (see Chapter 5 for details).	The bad consultant senses when internal knowledge about the IT landscape is low. This is a highly profitable situation, albeit only for the consultant. The bad consultant will push and push for more capabilities to be leveraged by the metadata repository that they are implementing because this results in more hours for the consultant to invoice. The metadata repository is pitched as the ultimate solution to the confusion illusion. The bad consultant will be able to strike a profitable alliance with the bad software vendor. If the software vendor has a license model that encourages edge-case usage of the technology—external capabilities—then, the bad consultant has a perfect ally. The bad consultant may not have a perfect ally in the bad employee because the latter will be focused on implementation deadlines at all costs—also at the price of truly functional technology. Creeping the scope of the metadata repository may not be in the interest of the bad employee.	The ugly consultant will be a regular in the company for which they deliver an implementation. The ugly consultant will assist with delivering a functional solution, although the metadata repository will not be used to fully leverage its core capability. The ugly consultant is common because it will rarely be profitable for consultancies to specialize in a good level of expertise, simply due to too high of a cost and too little understanding of the severity of the problem at the executive level.
Software vendor	The good software vendor will most likely make less aggressive sales pitches up front when companies are signing a new contract for their software than the bad or the ugly software vendor will. They will be focused on long-term customer relations, which entails realistic scoping from the sales team to ensure a smooth handover to the vendor's customer success team.	The bad software vendor will tell companies that their software is the perfect solution for whatever capability the company wants to leverage. The bad software vendor will find the bad consultant to be a good ally, although there is a subtle difference between the sales team and the customer success team within the software vendor's company. The sales team will push for high uptake from the customer, with less focus on the practical aspects of implementing and using the metadata repository than the customer success team will have. This team has as its mission to fight churn—customers abandoning a software application because it was pitched in a way that overpromised and underdelivered—which is often the case.	The ugly software vendor will tap into a plethora of capabilities that are to be leveraged with their software, in a relatively imprecise and unproductive way. However, such a solution will be acceptable and functional, just not to the extent that is possible if the software is used correctly and the employee and consultant understand how to leverage these capabilities.

CHAPTER 9

The Data Discovery Team

In this chapter, we introduce a novel team: the data discovery team. Before exploring this team's functions, we must address a common issue with metadata repositories for numerous teams: the proliferation of conflicting "single sources of truth" regarding the IT landscape. Hence, the necessity of the data discovery team emerges: to harmonize these divergent truths. We will address this as a Conway's Law for metadata.

In this chapter, we focus on the repository level, treating it as a cohesive technical entity. Subsequent chapters will delve into the repositories more deeply, examining specific metadata components. However, before venturing into that territory, it's crucial to grasp the necessity and functions of a data discovery team.

Let's dive right in!

Our Problem: Managing Multiple Truths Across Teams

The problem with all of the metadata repositories that I described in Chapters 3, 4, and 5 is that they all depict the IT landscape—and they all do it differently, each with its own focus, each from its own position in the organization, each by teams with different agendas.

As I previously emphasized, this is not a book about a specific type of technology designed to solve all issues with understanding the IT landscape, managing metadata, and creating the infamous "single source of truth"—which is a typical selling point for metadata repositories. Quite the contrary: this book argues that using a single technology to understand the IT landscape through metadata is impossible. Metadata is fragmented across multiple teams and technologies. This will never change. This fragmentation results in the creation of multiple "single sources of truth" about the IT landscape.

In this chapter, I'll shed light on how you can relate these truths to one another to the benefit of all teams working with them. You must embrace that plurality of single sources of truths in your company, not harmonize them, because that is politically impossible, and furthermore, it is useless. Data harmonization is about improving the flow in the value chain through *master data* management and more traditional business intelligence.[1] Achieving success in *metadata* management, as emphasized in this book, does not require this particular element.

Instead, what is feasible and beneficial is getting the full picture. Understand what your EAM tool holds, your CMDB, your IRs, your ISMS, your RIMS, and so forth—and then coordinate that. This is the role of the data discovery team.

All companies generally have an executive management team, with individual departments having one or more teams. Normally, it's at the team level that metadata repositories are managed. In Figure 9-1, you can see a generic diagram of this.

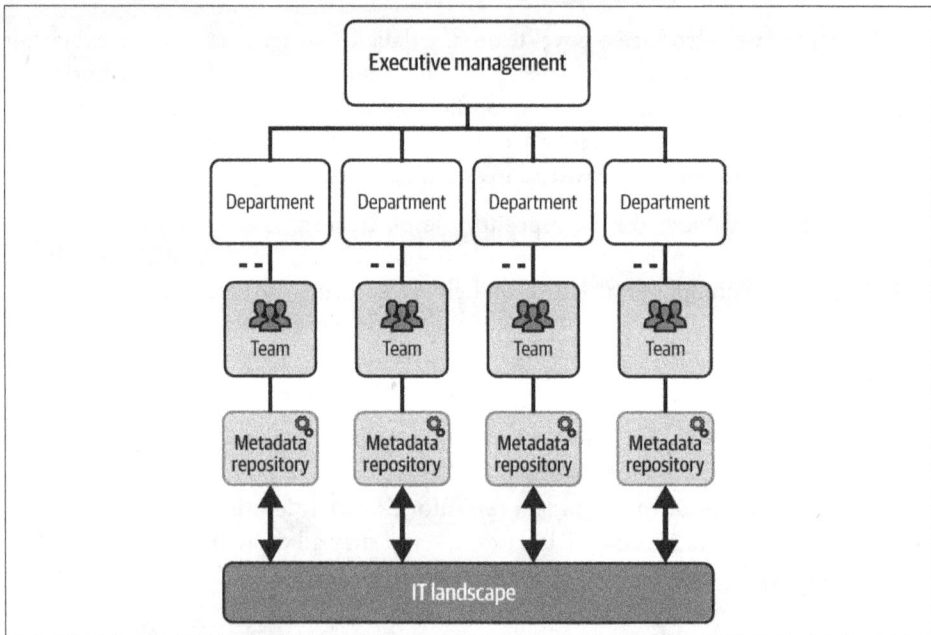

Figure 9-1. How metadata repositories are placed all over a company

However, the constellation of metadata repositories and teams will never be the same from company to company. Every company is different, and no two companies in the world will have the same organizational structure and collection of metadata repositories—or place those metadata repositories alike in their organization. So it's

---

1 See, for example, Chapter 4 in *Deciphering Data Architectures* by James Serra (O'Reilly).

important to stress that you can't find an authoritative example of how metadata repositories are distributed throughout a company. Figure 9-2 is an example illustrating all of the metadata repositories that I have discussed in previous chapters.

The situation in your company may not exactly match Figure 9-2, but it is likely to be just as complex as the reality depicted.

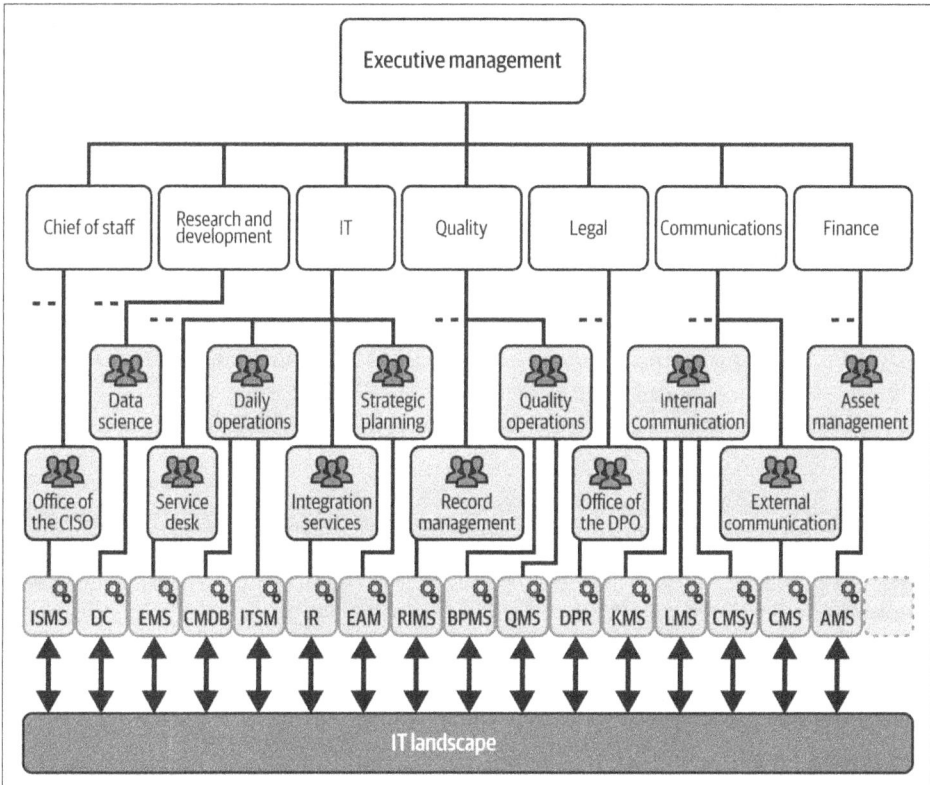

Figure 9-2. Specific example of how metadata repositories are placed all over a company

In Figure 9-2, you can see that the IT department runs the CMDB to handle incoming change requests to the IT landscape; the IR to document integrations; the EMS to keep control of servers, laptops, and phones and what is installed on them; the ITSM system to do IT management in a professional and smooth way toward a line of business; and the EAM tool to plan for the future IT landscape. All in all, the IT department has these repositories to carry out its daily operations while maintaining an overview of those operations in the past, present, and future. And all of these metadata repositories represent a vision of the IT landscape. In most organizations, it's likely that they are not aligned. This is because they are maintained by different teams within the IT department that are not necessarily in regular contact. Hence, they build different descriptions of the IT landscape in their metadata repositories, which they consider to be single sources of truth.

Furthermore, in Figure 9-2 you can see that the office of the CISO runs the ISMS— naturally, as this metadata repository is at the heart of what the CISO does, information security. Likewise, the office of the DPO runs the DPR because the DPO must ensure their function via a tool, which is the DPR.

Quality is responsible for mapping business processes in the BPMS; ensuring lifecycle management of the company's information and records in the RIMS; and performing overall quality management in the QMS. Finance has the AMS to gain control of the cost of everything inside the IT landscape. Communications has a CMS to control all knowledge that the company communicates outwardly, the LMS to ensure that all employees are properly trained, and the CMSy to maintain the corporate memory. Finally, the data science team in the research and development department has the DC because it wants to experiment with data to foster new innovation, and therefore, it wants to search for data.

As mentioned in previous chapters, these metadata repositories are integral components of software solutions that interact with the IT landscape to varying degrees. These repositories should remain accessible to the staff members who use them to carry out tasks effectively.

Yet at the same time, this causes a significant problem at the metadata layer because what you are looking at are 16 silos of metadata: 16 metadata repositories that are not loyal to anything else other than the vision proposed by the teams that own them and whomever those teams report to, upward in the organization.

The question is: what is the essence of this problem? Once we identify and comprehend the problem, we'll also possess the solution. Let's uncover the problem now.

Conway's Law

One of the most important truths about IT systems was put forward by Melvin Conway in his famous paper from 1968, "How Do Committees Invent?" (*https://oreil.ly/ bHcU-*). This is known as *Conway's Law*:

> The basic thesis of this article is that organizations which design systems (in the broad sense used here) are constrained to produce designs which are copies of the communication structures of these organizations.

The idea behind Conway's Law is that, instead of organizations designing IT systems that are fit for their intended purposes, these systems end up reproducing the communications logic of whatever organizational structure these systems are in. *System design copies communication design.* The people higher up in the organization push the managers of IT systems to report according to their needs, not for the purposes that the IT systems have. The main issue is that the design of the system shouldn't align with the communication design. In other words, the goals of the IT system and the existing communications structure it operates within aren't the same. At worst, the IT system ends up enhancing the already existing problems of the organization it serves, and for metadata, this results in siloed, opposing metadata repositories.

The Metadata Monolith

Conway's Law has been greatly applied since it was proposed. A recent example is *Team Topologies* by Matthew Skelton and Manuel Pais (*https://teamtopologies.com*), which sets forth an entirely new vision of how IT teams should be set up in a modern, cloud-based software world and is used for microservices and data mesh architectures. The thinking put forward in *Team Topologies* is also relevant for metadata repositories.

Metadata, which is stored within metadata repositories, has traditionally been managed in a way that resembles the monolithic model (a single view of the world) described in *Team Topologies*:

> A *monolithic model* is software that attempts to force a single domain language and representation (format) across many different contexts.[2]

Each metadata repository has this monolithic risk built into it: that its owners and users think it depicts the IT landscape and that it should be applied elsewhere. The problem with that assumption is that the depiction of the IT landscape inside these repositories may simply be wrong, be incomplete, or more subtly, be described with names, diagrams, and code that do not match other repositories with different depictions.

Look at Figure 9-2 and contemplate the issue of the multiple perspectives on the IT landscape present at the metadata level. You should consider that each metadata repository has its own definitions, groupings, and assessments of the same things in the IT landscape. It is evident that these metadata repositories serve the communications structure of the organization and thus that system design—defining metadata describing the IT landscape—copies communication design.

---

2 Matthew Skelton and Manuel Pais, *Team Topologies* (IT Revolution, 2019), 114.

For example, the CISO describes the IT landscape in the ISMS so that they can carry out their purposes, providing insights to their superiors; the head of enterprise architecture does the same with the EAM tool; and so forth for all other metadata repositories.

Conway's Law is also at play for metadata repositories. They are all used to provide insights to higher levels of management but never jointly, never harmonized, always in competition with one another; there is a strong incentive to divide so that the top can keep control. This is why metadata repositories all depict the same truth—the IT landscape—but in a way that opposes one another. And this is why that very truth—and with it the assertiveness of what the IT landscape actually is—seems to evaporate when metadata repositories are viewed holistically. With opposing truths it's impossible to know what the truth really is!

However, in the context of metadata repositories, Conway's Law presents a slightly different problem and manifests in a different manner than its effects on traditional IT systems. *Team Topologies* suggests that the teams that operate the totality of the IT landscape organize into different, more fluid team structures so as to better support the overall IT landscape with a rapid introduction of new services and a smooth maintenance of existing services.

A similar organizational change cannot be applied to metadata repositories—they are inherently tied to the teams that utilize them. The need for different kinds of metadata management does not warrant removing these technologies from their respective teams in this scenario.

The solution to the problem discussed here is different, albeit still inspired by Conway's Law, and it still necessitates an organizational change.

The Solution: The Data Discovery Team

In this section, I'll introduce a novel team type that I refer to as the *data discovery team*.

> The data discovery team is virtual. It consists of members of all teams that manage metadata repositories. To understand how it works in more detail, go to Chapter 13. It requires reading Part III to completely get the concept of the data discovery team.

The purpose of the data discovery team is to note, coordinate, and harmonize all metadata repositories in the company. This approach enables us to dismantle metadata silos within companies and gradually move toward a clearer comprehension of the IT landscape's reality within these organizations.

We can motivate the data discovery team through Conway's Law. To counter the effect of Conway's Law, organizations can reverse or inverse the law, as mentioned in the book *Accelerate*:

> Our research lends support to what is sometimes called the "inverse Conway maneuver," which states that organizations should evolve their team and organizational structure to achieve the desired architecture.[3]

Reversing Conway's Law means making adjustments to teams. However, in the context of metadata repositories, we cannot alter the existing realities of the organization. Metadata management is not a considerable enough element to ignore the vital tasks performed by teams that happen to own metadata repositories. Instead, what must be done is to allow for a coordinated understanding of metadata.

This is achieved not by changing the existing teams or removing their metadata repositories but by understanding their views of the IT landscape collectively and coordinating them. For practical advice on doing this, please consult the architectures laid out in Part III of this book.

Figure 9-3 illustrates that the focus of the data discovery team is on the views themselves rather than on the physical repositories. The data discovery team looks at the differences in views, understands them, and coordinates them, without taking the metadata repositories away and without replacing existing teams.

This is why the data discovery team is needed. Now, let's learn more about this team and what it does.

---

3 Nicole Forsgren, Jez Humble, and Gene Kim, *Accelerate: Building and Scaling High Performing Technology Organizations* (IT Revolution Press, 2018), 63.

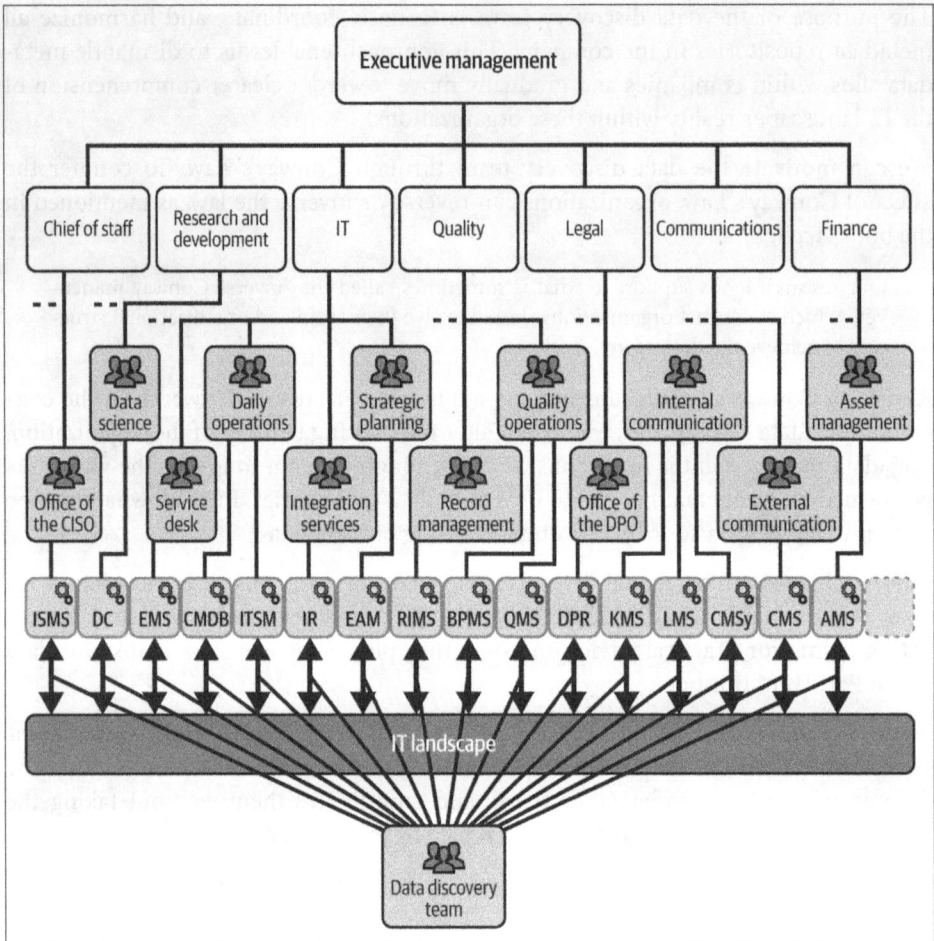

Figure 9-3. Understanding and coordinating the views represented in metadata repositories

What Is the Data Discovery Team?

Ultimately, the data discovery team should aim at building a meta grid. The meta grid is a structured, preferably automated way to coordinate metadata repositories. I'll describe the meta grid in Chapters 10 through 12 in Part III of this book, and the data discovery team is discussed again in Chapter 13. What we can do at this point is consider all of the teams to be constellations of domains that work together on shared metadata, as depicted in Figure 9-4.

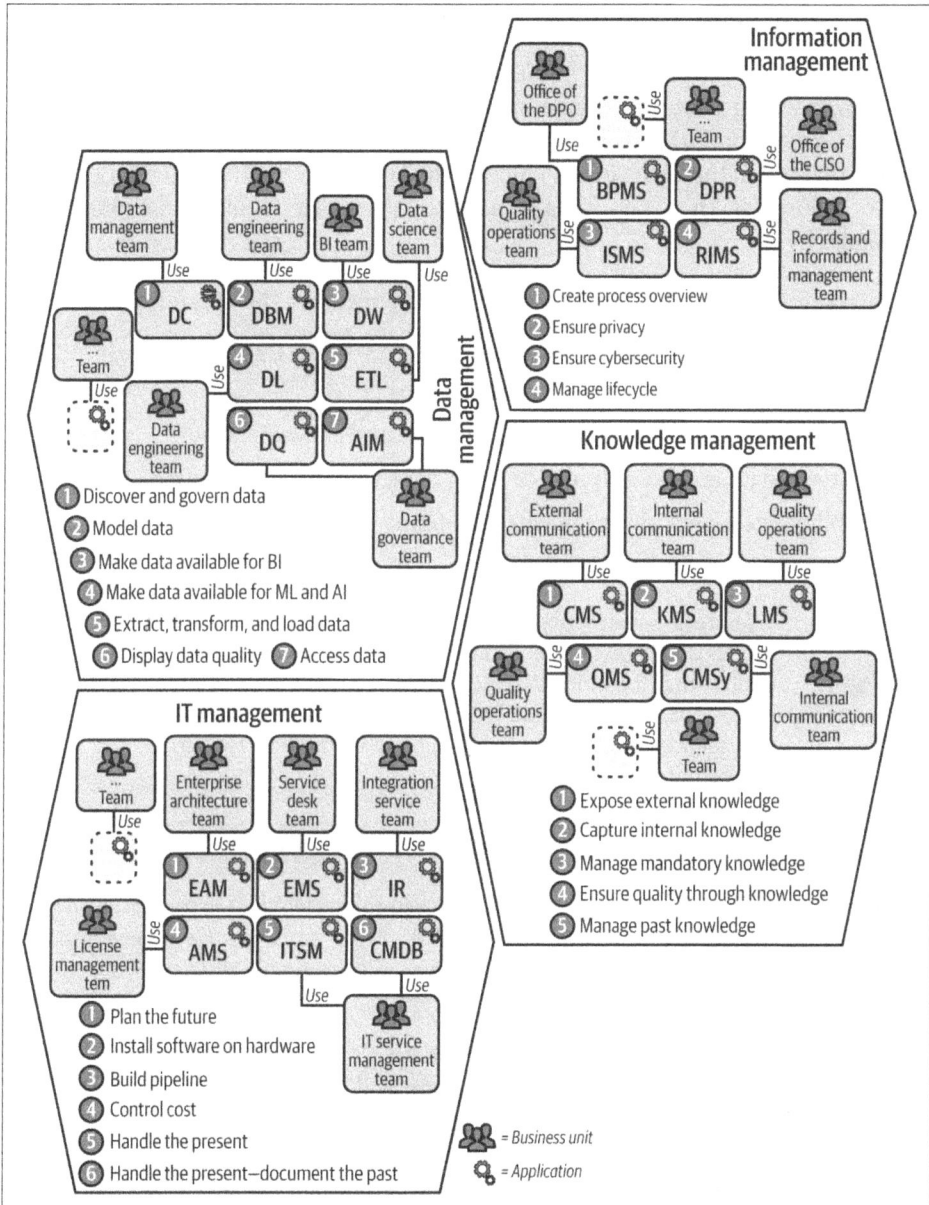

Figure 9-4. The four domains of IT, data, information, and knowledge management

These four domains can come together and exchange metadata internally and externally, as we will see from the examples in Part III. But let's first discuss some organizational challenges that the data discovery team must face to be able to push forward.

On the Political and Technological Mess of Companies

The data discovery team faces numerous constraints that must be acknowledged before progressing toward a deeper comprehension of the IT landscape. Layers of complex legacy from projects gone wrong and failed implementations lead to technical debt that is a natural part of any functioning landscape offering capabilities for all parts of a business. In certain cases, departments compete rather than cooperate on IT agendas by:

- Insisting on being right about definitions of elements in the IT landscape
- Pushing or ignoring new metadata repositories for new purposes
- Pushing or ignoring old metadata repositories
- Claiming that a new technological reality demands new metadata
- Insisting on an empirical approach when depicting the IT landscape
- Insisting on a logical approach when depicting the IT landscape

We are a constructive community of learners that wants to get things done! And that is also the case for this book—but we need to realize that the point of departure for aligning metadata repositories is not neutral ground. Different parts of a company have different agendas. We need to embrace them before they can change for the better.

Embracing the Multiple Truths and Providing a Way Forward

When the data discovery team begins coordinating the metadata repositories, it must keep in mind that this is a highly sensitive task. Many attempts have been made to create the correct depictions of the IT landscape, and they are all to a certain degree correct. However, they could also be incorrect.

Psychologically, it is very important that the data discovery team does not approach its task as an error-finding enterprise. The team will be exposed to all the complexities and flaws of the architecture, so it's important to focus on data discovery rather than critique. Mapping an IT landscape at the metadata level is very difficult, and all metadata repositories contain precious knowledge that must be preserved. Think of it as metadata coordination—not correction.

I want you to think back to the reference librarian I mentioned in Chapter 1. The data discovery team needs to foster mutual acknowledgment of a knowledge gap, which may involve bruised egos, by demonstrating kindness and curiosity and by treating all teams—each operating with its own metadata repository—equally. To quote a master from LIS, S. R. Ranganathan:

If you want to be a reference librarian, you must learn to overcome not only your shyness but also the shyness of others![4]

The data discovery team can't be shy—it's a fine balance to not be embarrassed and to not embarrass others—when asking delicate questions. Not being shy and understanding the shyness of others is the key to aligning metadata repositories.

How the Data Discovery Team Collaborates

In this section, I'll outline various scenarios illustrating collaboration between the data discovery team and specific teams that each manage their own metadata repositories. These examples are not exhaustive, encompassing neither all of the teams nor all of the specific metadata repositories. Each example showcases different approaches to organizing data effectively.

Collaborating with Enterprise Architects

The data discovery team collaborates with enterprise architects in three ways (Figure 9-5).

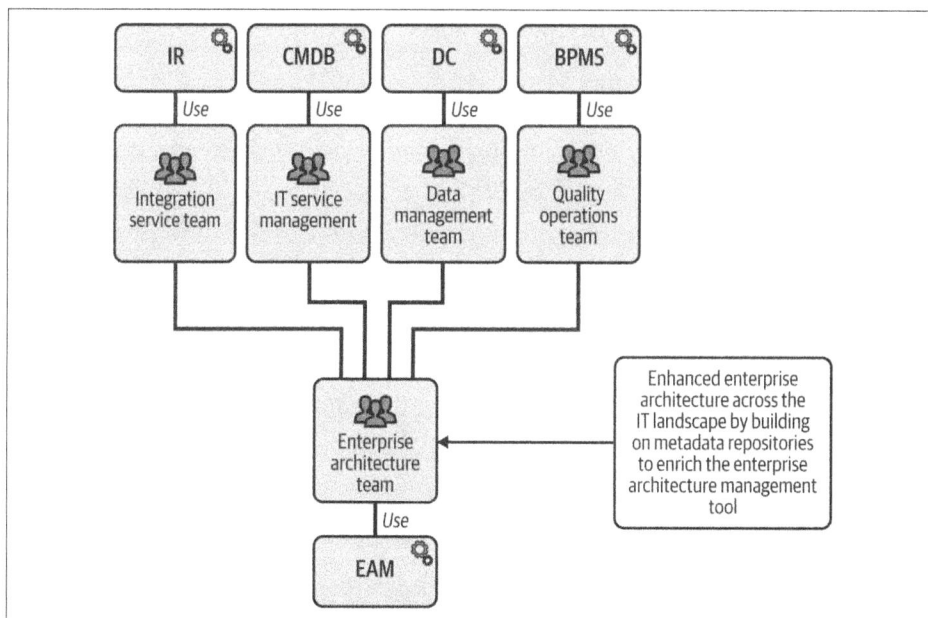

Figure 9-5. How the enterprise architecture team and the EAM tool relate to other metadata repositories

4 S. R. Ranganathan, *The Five Laws of Library Science* (The Madras Library Association, 1931), 65.

First, the data discovery team identifies all metadata repositories capable of supplying the EAM tool with pertinent metadata concerning the IT landscape. These are typically the CMDB for applications, the DC for data, the IRs for integrations, and the BPMS for processes. However, this can naturally vary from company to company.

Second, the data discovery team can leverage this situation to have the EAM tool influence other metadata repositories, particularly for naming conventions for applications, projects, and more. The EAM tool represents the future; therefore, numerous types of high-level metadata originate from it.

Third, the data discovery team can assist the enterprise architecture team by simply raising awareness of the collective set of metadata repositories available to them. Enterprise architecture teams typically come in two categories:[5]

Logical enterprise architecture
> This is based on framework thinking, like TOGAF, and is built on logical assumptions. Enterprise architecture teams following a framework tend to start very ambitiously, with certifications and a firm belief in doing it right, claiming that "if we all just follow the framework, we will make EA happen." And then, as the framework increasingly proves to not match reality, they fail. Logical enterprise architecture has a track record of not working.

Empirical enterprise architecture
> This is based on observing reality. It meticulously collects information about what the IT landscape looks like, slowly building a capability to provide more and more deep guidance for strategic decision making on the future of the IT landscape, without having to force an entire business into a single way of doing things.

For enterprise architecture teams working with an empirical approach, the metadata repositories presented by the data discovery team are vital sources for a deep understanding of the actual IT landscape. So, beyond the EAM tool itself, all metadata repositories can be consulted by empirical enterprise architecture teams, making the overall control of the IT landscape and planning for the future more robust—not a "single source of truth," just more robust.

Collaborating with the Data Protection Officer

The DPO oversees the processing of personal data by the company and must—by regulation—register how that data is processed in a dedicated metadata repository.

---

5 Svyatoslav Kotusev, *The Practice of Enterprise Architecture: A Modern Approach to Business and IT Management* (SK Publishing, 2018). For a quick introduction to Kotusev's ideas, read the preface of his book and check out my podcast episode with him (*https://oreil.ly/Gvfm_*).

The data discovery team can help the DPO in a very concrete way by surfacing other metadata repositories that the DPO may not know of (Figure 9-6).

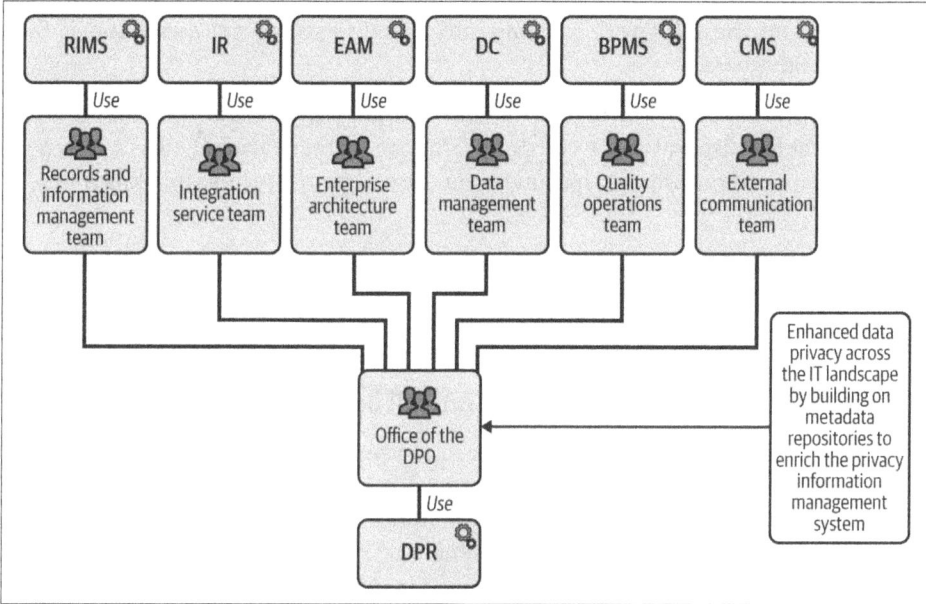

Figure 9-6. The teams that can typically assist the office of the DPO

As you can see, it's typically the CMS, the EAM tool, the IR, the DC, the BPMS, and the RIMS that can enhance the registration of how personal data is processed in the DPR.

In the EAM tool, integrations are generally mapped at a very high level, indicating if the integration is one-directional or bidirectional, and only at the application level, not at the instance level of the application. The integrations listed in the EAM tool can have data types linked to them, and if so, they may indicate if they are personal, sensitive information, such as Customer Name. When data types like Customer Name are sensitive and are included in integrations, then these integrations are processings of personal data that should be registered in the DPR.

The same is the case for the many IRs in each company: they contain documented integrations at the actual instance level with a deep level of details in service-level agreements. They should also indicate personal, sensitive data that can enrich the DPR.

The DCs of the company will delve deeper than the EAM tool and the IRs. They will document data lineage across multiple integrations between applications and storage solutions, ultimately providing detailed insights into the processing of sensitive data across entire data pipelines.

The BPMS will present at a higher level—specifically, the information management level—where data resides within various business processes. Hence, it's likely that the closest counterpart to the existing reality is found in the DPR. However, the BPMS can supplement the DPR with insights into already existing processes and if they include sensitive data.

The RIMS will contain sensitive data that the people this data belongs to have accepted is at the disposal of the company. This can further enrich the DPR with general information about which departments in the company process what kinds of sensitive data.

Finally, the CMS, as an outward-facing metadata repository, will further enrich the knowledge of how personal data is processed because it contains consent specifications and lists how that data is processed.

Collaborating with the Chief Information Security Officer

The CISO works to constantly reduce risk in the company, using the risk assessment component within the ISMS. The data discovery team can help the CISO by displaying metadata repositories to enhance information security. These include the EAM tool, the CMDB, the EMS, the RIMS, the QMS, and the CMSy, as shown in Figure 9-7. Note that—as in all cases discussed in this section—the relevant metadata repositories vary from company to company.

The EAM tool is central because it contains the future planning of the IT landscape. This is relevant because changes to the IT landscape mean a change in the overall risks and vulnerabilities for the company.

The CMDB is typically a more detailed list of instances of all applications and physical locations of servers. With the insights provided by the CMDB, the CISO can further detail the description of the IT landscape in the ISMS and what risks are associated with which parts of the existing IT landscape.

The EMS allows for a survey of what applications are installed on what devices and, ultimately, whether that can be coupled with otherwise suspicious behavior, such as monitoring the activity of specific employees.

The RIMS already contains a description of records that are highly confidential. The CISO in the ISMS must ensure that it is matched and monitored accordingly.

The QMS is primarily relevant in highly regulated industries. However, in such cases, its relevance is particularly significant. It will contain procedures and performance metrics of highly confidential spaces, such as production facilities that are of importance at a societal scale.

The CMSy will contain artifacts of high prestige for the company. As such, if these artifacts are stolen or destroyed, they can constitute information security risks.

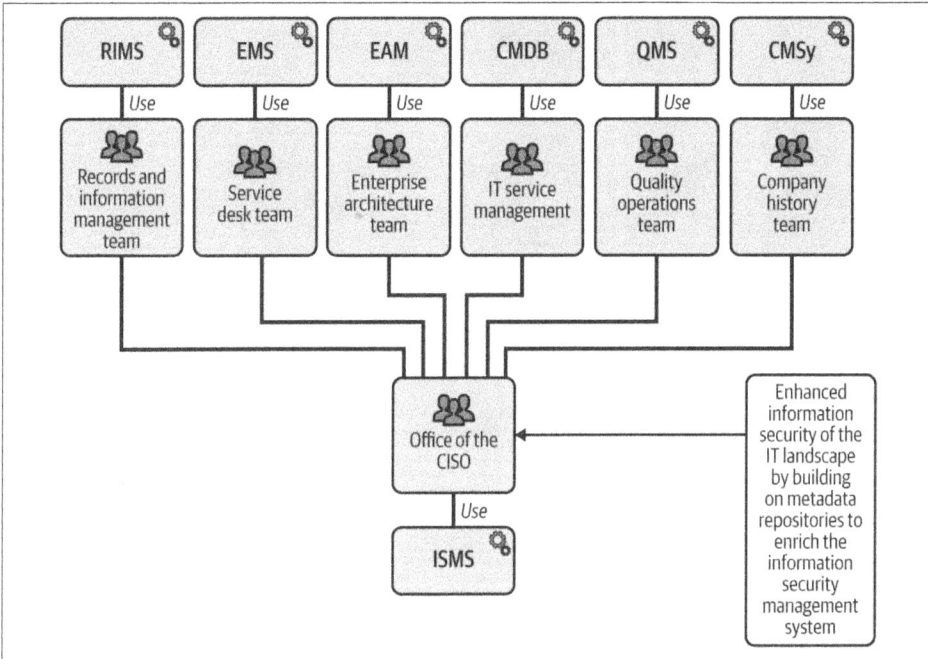

Figure 9-7. The metadata repositories that can enhance the ISMS managed by the CISO

Collaborating with Records and Information Management

The records management team works to keep records and information until the end of their retention periods. This team uses the RIMS to manage the information lifecycle. The data discovery team can assist the records and information management team with managing the information lifecycle by illuminating the existing IT landscape, primarily through the EAM tool, the CMDB, and the QMS. This makes it easier to identify the data sources that will later fall within the scope of management in the RIMS (Figure 9-8).

The EAM tool will help the records and information management department identify systems and future projects that will need to be collected by them. Ultimately, having the knowledge contained in the EAM tool will allow for a smoother plan for preservation of the past by looking at what is planned for the future.

The CMDB serves as the primary tool for identifying all relevant systems that are currently slated for representation in the RIMS. This is the running IT landscape, and at some point, the contents of the systems containing business-critical information will be transferred to cold storage solutions that are represented at the metadata level in the RIMS.

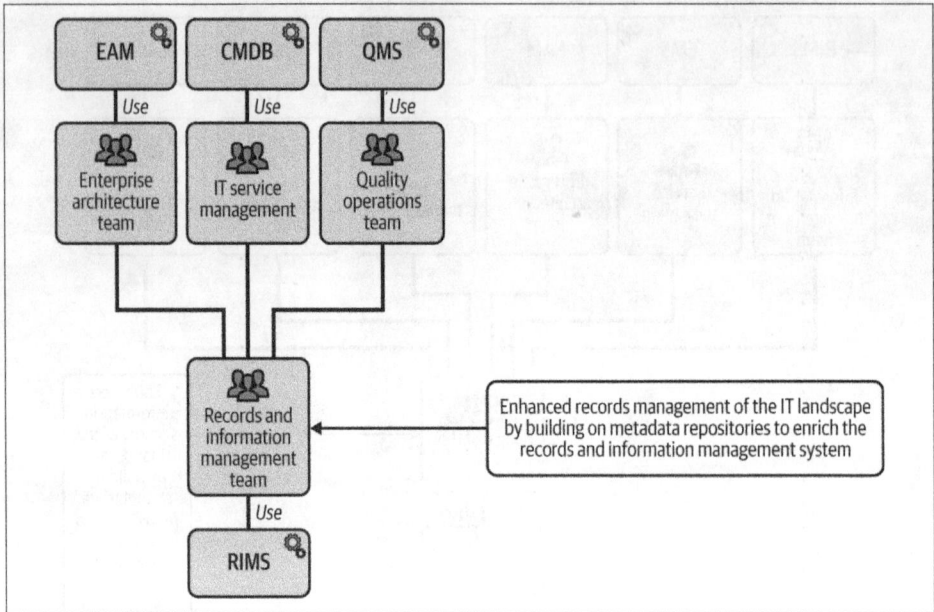

Figure 9-8. *The metadata repositories that can enhance the RIMS*

If a company has a QMS, then it will contain, by nature, the information that structures the RIMS, so it must be consulted when structuring the metadata in the RIMS.

Collaborating with Data Science Teams

A more advanced use case for the data discovery team is collaboration with data science teams. Data science teams use one or more enterprise DCs to explore the data sources that can be used for analytical use cases (also consider the opposite perspective: that the DC can hydrate the metadata repositories in the top layer).

> If this section appeals to you, imagine how you could describe this deeper and break this into three parts: collaborating with data science, collaborating with data analytics, and collaborating with data engineering.

The data discovery team may facilitate a deeper discovery of data sources for various data science teams by drawing attention to the EAM tool, the CMDB, and the RIMS. These metadata repositories can, of course, be consulted by the data science team, but the applications and storage solutions they describe can be crawled by the DC to further enhance their usage for analytics by all data science teams in the company, as illustrated in Figure 9-9.

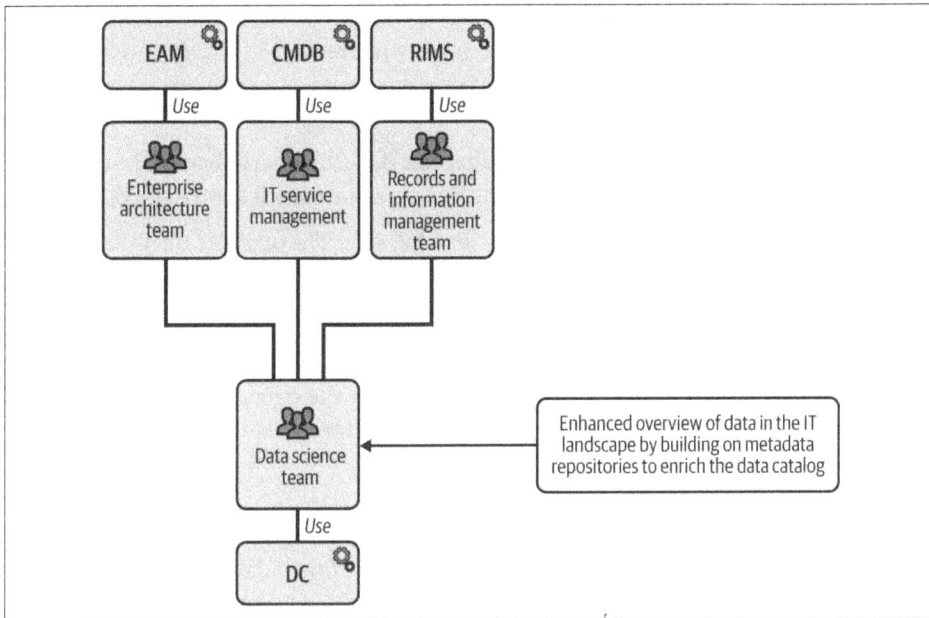

Figure 9-9. How the DC can be enhanced by other metadata repositories

Summary

In this chapter, we discussed the data discovery team. Here are the main takeaways:

- Many single sources of truths exist in metadata silos scattered all over companies; different teams create these truths because they use different metadata repositories for different things.
- Conway's Law describes a reality where system design mirrors communication design.
- Following Conway's Law, metadata repositories often end up as metadata monoliths: a single view of the world.
- The solution to this problem is the data discovery team.
- This is based on reversing Conway's Law—the ambition that companies must reorganize to allow for the most efficient IT architecture.
- The data discovery team coordinates metadata repositories to make it possible to organize and search metadata with maximum effect (this is demonstrated in Part III).
- It goes beyond the purpose of this book to fully unfold to what degree recognizing mess and embracing it are pivotal for the success of the data discovery team.
- Data discovery teams have to collaborate with all stakeholders.

- Collaborating with enterprise architects means that the data discovery team delivers insights that can increase the quality of the EAM tool from other metadata repositories and informs the enterprise architects of the contents of these metadata repositories.

- Collaborating with the DPO means that the data discovery team surfaces metadata repositories that can point to sensitive data and how it is processed.

- Collaborating with the CISO means that the data discovery team puts forward the metadata repositories that contain descriptions of confidential data.

- Collaborating with records and information management means that the data discovery team can surface metadata that will eventually end up in the RIMS.

- Collaborating with data science teams means that the data discovery team makes sources that are found via other metadata repositories available in the DC to be explored further.

- The collaboration patterns described in this chapter are nonexhaustive.

In the next chapter, we will look at the specific pieces of metadata in metadata repositories as we dive into a completely new vision for metadata management: the meta grid.

PART III

Metadata Repositories Should Be Connected in a Meta Grid

In this last part of the book, we explore the third—small!—wave of data decentralization: the meta grid.

I propose the meta grid because metadata is a "tribal" endeavor.

However flexible or beautifully architected they may be, metamodels in metadata repositories inherently depict the task at hand—they look downward into the IT landscape to identify the metadata needed for the desired capability. Metamodels are shaped for purposes, and rightly so. After all, no technology exists without a purpose.

However, an arabesque of intentions, spanning from the strictest controls to the most daring experiments, is expressed through these metamodels, which are domain and even capability specific. This leaves us with a monumental task of repetition: the endless repetition of mapping the same metadata to an infinite number of aspirations—at astronomical costs and with increasing confusion across the enterprise. But it doesn't have to be this way.

And that is why we need to stop looking only downward. We need to consider the context of our metadata repositories—to look sideways, to what surrounds us. Metadata is holistic and multidimensional. The metadata you seek to define already exists somewhere else, expressed slightly differently, serving a different purpose. I urge you to take a good, deep look at that. Do not ignore it. Do not begin at the whiteboard, assuming you can start from scratch with your impeccably crafted standards of the perfect metadata—along with the, I'm sure, highly functional technologies you plan to implement.

And do not preach to me about your single source of truth. I have endless empirical evidence that you are surrounded by the very metadata you claim to be the sole owner of. Instead, recognize that the enterprise you engage with is a living organism—with a history, a vision, and a language. Yes, it is scattered—I admit that—but it is stored somewhere, somehow, for a reason. So I suggest you don't start over. I suggest, instead, that you study and learn from what is already there.

Unlike data mesh, the meta grid architecture I am proposing is not something that companies decide to build. It already exists in every organization. You can use it and make it better. I have always implicitly followed a meta grid mindset: valuable metadata already permeates the enterprise. Look in the ISMS, the CMDB, the QMS, and many other metadata repositories. Logical, valuable metadata structures are there for the taking.

Don't *map* processes, capabilities, or data types—*find* them. Many software vendors surprisingly lack knowledge of enterprise realities. There's no shame in that, but it is a root cause of metadata repository failures: you can't build it in isolation, mapping a company from scratch. You must inscribe the metadata repository into the enterprise context that is already established. Then, it will work. In this final part of the book, I will show you how.

In Chapter 10, I introduce a new decentralized architecture for metadata management that brings together the teams and technologies discussed throughout this book. The meta grid is small, simple, and slow—and it will make the metadata in your company more robust.

In Chapter 11, we take a look at how the meta grid connects to the ambitions that organizations typically have and to other, more complex and demanding decentralized architectures, such as microservices and data mesh.

Chapter 12 discusses the organizational, financial, and technical benefits of the meta grid. In particular, it is worth noting that the meta grid holds a natural potential for generative and agentic AI.

Finally, in the short Chapter 13, we connect all the ideas put forward in the book as a team topology. The real enterprise reality is a hustle and bustle of metadata management throughout so many different teams with so many different agendas and technologies that I propose a data discovery team to unite them and a meta grid to empower them.

CHAPTER 10

What Is the Meta Grid?

This chapter presents the third wave of data decentralization: a decentralization of metadata. While I've aimed to explain the technical details in straightforward language, the concept of the meta grid is new and different, so I encourage you to keep an open mind. It can be a powerful architecture.

In this chapter, we dive into the four main points of the "Meta Grid Manifesto," followed by a closer look at what the meta grid is and what it isn't. We'll also explore how to document the meta grid using simple architectural decision records (ADRs), models, and lists. Finally, we will walk through a series of examples of meta grid architectures.

The Meta Grid Manifesto

In this manifesto, originally published on my website (*https://searchingfordata.com*), I introduced the concept of the meta grid in depth for the first time. The manifesto makes the case for a third wave of data decentralization, summarized in four key points:

- The meta grid is the third wave of data decentralization.
- The meta grid unlocks single-view-of-the-world monoliths.
- The meta grid is never finalized.
- The meta grid is simple, small, and slow.

Let's uncover what these principles mean, one by one.

The Meta Grid Is the Third Wave of Data Decentralization

The first wave of data decentralization came with microservices architecture, which liberated operational data from monolithic technologies supporting the value chain, propelling high-performing companies forward.

Building on this momentum, the second wave emerged with data mesh architecture. It freed analytical data from monolithic constraints, unlocking greater potential for data and AI innovations.

The meta grid architecture represents the third wave of data decentralization. By liberating metadata from traditional technologies used in metadata management, it aims to enhance the logic and cohesion of the enterprise IT landscape.

The Meta Grid Unlocks Single-View-of-the-World Monoliths

To fulfill its role, metadata must reside both at its source, alongside the entity it describes, and elsewhere, to ensure that the entity is searchable and discoverable. For example, metadata can be electronically stored with a data asset (a table or column or other asset) but also accessible elsewhere, such as via the browser and search UI features of a metadata repository or application/solution.

Enterprise IT landscapes are made searchable through metadata repositories, which are often implemented and maintained in isolation by various teams across the organization. This approach results in a multitude of conflicting, single-view-of-the-world representations of the enterprise IT landscape and the organization itself.

No single technology can serve as the ultimate metadata repository, nor can it resolve the issue of these fragmented views scattered across different metadata repositories.

Humanity will never fully rely on technology like that.

The Meta Grid Is Never Finalized

Instead of creating an ultimate monolith of metadata, we must do the exact opposite: strive toward the decentralization of metadata. While metadata repositories will continue to exist, *decentralization* in this context means recognizing that no single repository can provide a perfect view of the IT landscape. Instead, metadata types are managed within a grid, and this grid expands into a grid of grids as more types of metadata are added, forming new, previously unseen patterns. The meta grid, by nature, will always be incomplete.

The Meta Grid Is Simple, Small, and Slow

Microservices and data mesh architectures are complex, big, and fast. They are *complex* because they rely on sophisticated programming languages, *big* because they work with large volumes of data, and *fast* because they are intended for high-speed exchanges.

By comparison, the meta grid is simple, small, and slow. It is *simple* because it relies on spreadsheets, out-of-the-box connectors, and, occasionally, self-created APIs. The meta grid is *small* because the total amount of metadata is significantly lower in volume and number of entities as compared to data mesh and microservices. It is *slow* because it doesn't rely on real-time or frequent exchanges of data.

The true challenge of the meta grid is that it is both inevitable and unseen. It permeates the operational, regulatory, and innovative endeavors of the enterprise, spanning the disciplines of data, information, and knowledge management.

The meta grid transforms siloes of meaning into fragments of shared understanding.

What the Meta Grid Is and Is Not

The meta grid is an architecture for managing metadata. It enables the oversight of metadata repositories related to the IT landscape without relying on a single technology as the sole source of truth. The pursuit of one technology to provide a unified view has often led companies to a fragmented understanding of their IT landscapes. This approach has resulted in siloed, monolithic efforts that cannot be resolved by simply starting anew, regardless of how well funded or focused the new attempt may be.

Instead of suggesting *one* technology, the meta grid offers a set of practices and procedures that enable a consolidated view of the IT landscape across existing metadata repositories. The meta grid proposes that these metadata repositories are managed holistically. In the past and present, metadata repositories have been introduced one by one, implemented and managed in isolation of one another. This created a cacophony in the IT landscape, where multiple, opposing truths are maintained and defended by various parts of the organization. Instead, they must be managed collectively and share the truth among them.

The meta grid consists of four domains:

- IT management
- Data management
- Information management
- Knowledge management

Unlike with microservices and data mesh, the number of domains in the meta grid is small and not subject to substantial modifications (because the names of the domains do not represent the organization but rather quite static metadata domains: IT, data, information, and knowledge management). Therefore, the challenging task of mapping domains does not exist. However, this task has not been removed for convenience—it's not there because, unlike operational data in microservices and analytical data in data mesh, metadata is already organized in domains. Each domain in the meta grid represents an established management discipline that depicts the IT landscape by metadata, stored in metadata repositories.

Here are some further characteristics of the meta grid:

The meta grid does not need an experience plane
In data mesh, the *experience plane* is a portal to the mesh, a place to discover data products. This is typically a data catalog. The meta grid, however, does not need such an experience plane because all metadata repositories are the target of the meta grid—and should not be substituted by one technology. All of the existing metadata repositories are what we seek to improve.

The meta grid has producers
These producers are the members of the data discovery team who coordinate the metadata repositories depicting the IT landscape.

The meta grid does not have direct consumers
Since the meta grid is not located within a specific technology, no one consumes the grid directly. Instead, consumers benefit from it in all metadata repositories in the scope of the meta grid, as the quality of, for example, the EMS, ISMS, and QMS is raised with more certainty about the IT landscape.

The meta grid is discrete, invisible, and ambient
Ultimately, most users of metadata repositories shouldn't be able to sense the meta grid at all. It must be discrete in its methodology in the sense of being non-invasive for end users. It must be invisible because it shouldn't be flagged in metadata repositories that this particular metadata is part of the grid. Likewise, the meta grid must be ambient to really work—it is in the various metadata repositories that it improves.

The meta grid is small
Unlike microservices and, to a certain extent, data mesh, the meta grid is small. This is defined for the level of technical refinement that goes into the meta grid: large volumes of data require certain programming languages and integration types. That is not in the scope of the meta grid.

The meta grid is slow[1]

The meta grid has as its task allowing metadata repositories to depict the IT landscape. These repositories need to be built slowly and steadily. Unlike an ecommerce platform, for example, immediate updates will not be a primary concern.

The meta grid does not express an ontology

Even from a more conceptual point of view, the meta grid is not an ontology because it does not consist of related concepts.

The meta grid does not have distinct domain boundaries

Even though the meta grid has distinct domains in the examples in this chapter, interpretations of what metadata repositories reside in which domains may vary from company to company. That is not a problem as long as unity is achieved and metadata repositories are only placed and managed by *one* domain.

The meta grid is not a semantic layer

It can be tempting to compare the meta grid with a semantic layer. But it is not a semantic layer, for the simple reason that it does not contain any metadata but rather coordinates metadata among metadata repositories. Furthermore, the meta grid deals with types of metadata that are not relevant for a semantic layer.

Documenting the Meta Grid

The meta grid is documented in simple, lightweight records, models, and lists. These are quick to learn and easy to apply.

The meta grid is primarily documented in *architectural decision records* (ADRs): simple yet powerful written records that, as the name indicates, contain architectural decisions.

Would you want to search the ADRs that document the meta grid? Read on; it will be discussed.

ADRs introduce a context in which a problem or opportunity is addressed, leading to a decision aimed at achieving a specific outcome. To learn more about ADRs, consult the ADR GitHub (*https://adr.github.io*) and arc42 (*https://arc42.org*) and read *Release It!* by Michael T. Neygard (Pragmatic Bookshelf).

---

1 Alternatives to *slow* could be *comprehensive* or *gradually expanding*.

There are various ways to structure ADRs, with two overall designs: very short or short. The short format is used with this template:

> In the context of *<use case/user story u>*, facing *<concern c>* we decided for *<option o>* and neglected *<other options>*, to achieve *<system qualities/desired consequences>*, accepting *<downside d/undesired consequences>*, because *<additional rationale>*.

Each meta grid architecture can be explained in these records, and as such, these records constitute the body of knowledge of the meta grid because they are a source that documents and subsequently informs about the meta grid. But accessing this documentation will primarily be necessary for employees who are responsible for maintaining one or more metadata repositories. It is important to store these records securely, with version control and read-only permissions.

ADRs can be supplemented with models and lists or data storage solutions. In addition to the ADR and the model, there may be a spreadsheet, an API call, or even a manual upload of files, such as diagrams. This is the metadata itself, to be shared over the grid. Most metadata will not take up more space or complexity than what a spreadsheet can handle.

However, it will be easier to maintain the meta grid over time if it is simply API calls—APIs should be the long-term goal for this architecture. In rare cases, you would need large data storage solutions or databases.

In sum, the meta grid comprises four domains—IT management, data management, information management, and knowledge management—along with the metadata repositories that reside within each. They should all be open for communication with one another by standard connectors: simple export/import or API calls. This can be diagrammed, as you see in Figure 10-1.

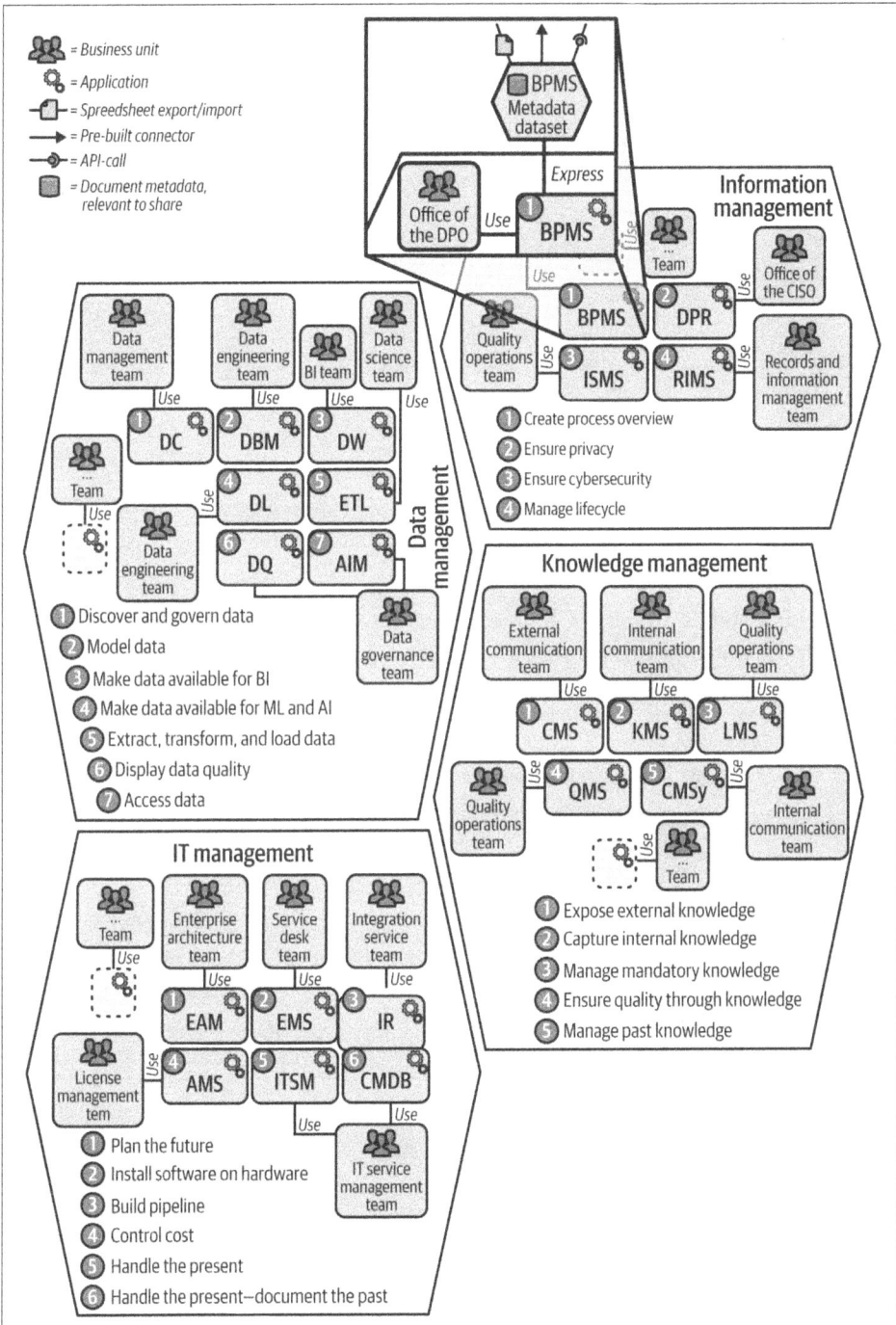

Legend:
- = Business unit
- = Application
- = Speedsheet export/import
- = Pre-built connector
- = API-call
- = Document metadata, relevant to share

Information management

BPMS Metadata dataset

Office of the DPO

Express

BPMS — Use

Team

Office of the CISO

BPMS · DPR

Quality operations team · ISMS · RIMS

Records and information management team

1. Create process overview
2. Ensure privacy
3. Ensure cybersecurity
4. Manage lifecycle

Data management

Data management team · Data engineering team · BI team · Data science team

Team · Data engineering team

DC · DBM · DW
DL · ETL
DQ · AIM

Data governance team

1. Discover and govern data
2. Model data
3. Make data available for BI
4. Make data available for ML and AI
5. Extract, transform, and load data
6. Display data quality
7. Access data

Knowledge management

External communication team · Internal communication team · Quality operations team

CMS · KMS · LMS

Quality operations team · QMS · CMSy · Internal communication team

Team

1. Expose external knowledge
2. Capture internal knowledge
3. Manage mandatory knowledge
4. Ensure quality through knowledge
5. Manage past knowledge

IT management

Team · Enterprise architecture team · Service desk team · Integration service team

EAM · EMS · IR
License management tem · AMS · ITSM · CMDB

IT service management team

1. Plan the future
2. Install software on hardware
3. Build pipeline
4. Control cost
5. Handle the present
6. Handle the present—document the past

Figure 10-1. Diagram of the meta grid domains and their metadata repositories

Examples of the Meta Grid

In the following sections, I will explain the meta grid through various examples. All of these examples are based on observations[2] and are not canonical, as they will vary from company to company. They provide guidance for building concrete instances of a meta grid and teach a methodology for creating meta grid architectures that precisely fit your company's needs.

Data Types

A very common question in most companies is, "What data types do we have?" As we have discussed throughout this book, depending on who you ask, you are likely to get different answers because the person answering will use their own metadata repository to provide that answer. Basically, chances are that the head of data will answer the question differently than the DPO.

In the meta grid architecture in Figure 10-2, you can see a coordination of data types across metadata repositories. In this way, data types remain consistent across repositories.

The core capability of the EAM tool is to facilitate planning the future IT landscape, including the eventual emergence of new data types. Therefore, in this example, the EAM tool is where new data types are listed. From this point on, these data types are sent in two directions to two clusters of repositories:

- To the ISMS and DPR simultaneously
- To the DC(s), IRs, DBM tool, and CMDB

From that point on, the data types are added to the RIMS and the QMS.

The logic of this architecture is that data types are listed and disseminated following their lifecycle: they emerge as high-level entities in the EAM tool and immediately thereafter, the data types are assessed in terms of their confidentiality (ISMS) and their sensitivity (DPR). Once that is done, the data types can transform from future to present state and can be brought to life in IT systems in production that are mirrored in the DC, IRs, DBM tool, and CMDB.

---

2 The observations stem from conversations with a large number of companies via my own consultancy, Searching for Data, as well as conversations with peers at conferences and in webinars.

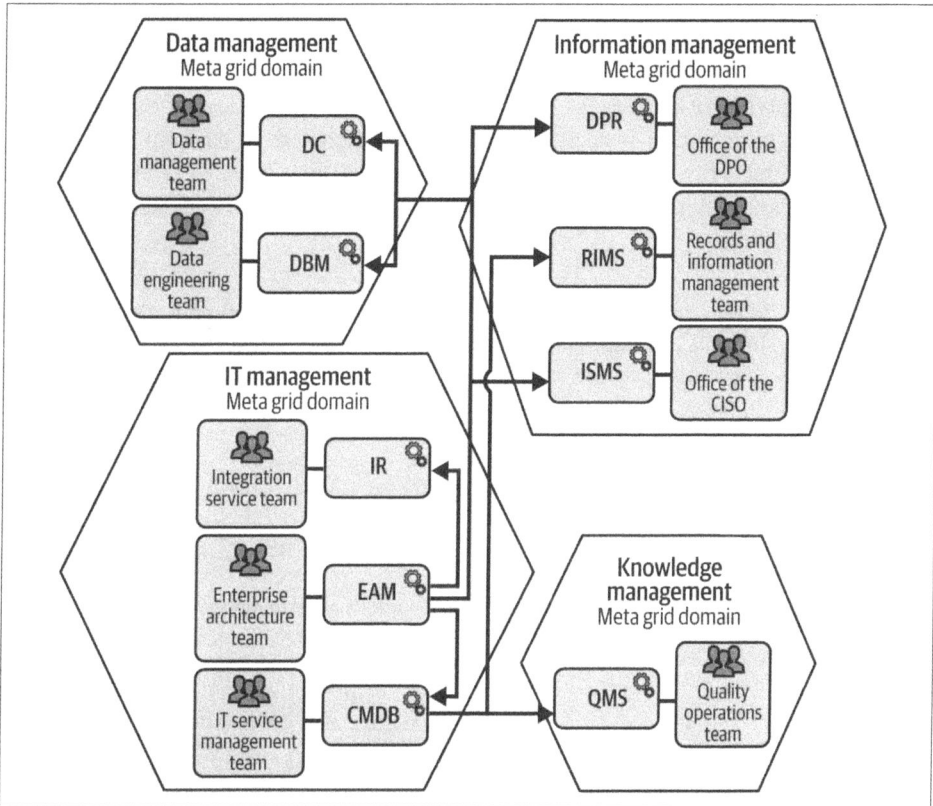

Figure 10-2. Meta grid for data types

When instances of a certain data type are archived, they can be firmly categorized in the RIMS after being flagged for archival from the CMDB. If no further instances of the data type are left in production, this is reported back to the DPR and ISMS from the RIMS. This means that the CISO no longer needs to conduct risk assessments for this data type, and the DPO is no longer required to perform data privacy assessments for it. Likewise, the CMDB will send data types to the QMS so that all regulatory compliance can be made with an updated view of the data types in the company.

> Note that this example does not include backups—backing up and archiving are not identical.

Applications

Another frequent debate among architects, developers, contract and category managers, and other types of employees is about the types of applications a company has. Typically, this information is scattered around in Microsoft SharePoint lists and in various technologically refined metadata repositories that serve different purposes within a company. These vary in drivers across all three types of regulation, innovation, and operation.

> Many companies do not have a complete view of their applications, and this is hazardous in terms of complying with regulations globally, controlling the cost of the IT landscape, and planning for the future.

In Figure 10-3, you can see a meta grid architecture that coordinates the metadata repositories listing applications.

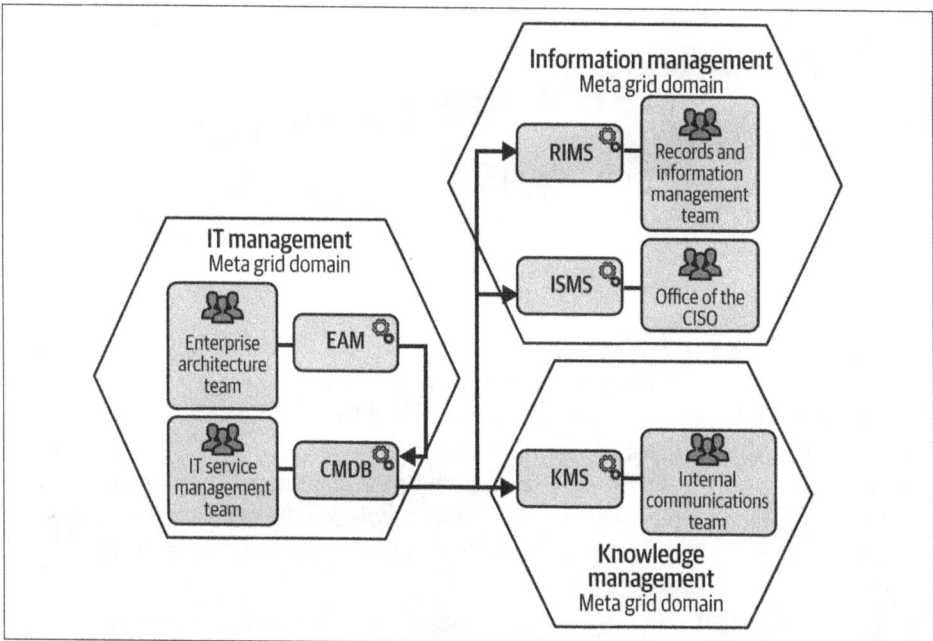

Figure 10-3. Meta grid for applications

As in the case of data types, the EAM tool is the repository that lists applications as they are considered prior to being put into production. Once they are placed into production, they are listed in three places, one of them being a cluster.

The CMDB will list all applications that the EAM tool recategorized from future state to present state. Contrary to the EAM tool, the CMDB will also list the *instances* of the applications, not just their names. Therefore, instead of merely listing, for example, Power BI and Tableau, the CMDB will list how many instances of Power BI and Tableau the company has, who owns them, and so on.

The RIMS and ISMS will list applications for regulatory purposes. It is of pivotal importance that the CISO provides risk assessments for new applications prior to their being put into production, while the applications are only registered as candidates in the EAM tool. This process can be automated for microservices and standard cloud applications. Once these assessments are done, the application is put into production, and only then is it registered in the ISMS and RIMS. The RIMS will list applications as records that will at some point be added to the RIMS from these applications for retention.

Finally, the KMS creates a high-level, company-wide introduction to the various applications by explaining their purposes, offering links to them, and specifying whom to contact for access.

Data Models

Data modeling has been called a *lost art* in the sense that much of modern cloud technology automates data modeling. This has contributed to a significant loss of understanding of how a given company is modeled in terms of the data it produces and processes. On top of that, data modeling is an activity that can take place in a variety of metadata repositories and tools, as discussed in Chapter 4.

The meta grid architecture proposed in Figure 10-4 is a constellation of metadata repositories for data models.

In this meta grid architecture, the database modeling tool is the primary repository for data models. It's an empirical source that depicts actual, physical data models. From this point on, the data models are sent in three directions, one of them being a cluster.

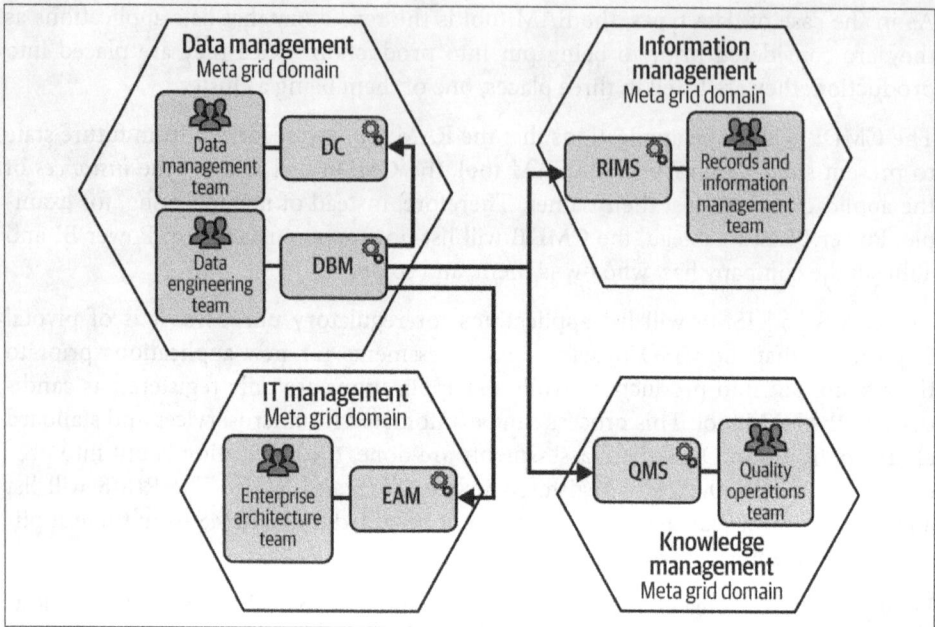

Figure 10-4. Meta grid for data models

The first direction is the cluster of the EAM tool and the DC. These each display the data models in the context of their purposes, planning for the future and depicting actual data in the company. The data models are also sent to the QMS and RIMS to provide the necessary context for data in a regulatory context.

> Data models are very likely to be floating around in PowerPoints across the company. Be aware that it is one of the most difficult types of metadata to actually capture in a metadata repository.

Integrations

Listing integrations in metadata repositories is one of the most challenging tasks in metadata management. It's inevitable that many IRs will exist in a company and that a holistic, simple overview of all integrations is difficult to obtain. A more realistic and useful approach is to take an architectural choice of depicting certain types of integrations in a centralized IR. Accordingly, Figure 10-5 depicts a meta grid architecture for integrations.

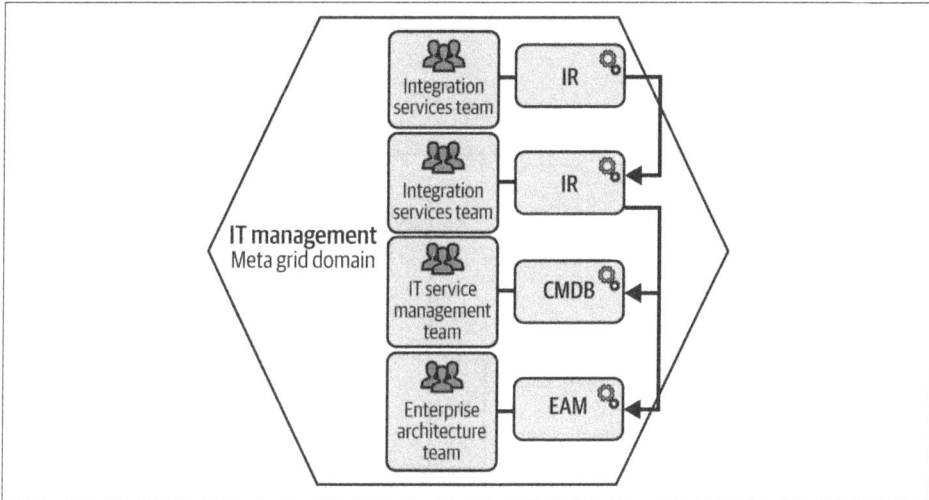

Figure 10-5. Meta grid for integrations

In this meta grid architecture, a centralized repository serves as the coordinating IR from which metadata about integrations goes in two directions. First, the IR sends integration metadata to the CMDB and the EAM tool so that these repositories can further process integration metadata in the context of their purposes. Then, a more subtle and two-way exchange of data takes place between the authoritative, centralized IR and the other IRs. They interact in the following way: the centralized IR is updated from the IR only in the context that has been defined for it. The other IRs are free to extend farther in scope regarding what they depict, as long as they respect the overall boundaries set up by the centralized IR.

Data Lineage

While integrations map the interfaces between two applications, *data lineage* describes the flow of data through multiple applications, layers, and storage solutions, illustrating how data progresses through various steps. There is not one single definition of data lineage. Instead, data lineage can be manually or automatically created at various levels of technological depth with different intended purposes in mind, from high-level business processes to conceptual, logical, and physical levels of data flow. An excellent resource on the multiple use cases for data lineage is Irina Steenbeek's book *Data Lineage from a Business Perspective* (Data Crossroads).

The meta grid architecture in Figure 10-6 depicts an empirical data lineage obtained through a DC.

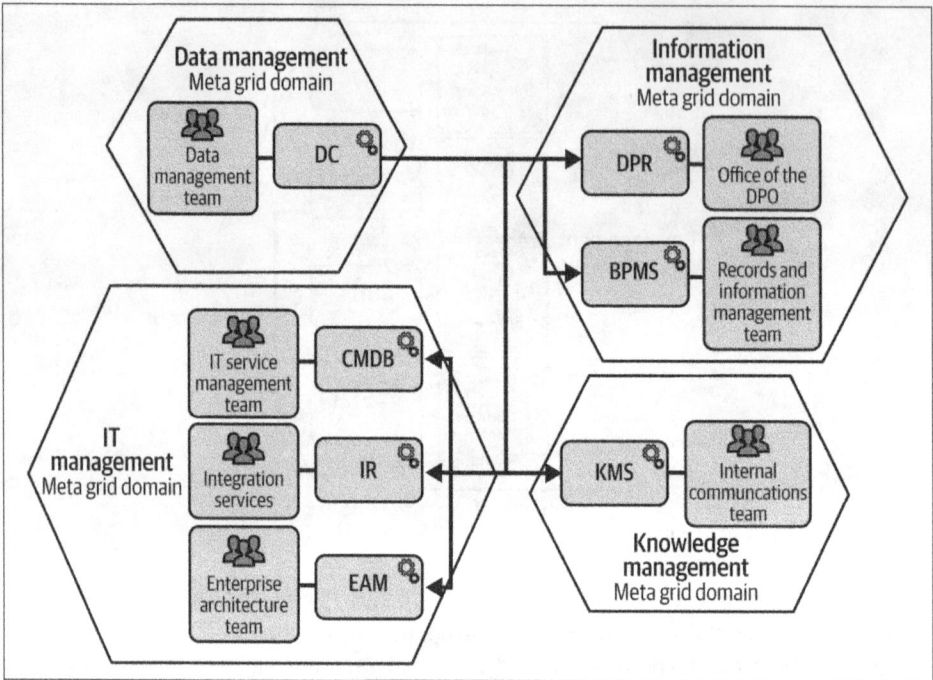

Figure 10-6. Meta grid for data lineage

In this meta grid architecture, the DC serves as the point of departure from which the data lineage is communicated in three directions. The DC updates an IT management cluster of metadata repositories with data lineage. These are the IR, EAM tool, and CMDB.

Servers

The locations, names, and responsibilities of on-premises servers in a company are of crucial importance. You can strive to be a cloud-only company, but the reality is that very few companies run 100% in the cloud. The meta grid architecture in Figure 10-7 depicts a constellation of metadata repositories with server metadata.

At the core of this meta grid architecture is the EMS that lists all on-premises servers in the company (along with what is placed on those servers, who owns them, their exact locations, etc.). From that point on, server metadata is shared in two directions:

- To the CMDB, which lists all servers with minimal metadata detail for the present. Unlike the EMS, which focuses on current configurations, the CMDB logs the historical configurations of each server.

- To the ISMS, which mitigates information security risks, including those related to servers. This type of metadata is necessary for the ISMS, but it does not need to be maintained within the ISMS itself.

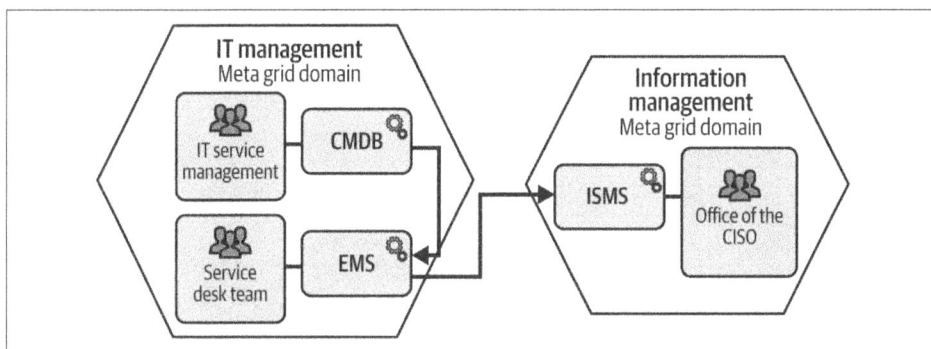

Figure 10-7. Meta grid for servers

Organization

Organizational charts are key to understanding your company and can be automatically generated by many tools. However, an authoritative organizational chart is maintained and updated centrally to truly reflect the groupings of teams in a company. In Figure 10-8, you see a meta grid architecture of metadata repositories containing organization metadata.

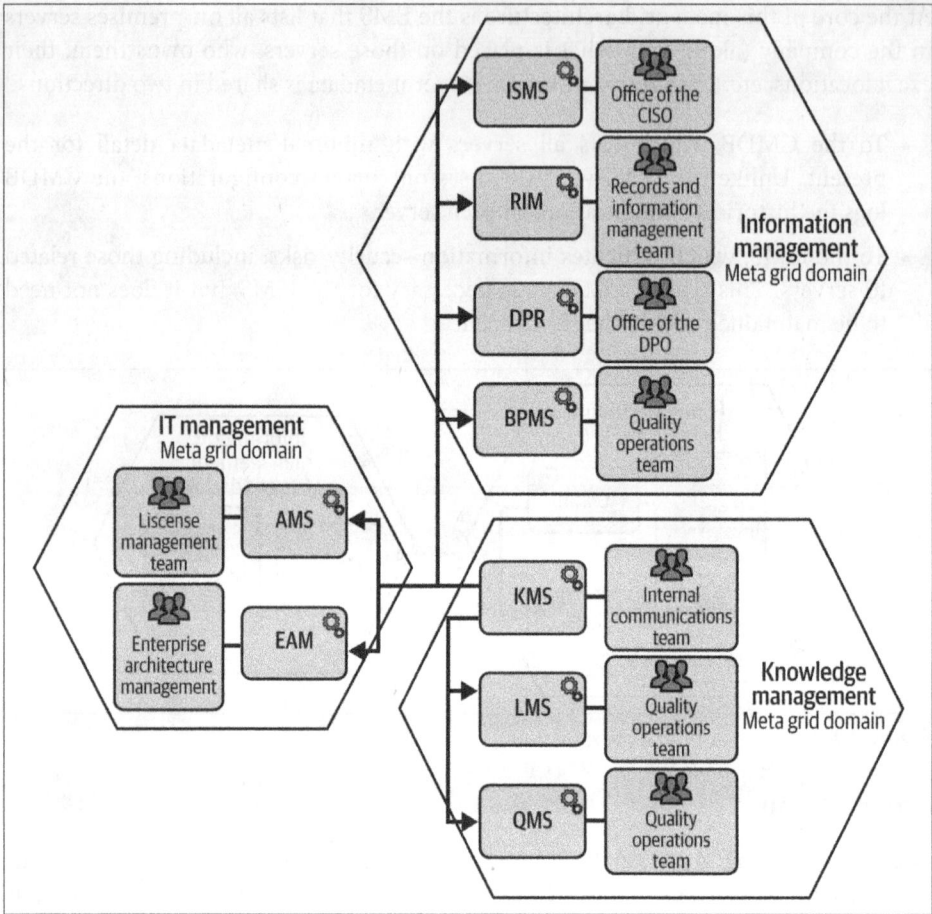

Figure 10-8. Meta grid for organization metadata

The organizational chart is maintained in the KMS, from which it is sent in clusters in three directions.

Internally in the knowledge management domain, both the LMS and the QMS receive the organizational chart for learning and quality management purposes.

In the IT management domain, the EAM tool and the AMS use the organizational chart to provide forecasts of strategic technology decisions for various parts of the organization and the costs of technology for the various teams in the company.

Finally, in the information management domain, the RIMS, ISMS, DPR, and BPMS need organization metadata. The RIMS's purpose is twofold: to assign records to the respective organizational unit and to archive past versions of the organizational chart.

Processes

Process metadata is used in an abundance of tasks in a company, and processes are one of the most common topics discussed in front of a whiteboard filled with arrows and boxes. Therefore, processes are often mapped in so many different ways that they overall can't be trusted. Figure 10-9 outlines a meta grid architecture for processes.

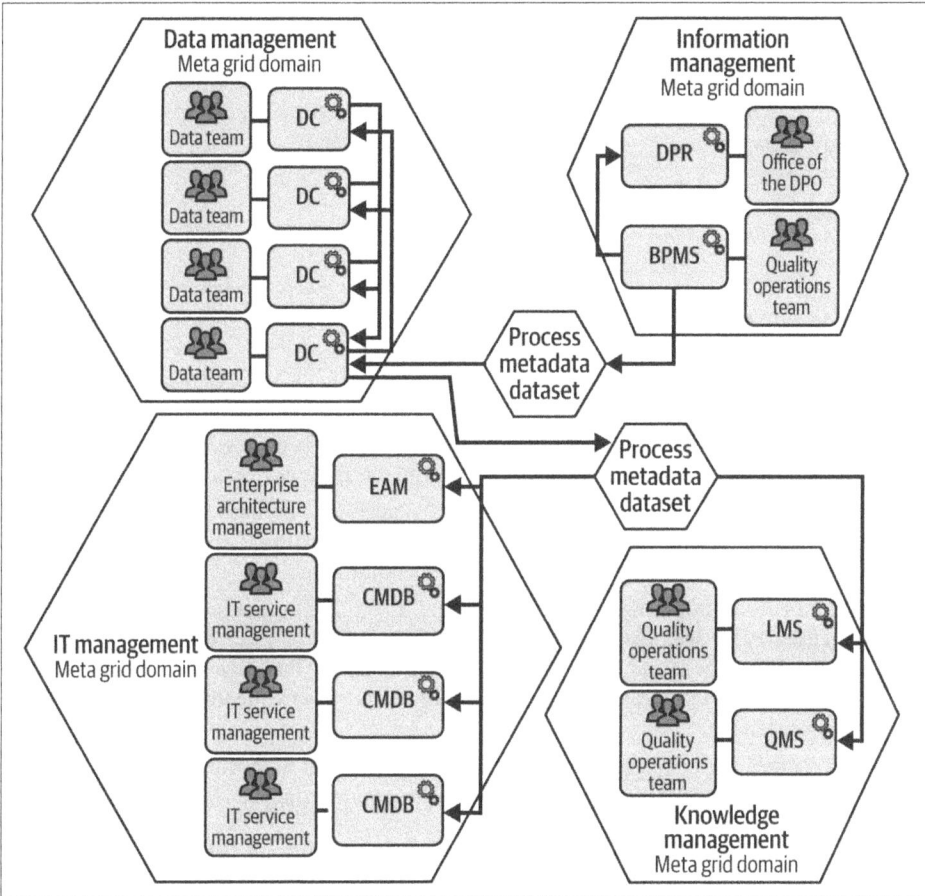

Figure 10-9. Meta grid for processes

The BPMS tool is the repository for processes. It lists and visualizes processes at the task level and up to more generic levels of processes. From that point on, processes are sent in three different directions. Within the information management domain, the DPR needs processes to depict data processing activities. Finally, the LMS and QMS contain process metadata. Process metadata is also sent to an enterprise DC, which then further distributes the metadata to three cloud data platform DCs. These return this process metadata with additional metadata to the enterprise DC. This metadata is then sent on to IT management, where the EAM tool and CMDBs also contain process metadata in their repositories.

A Real-World Meta Grid Architecture

While I was writing this book, many readers reached out to me because they had learned that the meta grid architecture is indeed found within their companies—because it exists in every single company in the world. I include here a message from one of my readers, a skilled architect in Scandinavia, who is asking questions about a specific meta grid architecture for information assets and business processes. I then provide my answer.

Questions

Here is the message I received:

> I really enjoyed your slides on the meta grid from Data Day Texas[3]—thanks for sharing them on LinkedIn!
>
> I'm currently working on integrating our data catalog with ServiceNow to manage information assets at the business process level. Our goal is to map these assets to the data exchanged between applications in lineage flows. To do this, we need to leverage capabilities from our data catalog, ServiceNow, and our business process repository.
>
> Would a systematic approach involve capability mapping (perhaps using functional decomposition) between our data catalog (data management) and ServiceNow (configuration management) to identify overlapping capabilities?
>
> As you mentioned, metadata often exists in multiple places, sometimes without clear boundaries. We've seen cases where Metadata Repo A provides metadata (A1) to both Repo B and C. Repo B and C then redistribute A1 alongside their own domain-specific metadata, leading to multiple versions of A1. If A1 changes frequently, this could create inconsistencies.
>
> Does this mean that clearly defined metadata domains and authoritative repositories are critical within the meta grid? Would love to hear your thoughts!

I think these questions are brilliant—this is a clear example of the endless meta grid architectures out there in all companies.

Answers

First, let me provide the diagram with the meta grid architecture in question (Figure 10-10).

---

3 I was invited to do the opening keynote at Data Day Texas in January 2025 (*https://oreil.ly/1Uh_B*) on the meta grid—these are the slides being referred to.

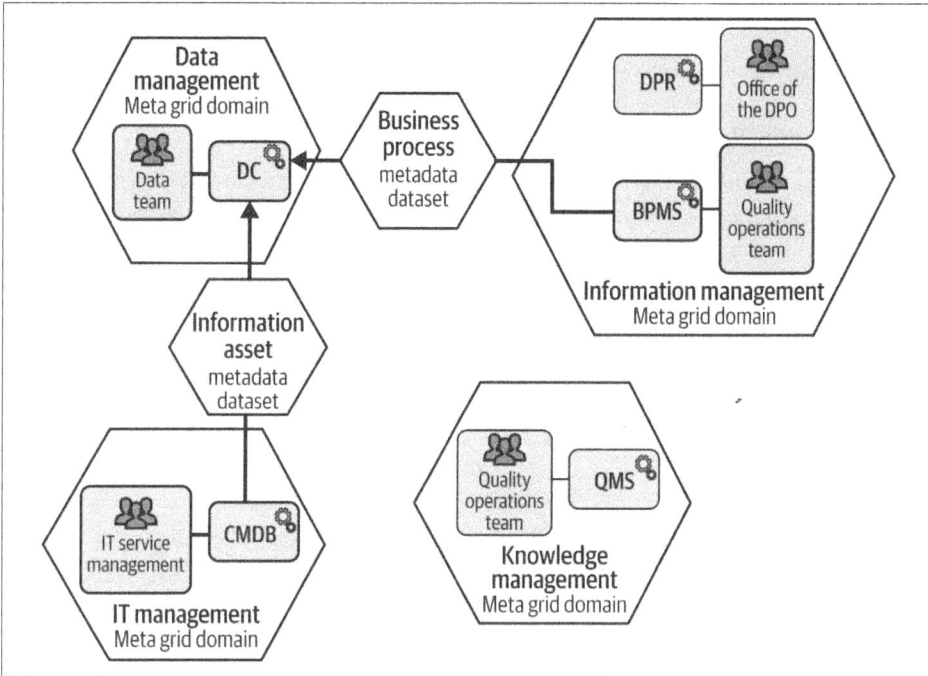

Figure 10-10. Meta grid for information assets

In this very simple meta grid architecture, two types of metadata flow from two different metadata repositories toward a third:

- (Business) process metadata (the business processes that exist in the company) flows from the BPMS toward the DC.
- Information asset metadata (the information assets that exist in the company) flows from the CMDB toward the DC.

In the DC, the metadata is combined so that information assets are linked to business processes. This metadata is then linked to the data lineage function inside the DC. Accordingly, the data lineage expresses a physical manifestation of a conceptual business process and a physical manifestation of the conceptual information types processed in it.

My overall comment is that this is a classical, useful meta grid architecture. I have consulted for several companies about exactly this pattern. It's simple and spot on.

Now, I will answer the questions.

The first question:

> Would a systematic approach involve capability mapping (perhaps using functional decomposition) between our data catalog (data management) and ServiceNow (configuration management) to identify overlapping capabilities?

I would recommend this. But honestly, I see the biggest confusion and potential in a capability mapping between the BPMS and the DC. The BPMS lists business processes but always at the conceptual level, even though these can be based on process mining. *Process mining* is a scanning technique that entails discovering business processes inside, for example, ERP systems and visualizing them, with the purpose of trimming them. The DC, on the other hand, always provides data lineage at the physical level because it is a scan of sources between which specific types of data travel. Accordingly, data lineage and business processes look almost identical, but they are not.

For example, it is often claimed by *bad* sales people (with reference to the good, the bad, and the ugly sociology that I put forward in Chapter 8) that data lineage is a capability that makes DCs a fit tool for financial auditing and thus to comply with, for example, BCBS 239 (see Chapters 3 and 4), but that is not correct. Data lineage is a feature so complex that it seldom works effectively across the IT data landscape. Accordingly, many begin to "invent" data lineage because they know this lineage exists but can't express it technically. It is easier to comply with BCBS 239 in a BPMS that does not depend on scanning data lineage but can be modeled freely, in BPMN, for example (see Chapter 5), and then audited and inspected at each step.

For CMDBs and DCs, I would argue that the capabilities are given like this: the CMDB manages past and present instances of software and hardware in the company by listing them manually or semiautomatically while the DC makes data across the present IT landscape searchable and discoverable by scanning data sources automatically and more deeply than what a CMDB would express. In this case, the information assets are managed in the CMDB—that's fine; there is no reason to change that. There may be a need to scope future information assets, but neither the CMDB nor the DC would be the proper tool for that—that would be an EAM tool or a project and portfolio management tool since these tools are dedicated to describing future states, not the present.

The second question:

> Does this mean that clearly defined metadata domains and authoritative repositories are critical within the meta grid?

Domains: yes. Do design clear domains in a meta grid architecture. It is not difficult; I suggest you do not use the thinking in domain-driven design. It is overly complex for the task at hand. We are, after all, not designing software but managing metadata.

Instead, I suggest domain-analysis thinking. Both ways of thinking are described in depth in my first book, *The Enterprise Data Catalog*.[4]

Authoritative repositories: this depends. Architecture is a moving target, and therefore, many kill the good solution for the unobtainable perfect solution. Most likely, information assets have been listed in multiple repositories, in various ways. The DPO is likely to have also compiled a list of business processes and information assets in the DPR, simply because the DPO needs this to perform their job. Embrace that. The same is almost certainly true for business processes that may be found in a QMS to conduct audits and training, if you are working in a regulated industry that needs a QMS to operate.

Summary

This chapter introduced you to a completely new kind of architecture: the meta grid. This represents a third wave of data decentralization specifically for metadata. The meta grid is designed to enable efficient and powerful metadata management, offering a range of positive outcomes. It primarily coordinates all metadata repositories, alleviating the pressure of providing a single, unified view. Instead, the meta grid integrates multiple metadata repositories into a cohesive architecture, with each repository representing a specific aspect of the IT landscape.

This chapter discussed the following key points:

- The meta grid is the third wave of data decentralization. It builds on the two previous waves: microservices and data mesh.

- The meta grid unlocks single-view-of-the-world monoliths. No single metadata repository can represent the entire truth about the IT landscape.

- The meta grid is incomplete in the sense that it will always expand as companies will need metadata for new purposes.

- The meta grid is simple, small, and slow, in contrast to the previous waves of decentralization, which were complex, big, and fast.

- The meta grid has four domains:

  — IT management

  — Data management

  — Information management

  — Knowledge management

---

4 I discuss this in more depth in the section "Understanding Domains" (pp. 25–32) in *The Enterprise Data Catalog* (O'Reilly).

- These domains all have a set of metadata repositories that describe certain aspects of the IT landscape.

- The meta grid does not need an experience plane. It is to be experienced directly in the metadata repositories it manages.

- The meta grid has producers that maintain the grid, but it does not have direct consumers. These are the users of the various metadata repositories.

- Therefore, the meta grid is discrete, invisible, and ambient.

- The meta grid is not contained in a technology.

- Nor does the meta grid express an ontology. Its elements have no mandatory connections that link it in a complete ontology.

- The meta grid does not have distinct domain boundaries—some metadata repositories can fall into multiple domains.

- The meta grid is not a semantic layer either because it is not focused on capturing the language of the business but rather on representing the IT landscape.

- The meta grid is documented in ADRs: models that depict the domains and metadata repositories in scope also mentioned in the ADRs as well as the necessary lists or APIs to connect the meta grid architecture in question.

- Examples of meta grid architectures include data types, applications, data models, integrations, data lineage, servers, organizational data, and processes. These examples are far from exhaustive.

CHAPTER 11

The Meta Grid Contextualized

In this chapter, we will discuss four key topics that contextualize the meta grid. First, I emphasize that you don't build the meta grid—you uncover it. Unlike microservices and data mesh, which are consciously designed, the meta grid is a decentralized architecture that already exists; it is something to be revealed and improved, but not to be constructed from the ground up.

Next, I describe the meta grid as a nuclear architecture. Although the meta grid is small in scale, it is densely packed with potential, both in terms of energy and risk. If mismanaged, it can be as volatile as a nuclear reaction—capable of exploding if things go wrong.

We will also examine the relationship between the meta grid and other architectures, such as microservices and data mesh, which connect to the meta grid in specific, intricate ways.

Finally, we will review the technologies that support a meta grid. While the meta grid itself is not a technology, it can be augmented by various tools—from ambitious broadscale platforms to more focused visualization or management solutions.

Before we dive in, it is important to understand that you cannot simply build a meta grid.

You Don't Build the Meta Grid—You Uncover It

In Chapter 2, I defined *metadata* as:

> A description that is both attached to what is described and placed somewhere else in order to make what is described discoverable and manageable.

Fundamentally, *metadata* is defined not by *what* it is but by *where* it exists: always in two places, not one, as we discussed at the beginning of this book. This definition has consequences. The key is that the *where* is not simply one place that mirrors another place. The same things can be mirrored in many different places. Therefore, we are not dealing with a double presence of something but rather with multiple, potentially unlimited presences of it.

When considering this in the context of a company's IT landscape, we must take into account that there are many metadata repositories that depict the IT landscape and that these repositories often overlap in the metadata they contain.

The absence of the definition also—in many cases—leads to the negative consequences that an awareness of the definition could have prevented. The quasi-religious discussions of whether there are three, four, or five types of metadata perform the philosophical fallacy of listing subcategories of a category in the attempt to define the category. However, examples of usage of something do not equal the essence of that something—in fact, they risk blurring the understanding of what is sought to be understood. Metadata is not just business, technical, or operational metadata. These subcategories lead to irrelevant discussions about how many subcategories a category has. Meanwhile, metadata expands into a wealth of technologies.

Whether it's business, technical, or operational data—or even analytical, social, and so on—metadata needs to exist both at the source, with the thing it describes, and in a designated repository, creating space to discover that thing. Metadata is, at its core, a link. That link will be created multiple times, using different logic each time, with the goal of leveraging the unique capabilities of each metadata repository. This is a consequence of the nature of metadata, as described in the definition.

Accordingly, the technology that claims to be the single source of truth, that sells itself to companies as the *ultimate* technology that will *finally* allow you to map and manage the IT landscape, is nothing but yet another single-view-of-the-world monolith alongside all the others. Likewise, the consultant who bursts into your office with declarations like "We will map your business processes once and for all!" isn't selling the ultimate business process map; they are creating yet another mirror, another collection of metadata, likely to be stored in a technology of their choosing.

The point is that there is nothing wrong with what these technologies and consultancies create. What is wrong is not the result, but the offset: the lack of understanding that they can never be single sources of truth and final versions of something—not because they are poorly conceived but because they fall short of understanding the nature of the thing they are working with. Metadata is in multiple places at the same time. Winning the game of the ultimate truth is lost before it begins.

Therefore, you must uncover your enterprise meta grid. You need to understand what already exists and where, often in multiple places, and then relate all of that in a cohesive grid. And no technology, no effort to harmonize everything, will ever change this reality. Only the acceptance of this condition and the meticulous mapping of the meta grid will make you rise to the top of metadata management.

It will be impossible to eliminate all the technologies and maps created over time, and it's not advisable, either—they all serve a purpose. What is possible is to relate them. That's what you should focus on as that will strengthen all of the metadata repositories within your company.

Uncovering Unconscious Meta Grid Architectures

Many tech books, whitepapers, and reports fall short of depicting the reality of IT landscapes in companies. They depict ideal *target states* or *end states*: well-functioning architectures that are logically composed, cost-effective, and highly performant. This is educational but is seldom the reality in companies. And there is something even deeper at play too: target states are illusions. The IT landscape changes over time. There is no end state. There is just the possibility of remaining adaptive to change and slowly making the architecture more logical and flexible accordingly.

This reality also goes for metadata repositories. They will never be implemented following the most ideal architectural advice available. Instead, they are implemented in siloes, gradually discovered and then—perhaps—coordinated to some extent. These kinds of architectures are what we discuss in this section: the *unconscious* meta grid architectures. They are not deliberately conceived but instead emerge as ad hoc solutions to ideas from various parts of the enterprise at various points in time. I cover three examples (though many more could be provided):

- Data driven (ambition)
- FinOps
- Intake funnel

The architectures discussed in this section are deliberately poorly conceived. They are not ideal target state architectures—instead, they depict the reality in many big industrial companies.[1] It's not a situation we can get out of. We need to start creating conscious meta grids, where metadata on applications, integrations, projects, processes, capabilities, and more flows consciously between these technologies so that they all perform faster and more precisely.

Data Driven (Ambition)

Most companies today declare that they are or want to be data driven. The ambition is to maximize usage of data for analytics, especially advanced analytics—meaning ML and AI—to have better decision making. That ultimately leads to a more appealing product portfolio and wiser judgments about trends in the market, creating a much-desired competitive advantage.

One central aspect of being data driven is implementing a collection of metadata repositories. However, unlike what target state architecture suggests, this typically occurs in isolated pockets across a company, at different times and often simultaneously.

In most companies of more than five thousand employees, it is common to have a handful of DCs implemented in the pursuit of being data driven. In our example, the company has decided to use several cloud providers offering their own DCs that connect with ease to the other applications in their specific clouds. These DCs are *best-of-suite* data catalogs, some with limited refinement. One of these DCs is connected to three instances of IRs that build pipelines and document them. Also, two standalone data lineage tools are added to the most tech-agnostic DC that is a best-of-breed, enterprise-wide *catalog of catalogs* sitting on top of the other DCs. One of the lineage tools is connected to a database modeling tool that provides empirical modeling and thus input to the lineage tool. Furthermore, two business process mapping tools are performing analysis and visualizations on two different parts of the business (using different tech stacks), and they are also connected to the authoritative catalog of catalogs. But for every metadata repository in this architecture, there are large quantities of metadata that are not shared between them and are managed in isolation. You can see this in Figure 11-1.

---

1 With my company, Searching for Data, I have consulted for numerous organizations across the globe. The examples I have created here are inspired by hundreds of conversations and presentations I have had with engineers and architects. None of the examples discussed here reflect a specific company.

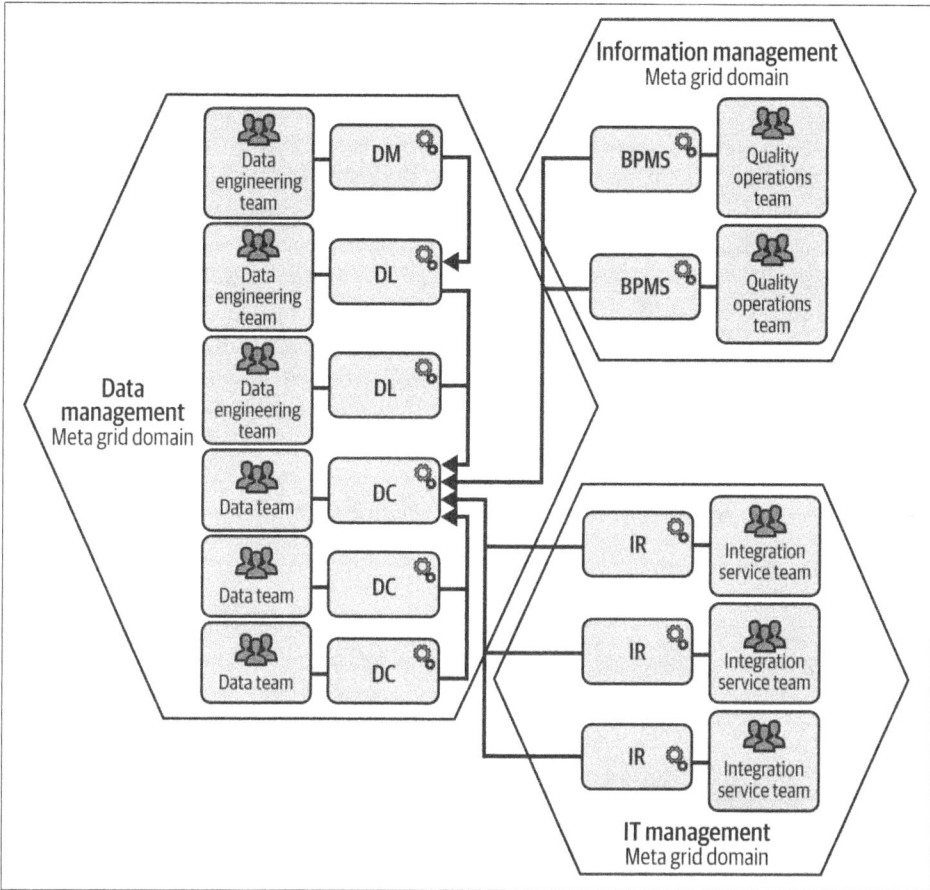

Figure 11-1. Data-driven (ambition) architecture

Is this a desirable architecture? No. It is too complex, too expensive, and most likely too underperforming. But chances are that this architecture resembles the architecture in your company significantly more than the reference architecture put forward in most tech books, whitepapers, and reports. Ask yourself: where is the truth about the IT landscape? The reality is, alas, that the truth dissolves in such an architecture. It is impossible to ask: What data types do we have? What domains? Processes? Applications? And so on. Vital enterprise metadata gets lost in a cacophony of over-engineered ambitions and insufficient organizational collaboration. This is the *unconscious* meta grid.

Once uncovered, you can alter this unconscious architecture. You can create a powerful meta grid and excel at metadata management.

FinOps

To control the cost of IT spending, companies use software that depicts the IT landscape in terms of who is spending what. This typically is an asset management tool. In our example, we have two asset management tools, where one is based on agents and another is agentless. Agent-based scanning installs a small agent on all company endpoints to examine what client applications are running on that specific endpoint. Agentless scanning looks at existing APIs and network communication to gather metadata directly from existing applications. Both offer details that the other excludes, and therefore, both AMSs are needed. The agentless AMS communicates with one of the two CMDBs that the company has (a merger with a second company five years ago created a reality of parallel CMDBs that were never integrated; they each represent their own part of the company). The agent-based AMS is connected to a data observability tool, maintained by a team in the data management domain for quality purposes—and as it runs on agents, the repositories share and exchange metadata on cost versus quality for mutual benefits. Figure 11-2 depicts this architecture.

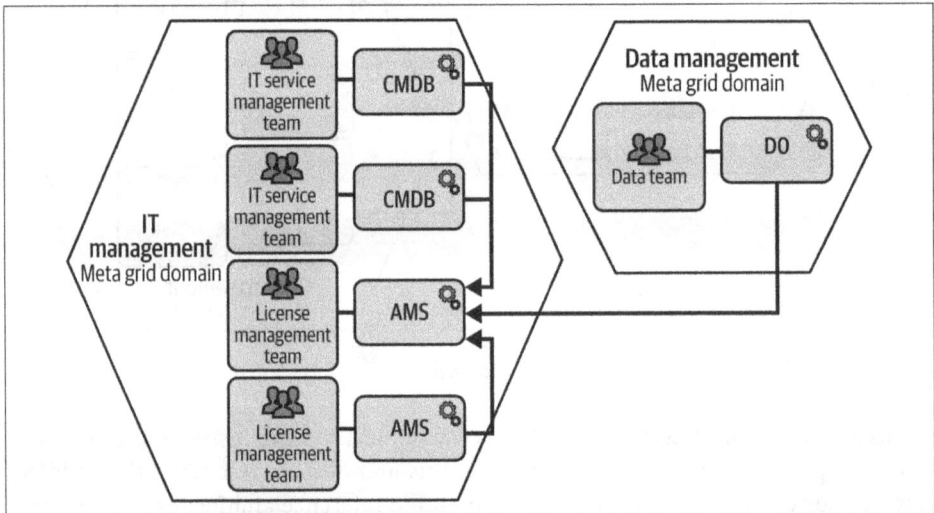

Figure 11-2. FinOps architecture

Again, is this a desirable architecture? No. But the point is that these architectures will never be perfect, in terms of the components that constitute them. IT landscapes have histories that make them irrational yet still functional. The meta grid is a pragmatic response to this, not an attempt to reach an illusory perfect end state that is too costly to obtain and will take too long to put into operation.

Intake Funnel

In this last example, we look at intake funnels in a company and, more specifically, how new IT applications are created in that intake funnel (and even intake of issues and new features). The company in question has two completely isolated intake funnels. In the first example, an EAM tool is used to register the applications, which are then subsequently registered in the CMDB and QMS when they go live for end users. In the other intake funnel, three parallel CMDBs are used to register the applications. One of them serves as the repository for particularly mission-critical, data-privacy-sensitive, and confidential applications. This CMDB integrates with a DC, which registers the applications and acts as the DPR while also being connected to an ISMS that performs continuous risk assessment. You can see this architecture in Figure 11-3.

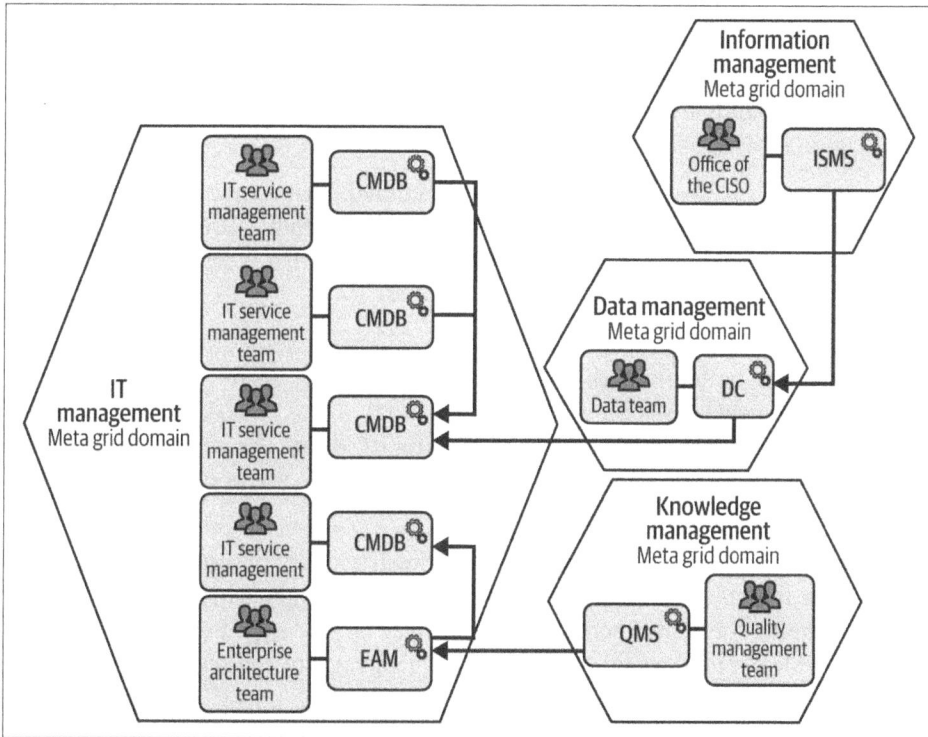

Figure 11-3. Intake funnel architecture

Is this a logical architecture? No! In fact, it is so illogical that you would have to create a link between the three CMDBs and the EAM tool to ensure that the applications listed in these metadata repositories are aligned. This example shows that the meta grid can handle illogical metadata repository architecture to the point where it becomes technically impossible to align the vision of the IT landscape; that is the point where illogical architecture tilts and becomes silos.

Now, let's look at the characteristics of the meta grid as an architecture.

The Meta Grid Is a Nuclear Architecture

In the vast majority of companies, meta grid architectures are *unconscious*, with only very few established relationships between the metadata repositories in use. As discussed in Chapter 2, metadata repositories come in waves, and as described throughout Part II, these metadata repositories are developed in isolation from one another, as monoliths of single-world views.

Metadata repositories developed in isolation will not break the company. But the many isolated metadata repositories will make it impossible to understand the actual IT landscape if they are managed poorly.

Unlike the other decentralized architectures—microservices and data mesh—the meta grid will never grow big. It will remain very small throughout its lifetime. However, what surrounds the meta grid is enormous: the entire IT landscape of a company (Figure 11-4).

Most company IT landscapes are deeply dysfunctional. They work, but they are full of extraordinarily expensive, underperforming IT solutions that gradually deteriorate as time passes—scrambling along with a logic of their own that is slowly lost to corporate amnesia.

Unlike microservices and data mesh, the meta grid is not something that companies actively decide to build. Instead, companies unintentionally create meta grid architectures whenever new legislation is passed, regulations are created, standards are developed, technologies emerge, or ambitions materialize within the company, across the three contexts of operation, regulation, and innovation, as waves of metadata repositories hit organizations again and again.

Meta grid architectures can be built consciously. If so, they become nuclear-fission-like vehicles: they allow the depiction of vital metadata elements in a coordinated way, cascading these coordinated activities deep into the IT landscape in various directions for a multitude of purposes rooted in innovation, operation, and regulation.

Meta grid architectures hold a lot of *energy* that can be used, if correctly understood. These architectures can hence *expand*—and they can *explode*. Let's look into these three aspects: energy, expansion, and explosion.

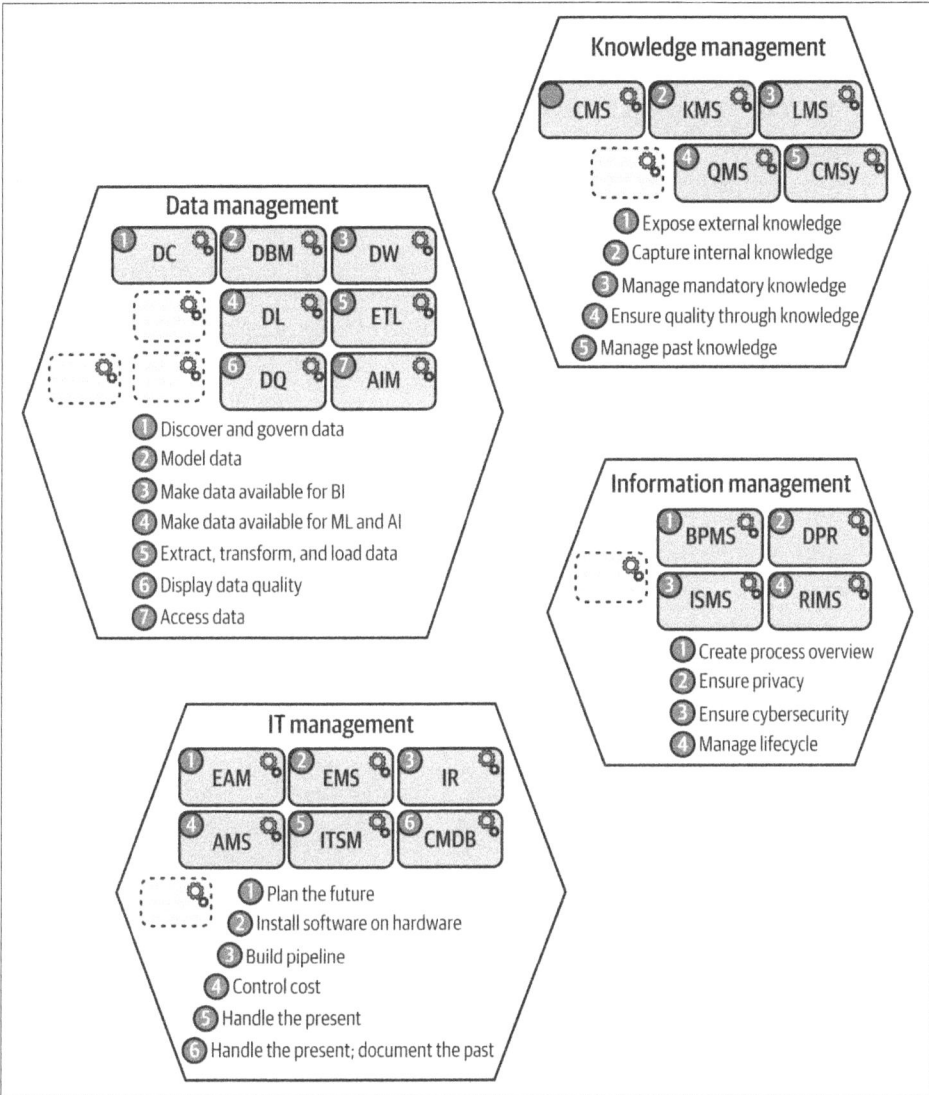

Knowledge management

- ① CMS ② KMS ③ LMS
- ④ QMS ⑤ CMSy
- ① Expose external knowledge
- ② Capture internal knowledge
- ③ Manage mandatory knowledge
- ④ Ensure quality through knowledge
- ⑤ Manage past knowledge

Data management

- ① DC ② DBM ③ DW
- ④ DL ⑤ ETL
- ⑥ DQ ⑦ AIM
- ① Discover and govern data
- ② Model data
- ③ Make data available for BI
- ④ Make data available for ML and AI
- ⑤ Extract, transform, and load data
- ⑥ Display data quality
- ⑦ Access data

Information management

- ① BPMS ② DPR
- ③ ISMS ④ RIMS
- ① Create process overview
- ② Ensure privacy
- ③ Ensure cybersecurity
- ④ Manage lifecycle

IT management

- ① EAM ② EMS ③ IR
- ④ AMS ⑤ ITSM ⑥ CMDB
- ① Plan the future
- ② Install software on hardware
- ③ Build pipeline
- ④ Control cost
- ⑤ Handle the present
- ⑥ Handle the present; document the past

Figure 11-4. The meta grid architecture and the immensity of the IT landscape

Energy

Let's take the example of a process like the one shown in Figure 10-9. In this meta grid architecture, *processes* are mapped and maintained across teams as *process metadata* is sent through the grid, instead of being maintained by six different isolated teams, in six different ways. Time spent on metadata management is significantly reduced and solidity is ensured, liberating time for the core capabilities of the technologies on the grid and the teams that use them.

As such, the meta grid can be considered energy that can be used functionally, when understood. The difference between an unwanted explosion of the IT landscape and the wanted energy liberated by the meta grid is rooted in the consciousness of the meta grid architecture as a logical expansion.

Expansion

The meta grid already exists as an unconscious construct in every company. But once a meta grid architecture approach is accepted even by the smallest number of employees, then it can gradually expand. There are four ways the meta grid can expand:

- Expansion of domains
- Expansion of metadata repository categories
- Expansion of the amount of the same repository category (e.g., many DCs)
- Expansion of meta grid architectures

Expansion of domains

The four typical domains—IT, data, information, and knowledge management—can expand into more domains if needed. That's not likely to be the case, though, and not likely to be useful; the number of domains must stay small. You may also find yourself in a situation where you are starting with two domains, such as IT management and information management, and then you gradually expand to data management. Figure 11-5 represents this expansion.

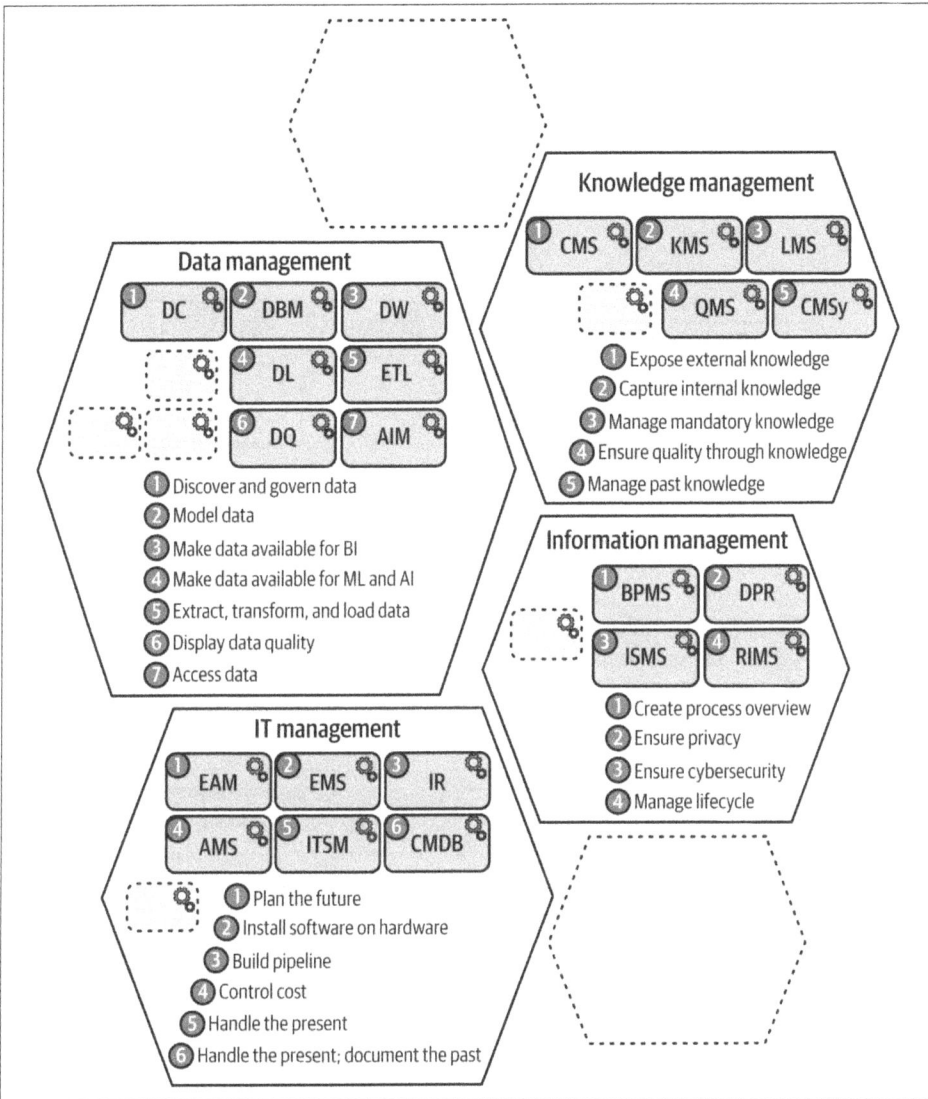

Figure 11-5. Expansion of domains

Expansion of metadata repository categories

This scalability is somewhat more difficult to control. After all, analysis of what is metadata about the IT landscape can be a slippery affair—ultimately, everything that mirrors anything may be interpreted as metadata repositories. A practical way to draw a line between what is and is not a metadata repository can be the categories of technologies that microservices and data mesh seek to split up (see Table 11-1). That said, there will be small metadata repositories inside these technologies, and these can be included in the grid, if deemed relevant. Figure 11-6 represents the expansion of metadata repositories in the meta grid.

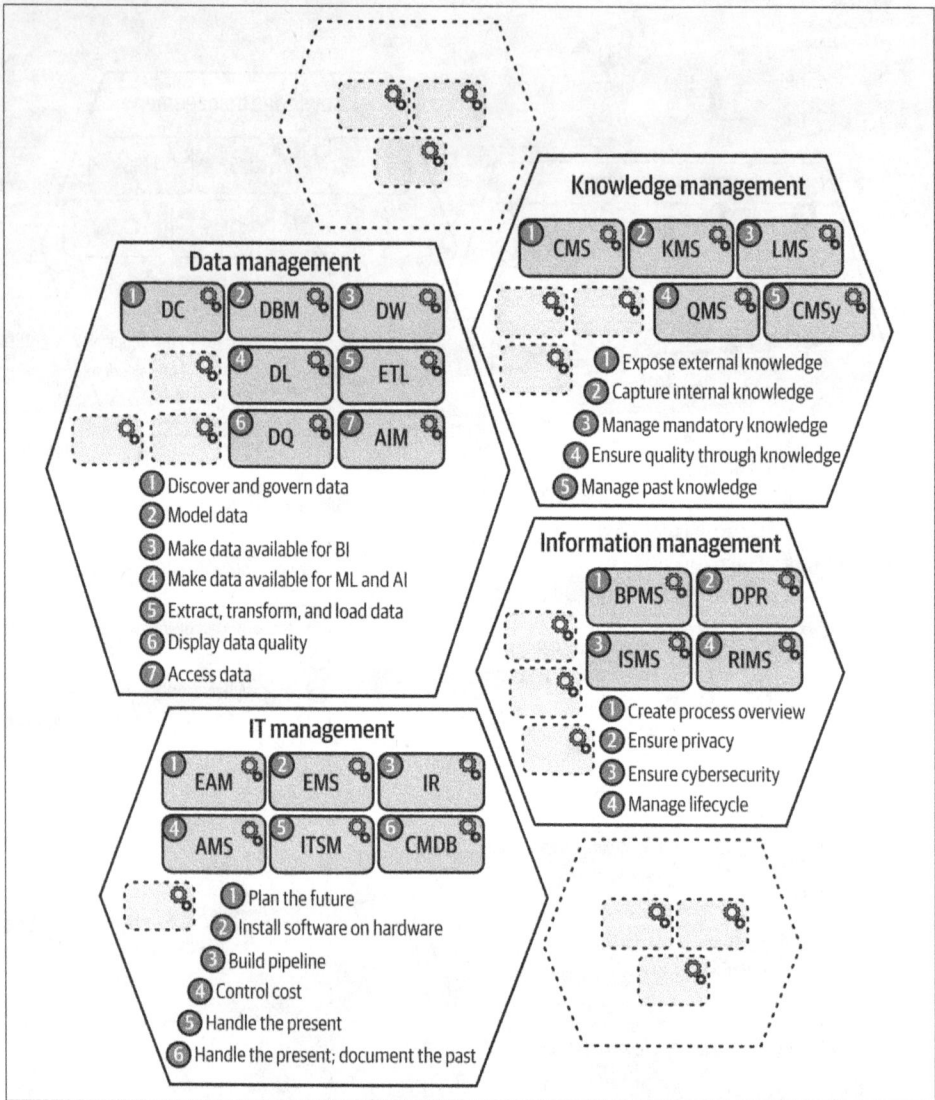

Figure 11-6. Expansion of metadata repository categories

Expansion of the same type of metadata repositories

Typically, working with meta grid architectures will uncover many of the same types of metadata repositories. In most companies, it is (unfortunately) the case that multiple DCs have been implemented across various business domains. As a result of mergers and acquisition, it is also often the case that multiple CMDBs and EMSs exist, as shown in Figure 11-7.

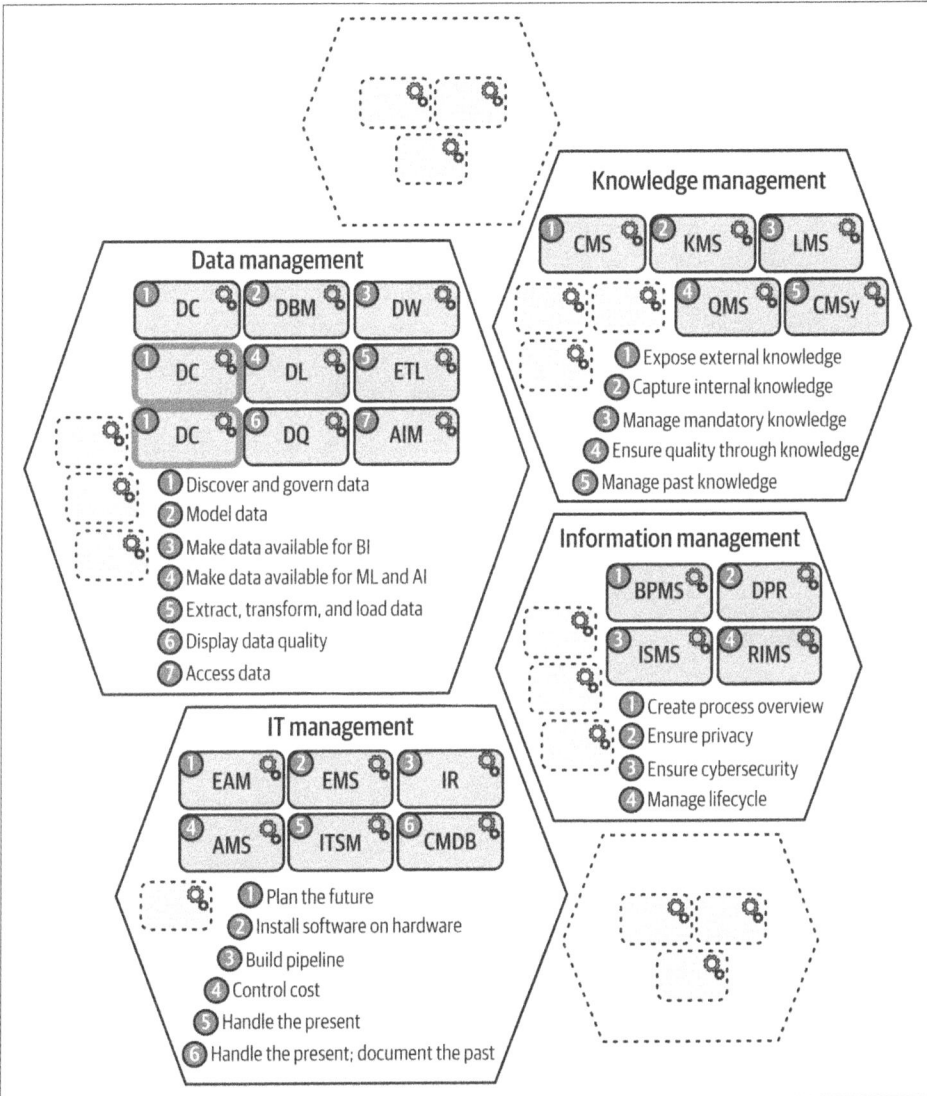

Figure 11-7. Expansions of the same type of metadata repositories (DC as an example)

Expansion of meta grid architectures

This is the most logical part of the meta grid to expand, and it should expand continuously. Every meta grid architecture adds another dimension to the total meta grid, creating a reality of a *grid of grids*. This grid of grids is not technically materialized in one unit; it is simply the sum of grids. It may be perceived if all meta grid architectures are documented as diagrams.

Explosion

Organizations all over the world suffer from what can be called meta grid nuclear explosions: metadata management gone haywire, imprecise metadata overviews of the IT landscape, and IT landscapes with skyrocketing costs and incomprehensible complexity. The root cause of this is not solely poor metadata management—as discussed in Part II, there is something poisonous at play in the triangle of external consultants, software vendors, and internal employees. Software is pushed by people with selfish motives. Sometimes this benefits the company, and sometimes it doesn't. Metadata repositories to manage the IT landscape are not exceptions. These metadata repositories may have been poorly maintained, but they can just as well have been implemented with great vigor to try to overcome an already catastrophic reality.

Here are some of the ways that meta grid architectures represent explosions:

- Numerous applications for the same capability
- Opaque integrations
- Poorly maintained cloud
- Poorly maintained on premises

Alas, meta grid architectures can also represent explosive, chaotic systems in and of themselves:

- Many of the same metadata repositories
- Multiplicity of metadata types

Microservices, Data Mesh, and Meta Grid

> If you aren't working in a company that focuses on microservices or data mesh, or you simply haven't studied these architectures, you can skip this section. If you still want to read it, go right ahead; just note that it may be a little dense without prior knowledge. I have added references where you can learn more.

Meta grid architectures also relate to the other decentralized architectures in a very concrete way. In this section, we will explore three relationships between microservices, data mesh, and meta grid:

- Microservices in the meta grid
- Data mesh in the meta grid
- Meta grid must not turn into microservices or data mesh

Microservices in the Meta Grid

In *Building Microservices*, Sam Newman writes that creating a microservice (by breaking down a monolith) can be done in several ways; this is called *decomposition by layer*:

> If we consider the traditional three tiers of a web-based services stack, then we can look at the functionality we want to extract in terms of its user interface, backend application code, and data.[2]

Ultimately, mirroring microservices in a meta grid architecture will consist of multiple metadata repositories because the decomposition of monoliths results in microservices of a different nature—some consisting of UIs, code, and data (databases).

> A meta grid cannot and should not replace a microservices architecture. What is explained here is simply that the microservice has to deliver metadata according to the metamodel or parts of the metamodel for the metadata repository. It is just an API serving metadata, as for more monolithic architectures.

There will be registrations of microservices in repositories such as the EMS, EAM tool, and CMDB, as depicted in Figure 11-8.

---

2 Sam Newman, *Building Microservices*, 2nd ed. (O'Reilly, 2021), 76.

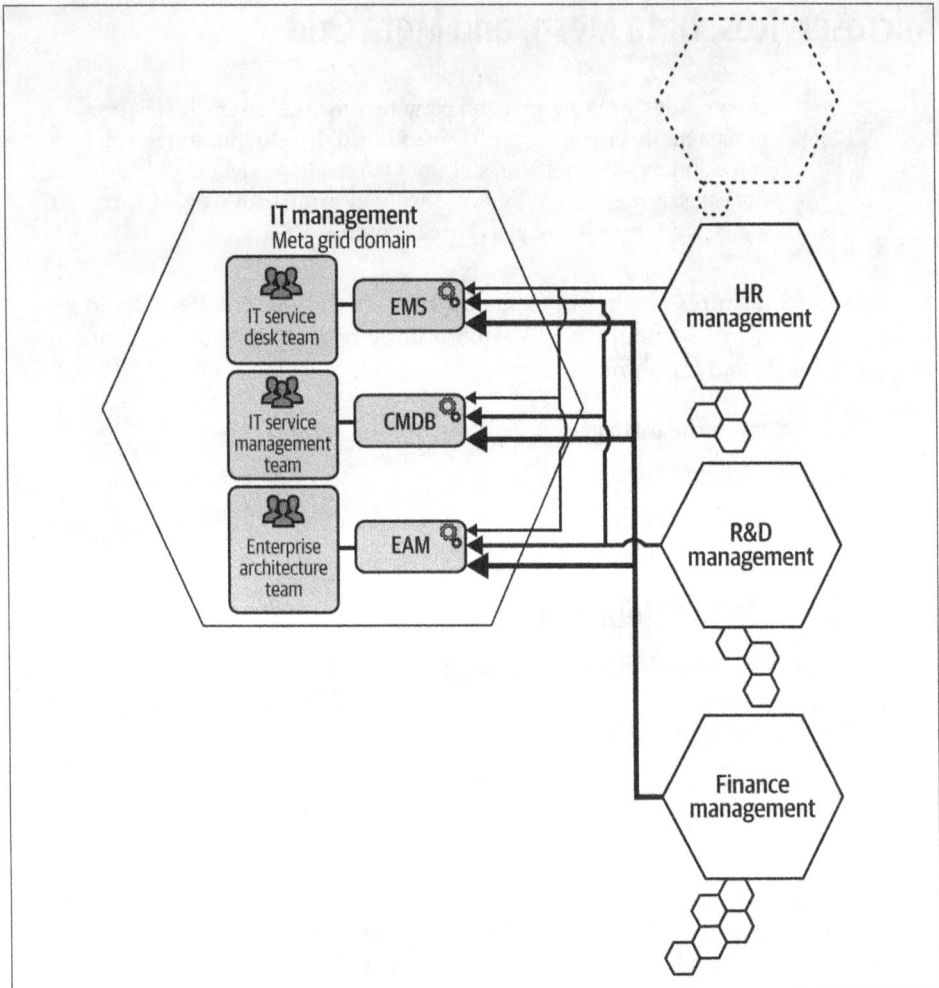

Figure 11-8. Microservices in the meta grid

Even though this may seem to be a rather abstract enterprise architecture discussion, it is not. Metadata repositories already allow for the depiction of microservices, such as LeanIX (*https://oreil.ly/ssFN6*). Your metadata repositories are ready to depict microservices today. Just remember two things:

- Microservices will land in various repositories depending on what kinds of microservices they are.

- Monoliths are broken down piece by piece. Your metadata repositories will need to faithfully depict the remaining monolithic structure until it is fully decomposed—or indefinitely, if only parts of the IT landscape will consist of microservices.

Data Mesh in the Meta Grid

The core idea behind data mesh is to break the monolith of analytical data and instead present data as a product, complete with relevant metadata for discovery. However, as we established in Chapter 2 and discussed in depth at the beginning of this chapter, the essence of metadata is that it is in two places at once. Metadata in a data mesh is no exception. Therefore, despite this big departure from monoliths of analytical data, data products in a data mesh are still to be made discoverable on the experience plane of the data mesh—more specifically, in a *data marketplace* using the data mesh vocabulary.

In *Data Mesh*, Zhamak Dehghani writes:

> The big departure from a traditional data architecture is that a data product itself is responsible for generating the metadata, as opposed to traditional systems where metadata is extracted, extrapolated, and projected by an external system—often after the data has been generated. In the traditional world an external system such as a central data catalog attempts to extract, collect, and serve metadata from all datasets.[3]

Eric Broda and Jean-Georges Perrin discuss data marketplaces in *Implementing Data Mesh*. They draw on the commercial marketplace architecture found in Amazon, for example, which is a *two-sided marketplace* in the sense that there is one user interface for consumers and one for sellers. The consumer interface is simple, fast, effective, and intuitive. The seller interface is more technical, allowing sellers to update their various products:

> We suggest a two sided marketplace....At the heart of the Data Mesh Marketplace is a user-friendly graphical interface designed to make the process of finding data as intuitive and straightforward as possible...it incorporates advanced search functionalities, leveraging the power of natural language processing and semantic search technologies.[4]

Modern data catalogs are constructed to leverage the two-sided marketplace tailored for a data mesh. I have pioneered one of the globally leading examples of this with Zeenea, now part of the Actian Data Intelligence platform. Its federated data catalog allows for the mirroring of the domain's data mesh within the marketplace. If you want to learn more about how to make this split between producers and consumers of data work, check out my book *The Enterprise Data Catalog* (O'Reilly). The idea behind the book is that how you organize data defines how you can search it—and that is exactly why you need a two-sided marketplace.

---

3 Zhamak Dehghani, *Data Mesh* (O'Reilly, 2022), 157.

4 Jean-Georges Perrin and Eric Broda, *Implementing Data Mesh* (O'Reilly, 2024), 148–149.

Just like with microservices, it is unlikely that your entire company will adopt a data mesh architecture for analytical data. Therefore, you will probably need to build a dual architecture consisting of a data mesh marketplace and a data catalog, which together make data available for analytical consumption, as shown in Figure 11-9.

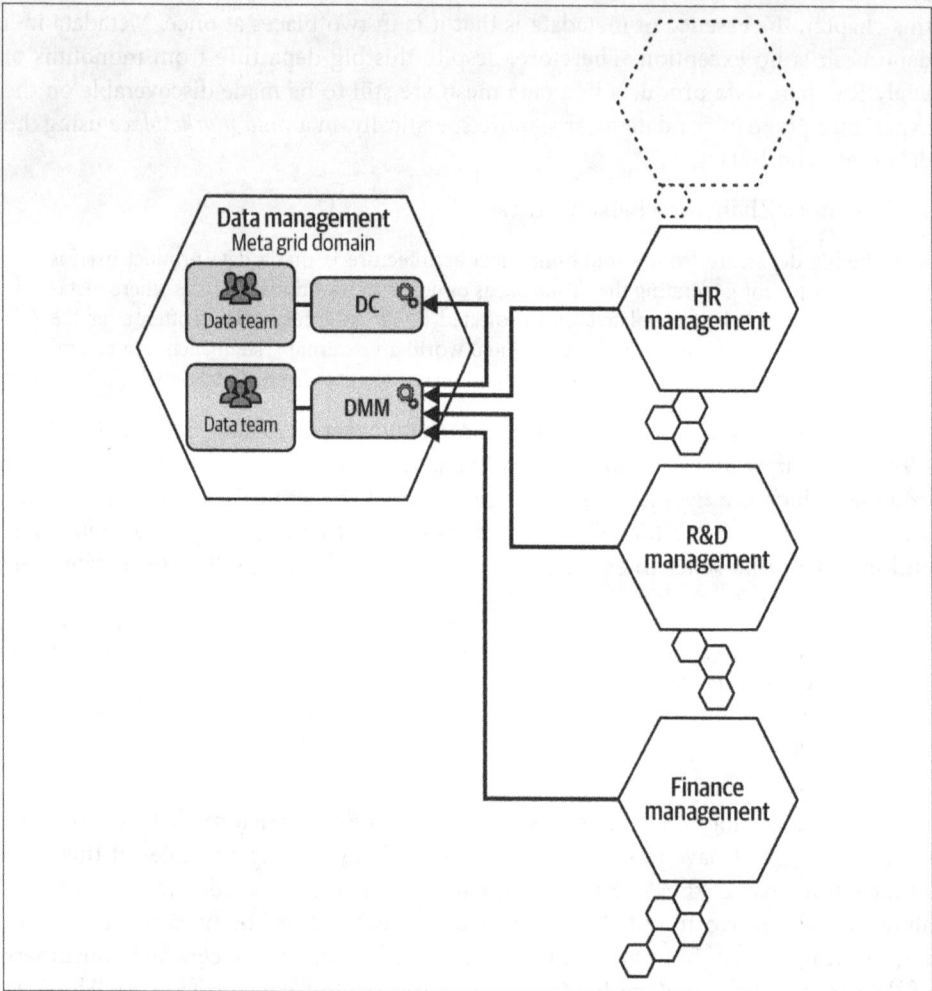

Figure 11-9. Data mesh in the meta grid

Meta Grid Must Not Turn into Data Mesh or Microservices

It is tempting to create more complete, deeper meta grid architectures because that is useful and effective for various purposes in the analytical or operative endeavors of the enterprise.

In the pursuit of powerful analytics, it would be obvious to go deeper and consider the meta grid datasets as data products. This would be extremely difficult to make happen because these cannot be considered golden sources: the metadata repositories wherein the metadata that is coordinated resides are the golden sources. But that would turn the meta grid into a data-mesh-like architecture. Furthermore, that would break the logic of an effective data mesh architecture because the meta grid does not represent the same degree of decoupling since it is a single-view-of-the-world monolith that has been broken.

Similarly, for complex operational tasks, it may be tempting to go beyond simply mapping types of integrations and applications. Instead, break them down further and let the meta grid manage the interoperability of these tasks. However, that would turn the meta grid into a—not very effective—microservices architecture.

It is important to remember that the meta grid is small, slow, and simple. You have to keep it that way. It is a light, intentionally high-level, and, one could even say, not very deep architecture. If you compromise that and tie the meta grid to analytical or operative agendas, it turns into something else: either a data mesh architecture for analytical data or a microservices architecture for operational data.

In Table 11-1, you can see how to distinguish between microservices, data mesh, and meta grid architectures.

Table 11-1. Comparison of microservices, data mesh, and meta grid

	Microservices	Data mesh	Meta grid
Purpose	Execute the value chain Purpose inside the architecture	Perform more and better analytics Purpose outside the architecture	Understand the IT landscape Purpose inside the architecture
Level of engineering	Very complex—very hard to obtain	Complex—hard to obtain	Simple—relatively easy to obtain
Order of establishment	Secondary or tertiary Building microservices alters the value chain, and this is difficult	Secondary Building a data mesh does not alter the value chain, merely analytics	Primary You have to know your IT landscape before anything else
Preexisting monoliths broken	ERPs, CRMs, and smaller software components to execute the value chain	Technically, none (the illusion of enterprise-wide data warehouses, lakes, and lakehouses is broken); in reality, these are not enterprise wide as both big data platform monoliths and siloes of smaller data platforms across business exist in all companies	Technically, none (the meta grid already exists, although it is very incomplete and, at the same time, too big)
Reason to decentralize	Staying adaptable and on top and changing quickly	Using better analytics to transform into a more modern product offering	Having a shared understanding of the IT landscape to better manage it

	Microservices	Data mesh	Meta grid
How to create it	Build Microservices replace existing solutions	Build Data mesh replaces existing solutions	Relate, don't build The meta grid strengthens relationships between existing repositories
Data types	Operational data	Analytical data (avoid master data creep)	Metadata No master data—only reference data
Domain granularity	Fine grained	Fine grained or coarse grained	Coarse grained
Rules of scalability	Aim for as big as possible	Aim for as big as possible	Aim for as small as possible
Speed	Extremely fast	Fast	Slow
Relationships between the three architectures	Microservices and data mesh intermingle.	Microservices and data mesh intermingle.	Stay light, don't go deep; then it turns into microservices and data mesh—this specifically means that meta grids do not serve the value chain or analytics.

The meta grid contradicts the usual reasons to decentralize. Typically, If you are decentralizing, it's to enable scale of either operational data or analytical data. Microservices are intended to scale your operations in the value chain, and data mesh is intended to increase analytical use cases for data. In those cases, you decentralize to scale because scalability is the power to execute. And honestly, that is what distinguishes modern companies from legacy companies.

For metadata, however, scalability is a risk, not an advantage: you decentralize to avoid a certain type of scalability (creep of metadata repositories). Let's take the overview of integrations running between applications. How many integrations are there? Where are they stored? How are they registered? Manually? Automatically when building pipelines? By scanners? By accepting that this overview is not contained in one metadata repository (it never will be in big corporations), we can control and limit the scale of that type of metadata, and possibly even reduce it, while making it more robust, to agree on what metadata should flow through the grid to the various repositories.

Technologies That Support the Meta Grid

A meta grid can never be a technology. A meta grid is a response to technology and a practice of metadata management that has been siloed *because* of technology. Therefore, more technology is not the answer to siloed metadata. However, there are solutions that can support a meta grid.

The most ambitious metadata management solution is the Egeria Project (*https:// egeria-project.org*). The meta grid shares the problem statement with the Egeria Project; however, the answers are different. Briefly explained, the Egeria Project believes that there is a technological answer to the problem that the meta grid addresses—even though the Egeria Project realizes the limitations of its platform (*https://oreil.ly/0q4oS*).

Technically, Egeria works as a distributed platform. It will set up servers in the various cloud environments used by a company, allowing metadata to flow to and from the metadata repositories in the different cloud environments (Figure 11-10).

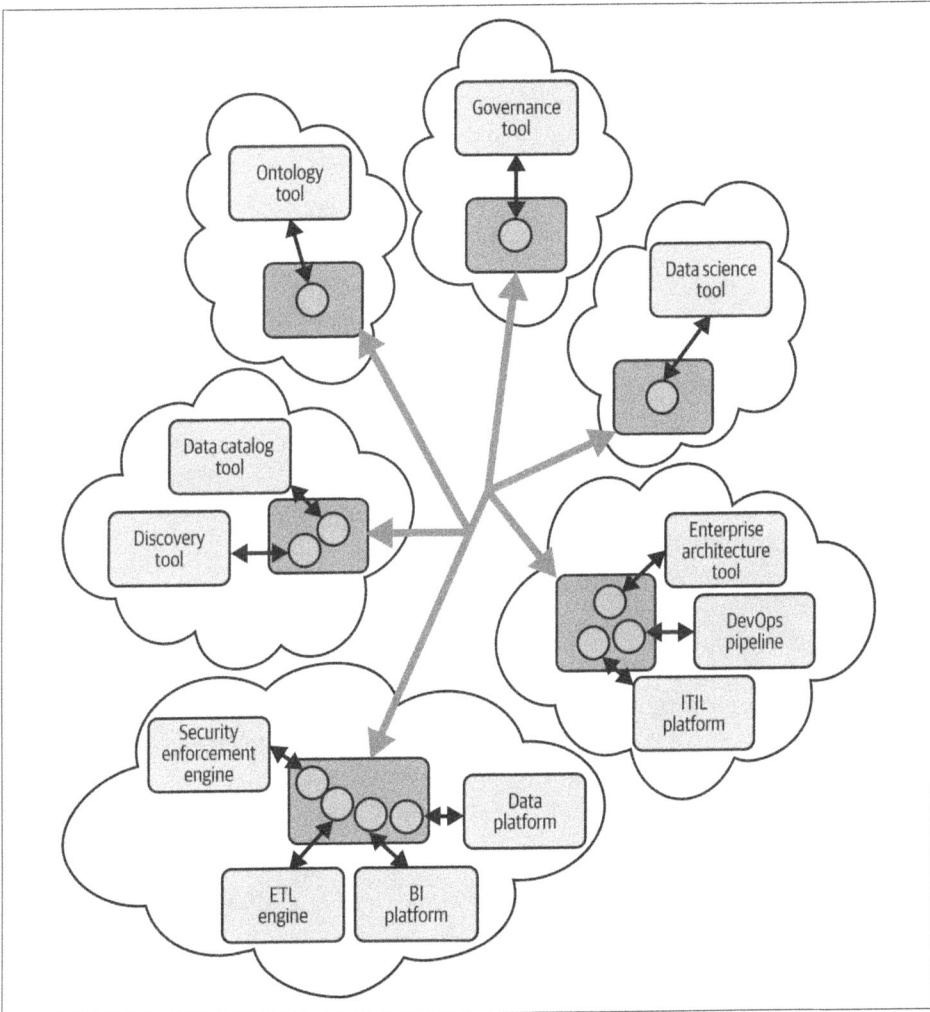

Figure 11-10. Technical overview of the Egeria Project

The Egeria Project argues that it is not a centralized solution on the basis that it only connects between various existing environments. However, it is a *complete* solution. In many cases, the Egeria Project will be overengineering; more specifically, the totality of means of transportation of metadata is likely not to take place in one and the same solution.

The Egeria Project will find users in very disciplined companies that are able to cooperate at a level that is not a given in the majority of companies. It's a great solution—but it is not an expression of the pragmatism intended with the meta grid.

Specific data platforms have the means to exchange data—and metadata—in a closed environment of what could be called a *platform-specific meta grid*. A compelling technology in this space is Palantir Ontology (*https://oreil.ly/GPZgb*).

It must be noted though, that as a platform-specific ontology, Palantir Ontology belongs in the IT management/data management domains of a meta grid, and it is unlikely to represent the collective body of metadata repositories in a company. But within its platform, Palantir Ontology represents a great advantage for metadata management.

Another platform in the IT management/data management domain is Microsoft Fabric (*https://oreil.ly/oUTgf*), which also offers an opportunity to create a platform-specific meta grid (like architecture) alongside the core capabilities of data analytics.

Furthermore, a meta grid can be visualized and managed—but not automated—via graph-powered DCs. Using such technologies to visualize a meta grid is not the primary use case but will be helpful for keeping an overview, especially as the meta grid expands.

Summary

In this chapter, we discussed topics that allow you to contextualize the meta grid. Perhaps most important is the fact that the meta grid is there—whether you like it or not. There is a shared pool of metadata already residing in various metadata repositories, in every company, and it is unconscious in most cases. To perform metadata management really effectively, this meta grid needs to be made explicit. That will allow you to effectively coordinate metadata across metadata repositories. Here are the key takeaways:

- Unlike microservices and data mesh, the meta grid is a decentralized architecture that already exists.
- This reality is most likely unconscious—metadata repositories are scattered all over the company and are not coordinated to a large extent.
- The meta grid is a nuclear architecture. It is extremely small and full of energy.
- Practiced unconsciously and poorly, meta grid architectures represent catastrophic realities—IT landscapes spin completely out of control.

- Practiced consciously and cleverly, meta grid architectures turn into a strong architecture for metadata.

- The meta grid can expand—in the number of domains, number of metadata repositories, and number of the same types of metadata repositories.

- Meta grid architectures can represent microservices architectures and data mesh architectures.

- Microservices are typically managed in EAM tools, EMSs, and CMDBs.

- Data mesh is managed in an experience plane connected to a DC.

- Meta grid architectures must not turn into microservices or data mesh.

- Meta grid is not a technology in itself, but it could be supported by several types of technologies from very ambitious solutions, ranging from more platform-specific solutions to more visualization- or management-supporting solutions.

Finally, never forget that you cannot simply build a meta grid. It is already there.

CHAPTER 12

The Benefits of the Meta Grid

In this chapter, we unfold the fantastic benefits of the meta grid! The meta grid can enable an enterprise IT landscape that is secure, rational, cost-effective, understood, searchable, configurable, adaptable, and more—all through meticulous metadata management, performed via metadata repositories. The meta grid is even an obvious use case for conversational and agentic AI, as you will see by the end of the chapter.

In fact, the meta grid is a little bit of a hidden treasure that can easily be enabled when first understood. In this chapter, we will run through two sections:

- The meta grid is not a technology.
- The meta grid is a technology.

Does this sound confusing? Don't worry, it's really not.

The Meta Grid Is Not a Technology

In this section, we discuss what the meta grid can do for your enterprise—without considering the meta grid itself as a technology but rather as simply a collection of documents, pictures, and data that improve the precision and search features in existing technologies.

There are many benefits to creating a meta grid architecture—more than are covered in this book because new use cases keep popping up once you see the potential of the meta grid. But here are the most vital and obvious:

- Better overview of the IT landscape
- Smoothly implemented metadata repositories
- Empowered owners of metadata repositories

- More secure data governance for both risk and privacy
- A stronger possibility of data-driven innovation
- Reduced cost of the IT landscape and consultancy support
- A greener IT landscape

There is a causality in these bullets, as you'll discover while going through them one by one!

Better Overview of the IT Landscape

The most fundamental benefit of the meta grid architecture is a better overview of the IT landscape. The situation in most companies is that metadata repositories are scoped, implemented, and operated in isolation—as we have discussed throughout this book. This is an unfortunate reality with significant negative consequences. Ultimately, the meta grid architecture is about getting a better overview of the IT landscape by rethinking metadata management more holistically, across hitherto siloed metadata repositories. This will solidify the company-wide vision of the IT landscape, but it will also solidify each metadata repository as it will be more consistent and reflect a commonly shared reality throughout the enterprise.

Smoothly Implemented Metadata Repositories

With a better overview of the IT landscape, thanks to the meta grid architecture you have put in place, your company can now implement each metadata repository more smoothly. Imagine a situation where, for example, a CISO implements an ISMS, or a CDO decides to make a data catalog the cornerstone in a new data and AI strategy. What is the first thing that happens? A mapping exercise begins: you determine what data you have, what applications you use, what processes you have in place, and so on. Substantial time and money are being spent on this activity, and it often occurs in isolation from the rest of the organization. However, thanks to the meta grid, the CISO and the CDO can consult a body of:

- Text (ADRs)
- Diagrams (domains architectures with metadata)
- Data (data samples, datasets, or data types)

This documents the metadata that's used across the organization and in multiple metadata repositories. This is a game changer! To proceed deeper with the meta grid, consider:

- Machine-readable data models
- API-first approach

> This reality is exponential. As more metadata repositories become part of the meta grid, it becomes exponentially easier to on-board new metadata repositories.

Empowered Owners of Metadata Repositories

Smoothly implemented metadata repositories lead to empowered owners of metadata repositories. The primary task of an owner of a metadata repository should be to deliver on a strategic capability: the intended core capability of the metadata repository they manage. However, that primary task is pushed aside by siloed metadata management, where no teams are learning from one another. Instead, the owners of the metadata repositories spend their time trying to understand the IT landscape, basically mapping the same data sources again and again, in isolation from one another and with uncoordinated outcomes, as shown in Figure 12-1.

This illustration can of course be accused of being the exact same type of "confusion illusion" that we discussed in Chapter 8. However, where technologies often offer a dubious way out of a dubious defined problem—when they are pushed by *bad* people, not *good* people—Figure 12-1 depicts the actual reality in companies. And the answer is not another technology, but a decentralized architecture: the meta grid. This reality is precisely what the meta grid addresses: multiple teams, each managing their own metadata repositories, are trying to leverage a unique capability—but the only thing they have time for is trying to understand the IT landscape. And they each do that in isolation.

Also take into account that many of these teams are multiplied across the enterprise—for instance, data teams, BI teams, and data science teams. The actual meta grid architecture is most likely bigger and more complex than what is shown in Figure 12-1.

> Consider the enormous waste of time and money that Figure 12-1 represents. Unfortunately, this is the reality for many companies! But with the meta grid, you can change this. Refer back to Figure P-2—you've now come full circle. This is the concrete reality of what was described in general terms in Chapter 1.

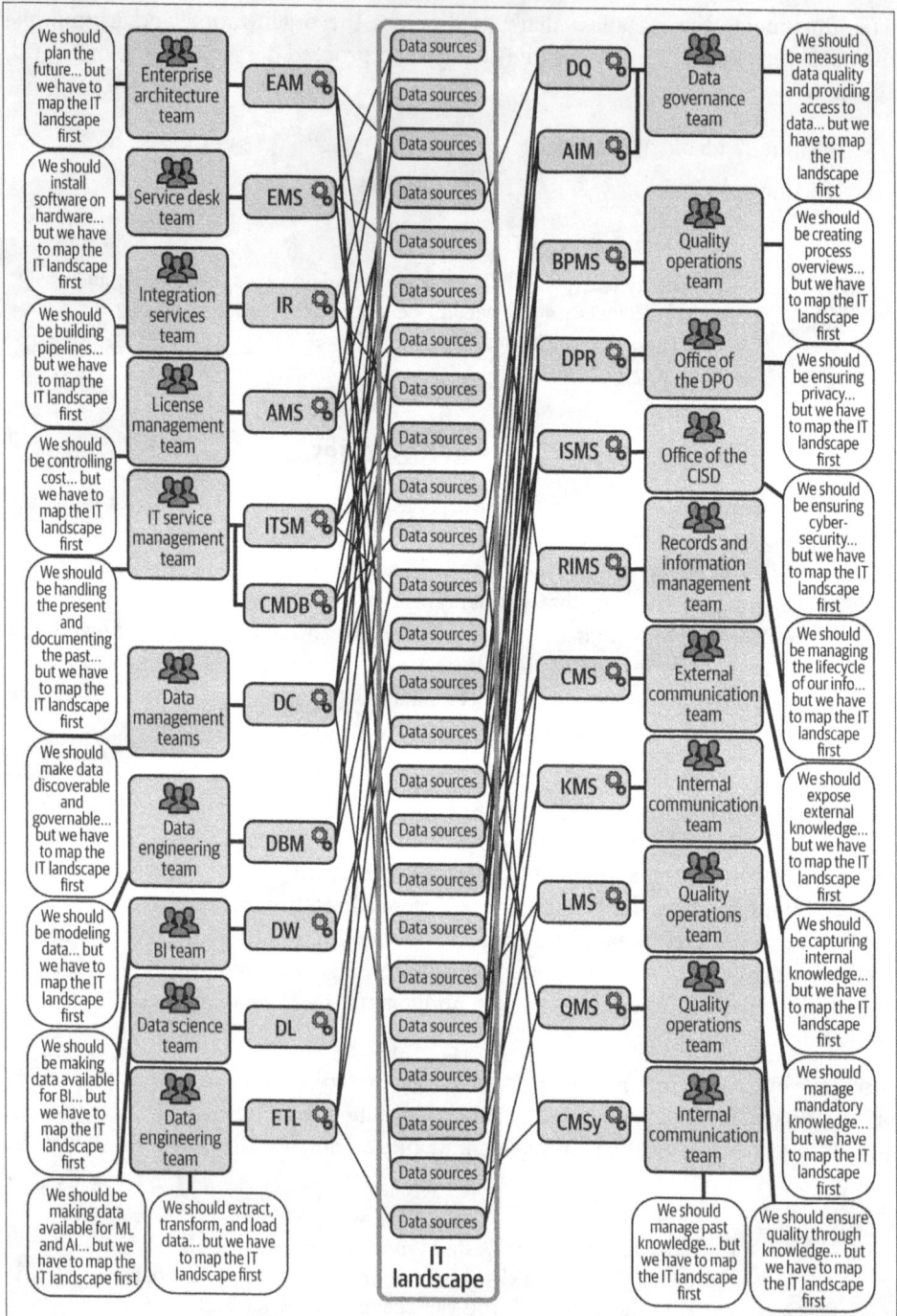

Figure 12-1. Multiple metadata repositories mapping the same IT landscape in isolation

More Secure Data Governance for Both Risk and Privacy

Empowered owners of metadata repositories lead to more secure data governance. The meta grid reduces and simplifies the task of understanding the IT landscape. This means that the teams ensuring data governance are liberated from this time-consuming and basic task. Instead, they can use their time as was intended—on data governance.

In Figure 12-1, three of the teams are working with data governance: the data governance team itself, the office of the CISO, and the office of the DPO (the actual constellation of teams working with data governance will differ from company to company). Let's take the CISO as an example. The CISO, as we discussed in Chapter 5, is focused on making strategic decisions about which risks to information security must be mitigated. This is a deep, technically challenging task, but most CISOs of the world are unfortunately not spending a lot of time on it—they are trying to understand the IT landscape instead and get it correctly described in the ISMS. The meta grid changes this by designing metadata architectures that make the ISMS a more complete, functional solution. This liberates the CISO to spend more time on what matters: mitigating risks to information security. The same goes for the DPO, the actual data governance team, and other teams that focus partly on data governance.

A Stronger Possibility of Data-Driven Innovation

More secure data governance leads to a stronger possibility of data-driven innovation because data governance facilitates secure access to data that would otherwise be inaccessible. When the entire IT landscape is more solidly governed across all aspects, including data quality and access, information security, and privacy, organizations have more opportunities to make strategic use of data and perform data-driven innovation. The biggest challenge remains the data engineering task at hand: setting up the actual infrastructure to transport, transform, and analyze data. This is a challenge that hinders many organizations from innovating with data. However, once you have a more complete data governance program running in your company, supported by a meta grid, you have removed a substantial barrier to data-driven innovation.

Reduced Cost of the IT Landscape and Consultancy Support

All of the factors previously described mean that money can be saved on the IT landscape and on consultants—and the costs of the company IT landscape and projects carried out by consultants are substantial in most companies. Basically, you can expect the core capabilities of each metadata repository to be exponentially enhanced by the meta grid, hence reducing the cost of the IT landscape. This is shown in Figure 12-2, where a siloed approach creates multiple, constrained views of the IT landscape on the left compared to a coordinated, complete overview on the right.

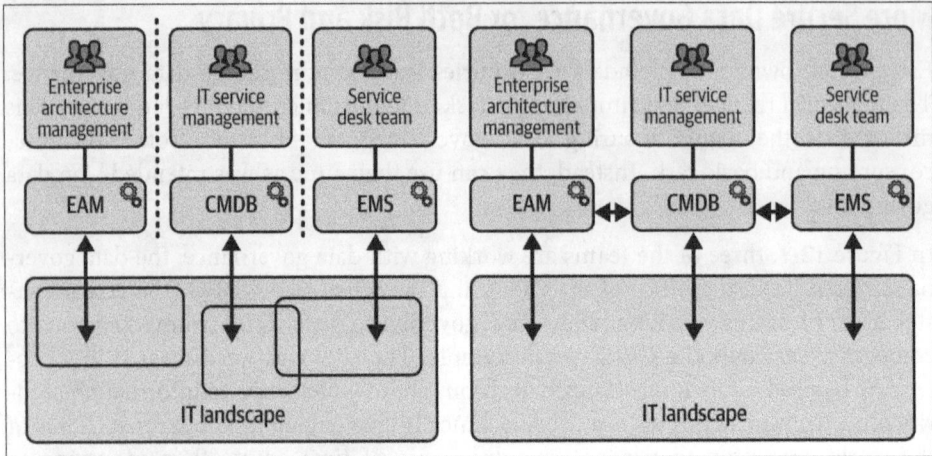

Figure 12-2. Accumulated effects of coordinated metadata repositories

Examples of Cost Reductions

You can translate the capabilities of metadata repositories into specific types of reduced costs. Cost reductions are hard to estimate, but you can expect many, many hours to be saved by providing self-serve access to knowledge about data, processes, applications, datasets, domains, teams, roles, rules, and everything by better metadata repositories that are trusted and of good quality. Whereas today, you have to be an archeologist and dig for hours to find certain types of information.

Accordingly, here is a short, nonexhaustive list of economically severe realities about the IT landscape that can gradually be countered by meta grid architectures (the complete list of all the economic severities that the meta grid can handle is infinitely longer):

Redundant software as a service
> According to Gartner research in 2024 (*https://oreil.ly/2fzRr*), companies spend approximately $1,370 per employee on SaaS applications (the total cost of IT per employee is significantly higher). What's more, 25% of the licenses of these SaaS applications are unused. Furthermore, as few as 40% of all SaaS applications are known throughout the company. This obviously creates a reality of redundant SaaS, which is typically addressed by AMSs and EAM tools. With a meta grid architecture, these tools don't operate in isolation but rather rely on metadata input about applications from other metadata repositories, which helps them eliminate redundant SaaS faster than they could have alone.

Fines for noncompliant data processing
> In most companies, the DPO works in isolation to try to capture how data is processed throughout the enterprise. The stakes are high: the European Union can

issue fines up to €20 million or 4% of annual revenue if sensitive data is misused. What the meta grid offers in this context is support for the DPO working with the DPR by enhancing the DPR with metadata from the BPMS and the lineage functionality inside one or more DCs. This will reduce the time spent by the DPO on understanding data processing and solidifies compliance significantly, ultimately reducing the risk of getting fined for noncompliant data processing.

Data breaches

This is essentially the same reality as for the DPO, but for the CISO it involves using the ISMS. CISOs should spend their time making strategic assessments about which risks against the IT landscape to mitigate, not in simply trying to understand the IT landscape.

Technical debt

Technical debt is deep uncertainty about the actual working of the IT landscape, all the way down to the code level. McKinsey has reported (*https://oreil.ly/KFOlu*) that technical debt constitutes 20%–40% of the costs of all IT projects in companies with a substantial IT legacy. While the meta grid will not solve all of the problems associated with technical debt, it will reduce them by creating a better overview of the IT landscape.

Application ownership

A data governance function will typically be tasked with the responsibility of assigning ownership of all applications throughout the enterprise. This is a task that almost always fails—the line of business is busy and typically fears the technical perspective of owning an application. With no established owners of applications, no decisions can be made about them: they become forever-applications. A meta grid architecture can resolve this. By pulling all created knowledge from sources like the CMDB, AMS, and others, a robust overview of application owners becomes accessible to the data governance team without disturbing too many people in the line of business.

Now that you've made it this far in the chapter, consider how the meta grid architecture can reduce the cost of your company's enterprise IT landscape.

A Greener IT Landscape

And finally, let's not forget that a meta grid architecture will enable a greener IT landscape when it has begun working by rationalizing it. In this context, *greener* means energy efficient. This is a long-term return—and it should also be a long-term goal for each company!

The Meta Grid Is a Technology

The meta grid is an architecture that stitches together existing technologies within companies through small but powerful and strategic integrations. This stitching is a process of integration and transformation that will never fully take place in a single technology but rather in a mix of standard connectors, API calls, and spreadsheets.

However, the meta grid is documented in ADRs, diagrams, and datasets, and that documentation can be supported and enhanced by technological solutions. There are three technological perspectives that can support and enhance the meta grid:

- Create a knowledge graph of metadata across metadata repositories
- Search the meta grid conversationally with generative AI
- Perform the meta grid automatically with agentic AI

> If you think these points contradict the overall point of the meta grid, then you are on to something. What is discussed in this section is an evolution of the meta grid that can only be enabled after uncovering it as advised in the previous chapters. Trying to obtain these solutions without the preceding work is impossible.

Create a Knowledge Graph of Metadata Across Metadata Repositories

Arguing this point is the most delicate in the entire book. You can think of the potential of the knowledge graph powering a meta grid like this: a meta grid is naturally an ontology[1] and, therefore, a knowledge graph. However, the meta grid does not need to be conceived as a knowledge graph. All it needs to be are integrations of specific types of metadata between metadata repositories. There is no need for these integrations to make ontological sense in their totality—but they can, if you have the organizational setup to define it. There are risks to this approach that are not linked directly to knowledge graphs as a technology but rather to the organizational aspects of their implementation.[2]

---

1 The term *ontology* is understood in LIS as a semantic, conceptual structure of connected words, with the connections being explicit. When I was writing this book, many of my readers asked me if the meta grid is or isn't a knowledge graph. A handful of these readers are from Fortune 500 companies that have an ontology, manifested in a graph database, as the heart of a meta grid. This is an impressive reality. And it exists; therefore, I obviously acknowledge it. It is—let there be no doubt—extremely difficult to obtain a meta grid powered by an enterprise-wide acceptance of *one* knowledge graph.

2 For a great introduction to knowledge graphs, see *Designing and Building Enterprise Knowledge Graphs* by Juan Sequeda and Ora Lassila (Springer Cham).

There is a risk associated with turning your meta grid into a knowledge graph: that the metadata repository of your choosing becomes the "single source of truth" that it never can become in reality (the meta grid is always incomplete). Read this section very carefully if you are interested in making a graph of the ontological heart of your meta grid.

The point of the meta grid is not, and should not be, to build a graph database. That is not its purpose. The meta grid is an extremely small but powerful integration architecture between *existing* metadata repositories. That's *all* it is. And it is documented in text, pictures, and data, as mentioned previously.

If you think you should build an enterprise-wide ontology in a graph database when setting up the meta grid, you're building highways before inventing the car. The reason why I warn strongly against knowledge graph thinking in a meta grid architecture is not because I don't find knowledge graphs useful. It's because they are useful in extremely precise contexts:

- Data catalogs powered by knowledge graphs are great at creating an ontology for data and analytics that is accepted by a community of data engineers and data scientists.
- EAM tools powered by knowledge graphs, such as Ardoq (*https://oreil.ly/vJRPp*) and SAP LeanIX (*https://oreil.ly/h_mma*), are great at creating an ontology for application management that is accepted by enterprise architects, domain architects, and solution architects.

If you think that one of these metadata repositories, the DC or the EAM tool, will *also* serve as the heart of the meta grid, you are wrong. You are doing the exact opposite of what the point of the meta grid is: you are centralizing instead of decentralizing. Remember that the meta grid is not an academic discussion—it's the reality in industry and in most big enterprises.

Even though a metamodel in a metadata repository is flexible, this does not solve the challenge. Even flexible metamodels are shaped by the core capability they serve. If LIS has taught us anything at all, it is that absolutely no ontology is without intention. Only naive (or cynical) technologists would argue otherwise.

Go back and browse the chapters in Part I to review the core capabilities of the metadata repositories I discuss. These core capabilities will always affect the metamodel of the metadata repository. Therefore, using one of these metadata repositories to power the meta grid—if it is based on a knowledge graph—risks becoming skewed.

To succeed with a knowledge graph powering your meta grid, you need to make sure that the knowledge graph is 100% detached from leveraging the core capability of the metadata repository to which it is attached. You can also use a graph database with a custom-built application to express the meta grid. Examples of graph databases include Amazon Neptune (*https://oreil.ly/Dfwdp*) and Neo4j (*https://neo4j.com*); a substantial list of graph databases is maintained on Wikipedia (*https://oreil.ly/LxnxH*).

Two additional elements challenge a knowledge-graph approach for a meta grid: transformation and time.

Transformation

While it is certainly possible to build an architecture of a graph database connecting to a selection of source systems, a graph database in itself does not allow for data transformation and transportation, known as ETL/ELT. Therefore, in scenarios where a meta grid would entail data transformation and transportation, the graph in itself falls short of leveraging a meta grid. This is, as we discussed in Chapter 10, often the case. In these instances, a knowledge graph risks becoming an overengineered, underperforming meta grid. But you can address the challenge of lacking ETL/ELT in a graph; see Chapter 5 of *Building Knowledge Graphs* by Jesus Barrasa and Jim Webber (O'Reilly).

Time

A knowledge graph can represent a complete ontological vision of an enterprise universe. However, a knowledge graph will have challenges with time; the ontological vision is subject to change, and this change is not necessarily possible to synchronize meaningfully with the metadata that must be stored in and shared between metadata repositories.[3]

In sum, knowledge graphs hold great potential for a meta grid architecture—but also great risks. This is expressed in Table 12-1, which includes the Egeria Project that was discussed in Chapter 11.

---

3 See p. 192 of *Building Knowledge Graphs*.

Table 12-1. The meta grid alone, with knowledge graphs, and with the Egeria Project

	Meta grid	Meta grid powered by knowledge graphs	Meta grid powered by the Egeria Project
Solution	Isolated elements of metadata Documented in text, pictures, and data Transformed in metadata repositories and/or spreadsheets Transported with standard connectors, API calls, and simple export/import of .csv and .xlsx files	All metadata documented in one graph The graph must be supported by ETL/ELT tools	All metadata documented, transformed, and transported in one solution
Prerequisites	None	A documented meta grid	A documented meta grid
Pros	Easy to obtain Only needs buy-in from the involved teams in the data discovery team Adequate engineering	A smooth way to overlook the IT landscape in one solution	A very smooth way to overlook the IT landscape in one solution
Cons	Can become difficult to maintain and oversee	Difficult to obtain Needs buy-in from the entire enterprise up front Likely to be overengineered	Very difficult to obtain Needs buy-in from the entire enterprise and all technology vendors up front Very likely to be overengineered

Search the Meta Grid Conversationally with Generative AI

This use case for the meta grid is based on the idea that you can automate and scale the capabilities of the data discovery team discussed in Part II. Instead of having a group of people answering every single question about the IT landscape, generative AI can facilitate a conversational search about the IT landscape. This vastly expands the potential of the data discovery team and gives it a reason to exist in the first place.

The meta grid is a set of documents, pictures, and data. As such, it constitutes a great source for generative AI. Just as certain technologies offer to "talk to your data," with generative AI you can "talk to your IT landscape" using the meta grid documentation.

Technically, this is doable by creating what can be described as meta grid retrieval-augmented generation (RAG). RAG is a way to specialize and fine-tune the output of a large language model (LLM) by supplying it with additional context on an enterprise-specific set of sources.

> Generative AI is too vast a topic to cover here. This is merely a super short introduction to set the stage for the use case proposed: the meta grid RAG. To explore further, see *Essential Math for AI* by Hala Nelson (O'Reilly) and *AI Engineering* by Chip Huyen (O'Reilly).

RAG has four stages of development and usage:

- Indexing
- Retrieval
- Augmentation
- Generation

Basically, sources must be *indexed* (using vector embeddings) to be made retrievable. Once they are *retrievable*, the LLM can be *augmented* by prompting—searching—it through a user interface such as a chatbot. After a thorough augmentation, it is ready to *generate* answers.

> Let's now (re)introduce the fictitious company from my first book, *The Enterprise Data Catalog*: Hugin & Munin is a Scandinavian architecture company that specializes in sustainable construction. I will use it to demonstrate how the meta grid can be searched conversationally with generative AI.

Hugin & Munin has enabled a chatbot called Ratatoskr (after the small, fast messenger squirrel from Nordic mythology—a perfect symbol for a chatbot!).[4] The chatbot sits under a search interface for the meta grid. The employees at Hugin & Munin are eager to ask Ratatoskr all kinds of questions. You can see Ratatoskr below the search bar in Figure 12-3.

---

4 I first mentioned Ratatoskr in my newsletter *Enterprise Wide Search* (*https://oreil.ly/QFHyt*) when discussing AI chatbots in DCs. As discussed in this chapter, it is important to architect an ontological heart of the meta grid very cautiously, if using a DC—and to assess if such an ontological heart is desired at all. The thing to remember is that such an instance of a DC can in no way serve as a traditional DC as well—it needs to focus only on the ontology behind the meta grid. The same goes for an EAM tool used as an ontological heart for the meta grid.

Figure 12-3. The search interface for Hugin & Munin

Imagine the following situation: Joe, a brilliant data engineer—one of the best globally—works for Hugin & Munin. He believes deeply in the company's mission: sustainable architecture. One day, he talks to the CISO, Jenna, over lunch. She's incredibly smart, too, but as someone new to Hugin & Munin, she still feels a little isolated within the company. Jenna tells Joe that she is mapping business processes in the newly acquired ISMS her team manages—and that she needs to do this because these processes are a key component of mitigating information security threats. Joe listens quietly and is interested in the vulnerabilities of Hugin & Munin as he has been thinking a lot about them. Later, while getting coffee alone after lunch, Joe has a thought: aren't business processes already mapped somewhere other than in the ISMS? He begins a conversational search with Ratatoskr, as shown in Figure 12-4.

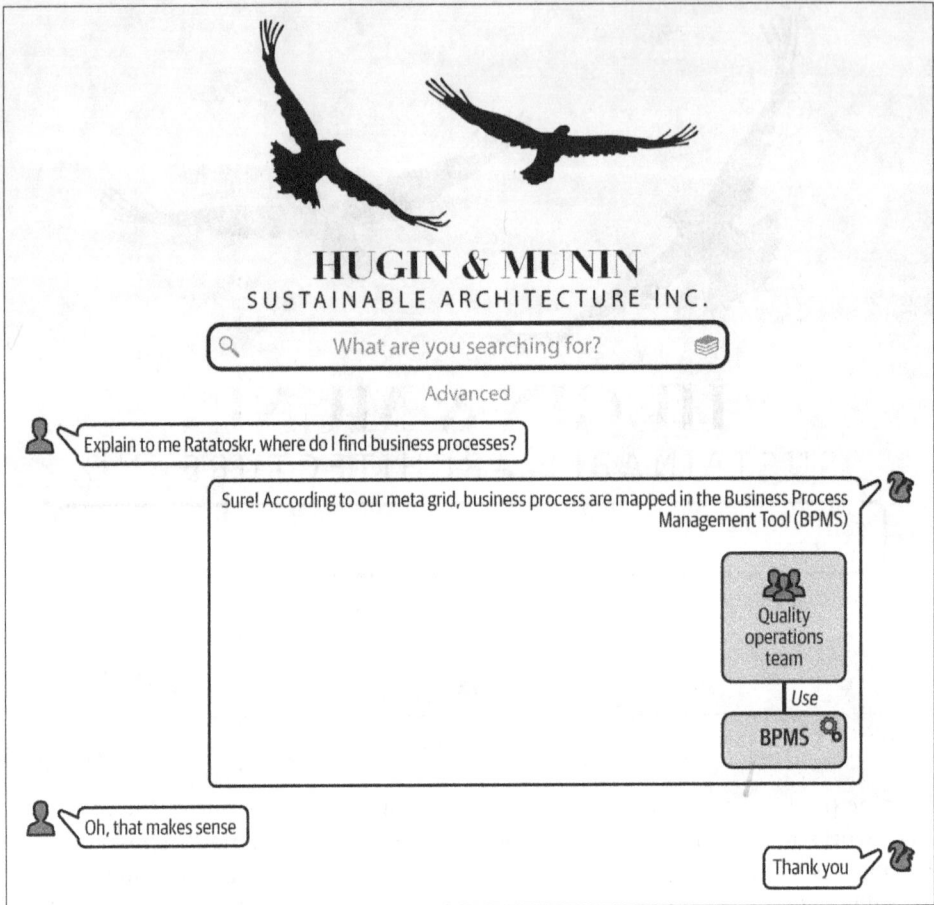

Figure 12-4. Conversational meta grid search about business processes (part 1)

As Joe anticipated, business processes are already mapped in the BPMS. It's only fair that Jenna wasn't aware because it's still early days for her—and for Ratatoskr, too. Having conversations about the meta grid is not widely adopted yet since this functionality is still very new.

Joe has seen this before: high-level leaders who report upward loyally and map the metadata they need to do that. He informs Ratatoskr about this (Figure 12-5).

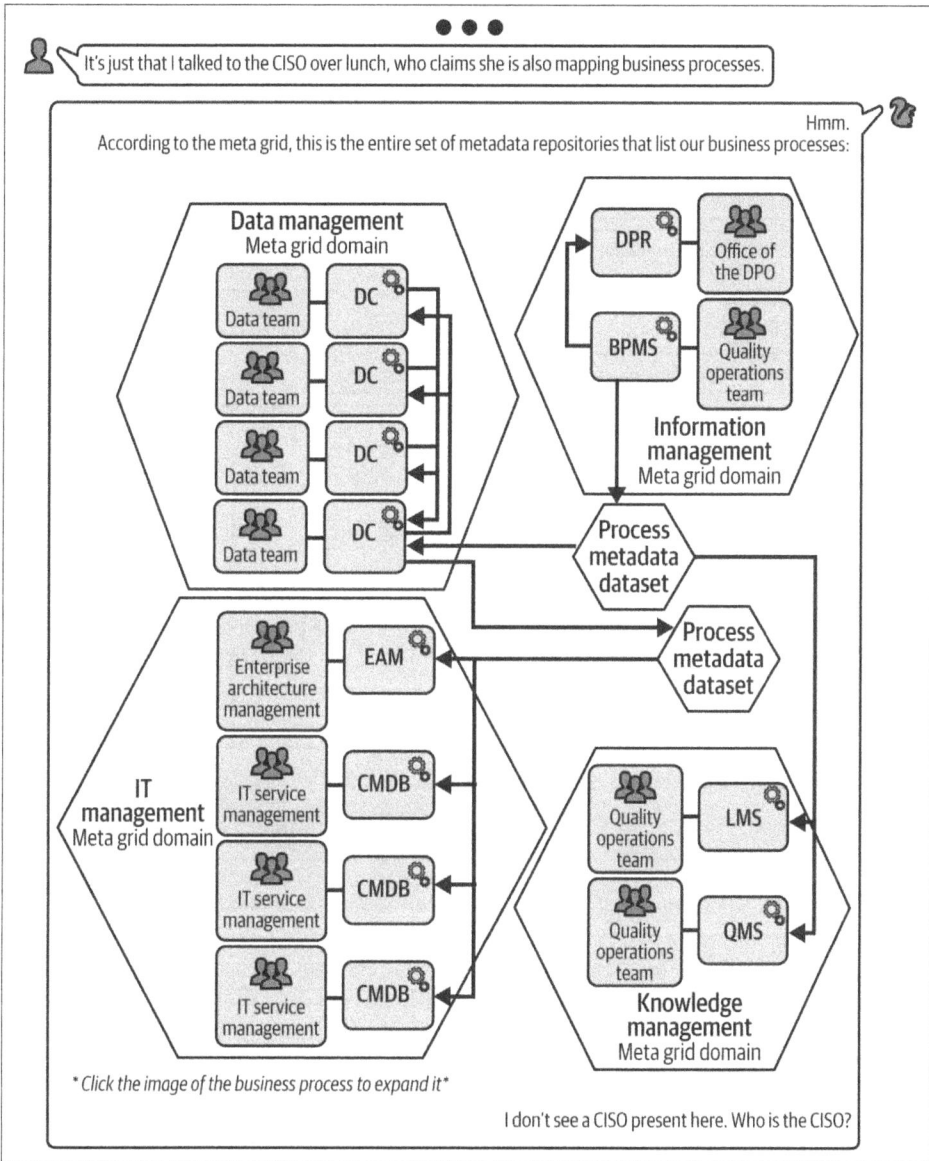

Figure 12-5. Conversational meta grid search about business processes (part 2)

This prompts Ratatoskr to inform Joe that the CISO is not present in the meta grid architecture diagram for *processes*. Ratatoskr then asks Joe who the CISO is, to which Joe responds, as shown in Figure 12-6.

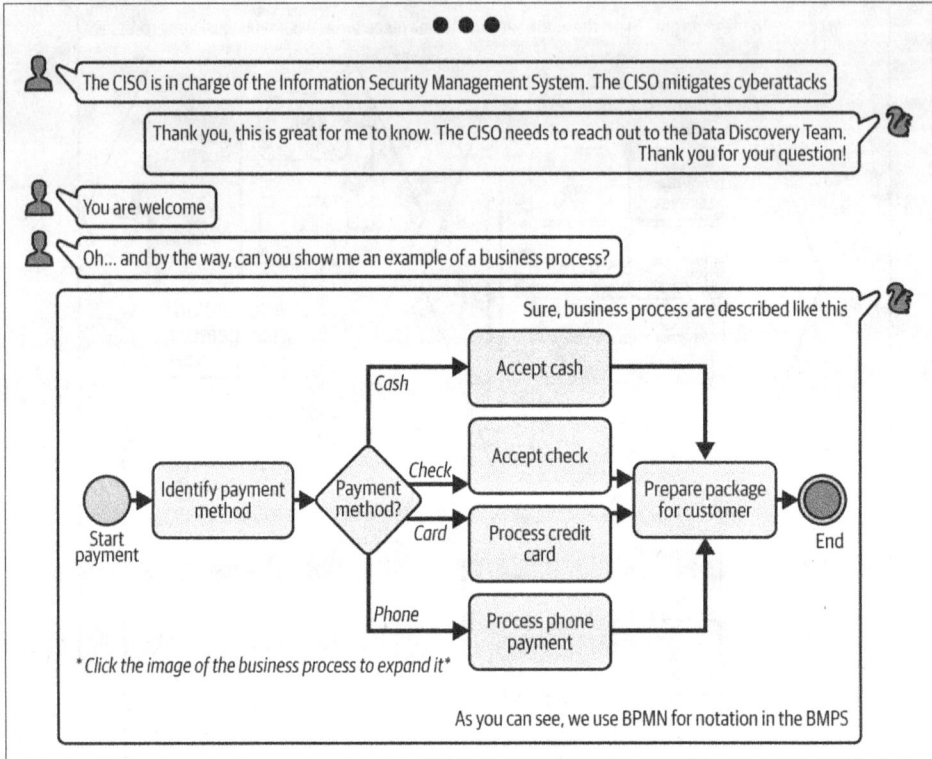

Figure 12-6. Conversational meta grid search about business processes (part 3)

Joe has a final question: he wants to see how business processes are actually modeled in Hugin & Munin. Ratatoskr provides him with an easy-to-follow example from the BPMS—namely, the business process "payment."

As shown in this example, the meta grid can be searched conversationally with generative AI. The potential is great: more people can be informed about the various metadata repositories and the metadata they share, and the meta grid can even be improved through augmentation of the LLM behind the chatbot—Ratatoskr, in our case. Imagine the ultimate potential of a meta grid amplified through a chatbot powered by generative AI: all new employees and external consultants can save the enterprise they serve a lot of money by not repeating the same exercises over and over, creating too many low-quality depictions of the IT landscape again and again.

Perform the Meta Grid Automatically with Agentic AI

Performing the meta grid automatically with agentic AI leverages the new path for AI introduced by Andrew Ng (*https://oreil.ly/hs-MX*) and designed as a response to generative AI's lack of actionability. The vision for agentic AI is to carry out tasks normally performed by employees, ultimately reducing the need for SaaS applications.

It is still too early to say if agentic AI will be an important technology for enterprises. An early indication of agentic AI as a real innovation is Operator, which was launched by OpenAI in 2025. While Operator is interesting, it is not a convincing use case for adoption at an enterprise level.

Nevertheless, a simple use case for agentic AI would be to perform the meta grid. Once the substantial redundancy of metadata management has been addressed by the meta grid and *understood* by generative AI, it is possible to imagine that agentic AI can *perform* the meta grid. In this reality, the capabilities leveraged by the various metadata repositories at play will happen without SaaS applications, as discrete communications between AI agents. The meta grid is small and simple—that makes it a good use case for agentic AI because it is not data intensive and does not require intricate, human-based context.

Summary

In this chapter, we discussed the many benefits of the meta grid in itself, in the sense that it is *not* a technology. Furthermore, we looked at the meta grid as a technology in three respects: the meta grid as a knowledge graph, the meta grid as conversational search, and finally, the meta grid performed by agentic AI. Key takeaways are:

- The meta grid is not a technology but rather a large set of existing technologies: metadata repositories that leverage a plethora of capabilities for regulative, operative, and innovative purposes.
- The meta grid comes with these benefits:
  - Better overview of the IT landscape by an exponentially strong and shared understanding of it across metadata repositories
  - Smoothly implemented metadata repositories because of the existing knowledge in the meta grid
  - Empowered owners of metadata repositories because they don't have to spend time understanding the IT landscape but can rather focus on the strategic capabilities they are tasked with, such as information security
  - More secure data governance for both risk and privacy—with a meta grid, data governance is performed more holistically, with maximum impact through multiple repositories, guaranteeing various aspects of data governance

— A stronger possibility of data-driven innovation—all data sources are made more discoverable as the meta grid connects, for instance, data catalogs in a grid of shared metadata

— Reduced cost of the IT landscape and consultancy support, which can be divided as follows:

   — Redundant SaaS—the meta grid will help identify redundant SaaS and therefore reduce costs

   — Fines for noncompliant data processing, as the meta grid will enhance data governance

   — Data breaches, for the same reasons

   — Technical debt—although it's difficult, the meta grid can reduce the uncertainty of technical debt and therefore reduce its cost

   — Application ownership by coordinating knowledge about applications across metadata repositories

— A greener IT landscape

- The meta grid is a technology in the sense that its capabilities can be enhanced and made easily accessible:

   — The meta grid can be given an ontological "heart": a knowledge graph that relates all types of metadata and how these are exchanged and expressed in various metadata repositories. This type of ontological heart is difficult to achieve and requires simple meta grid documentation up front—but the outcome is very powerful.

   — The meta grid can be made searchable and interactive with generative AI. This would provide an easy, simple solution for everyone to examine the IT landscape.

   — The meta grid can be performed by agentic AI.

CHAPTER 13

The Data Discovery Team and Meta Grid As a Team Topology

In this short chapter, I will conclude my thoughts on metadata management and the meta grid. I'll present a team structure and platform thinking for a meta grid that builds on everything discussed throughout the entire book. This chapter brings everything together from Part I about metadata repositories, Part II about the organizational aspects, and Part III about the meta grid itself.

Keep in mind that fundamentally, a meta grid is a simple architecture for improving metadata management. Metadata management is performed in a wealth of metadata repositories that all describe the IT landscape for various purposes, each leveraging a unique capability by understanding the IT landscape. We have only discussed a handful of repositories in this book, so remember that this is a methodology, a way of thinking—and more repositories specific to your enterprise reality can and should be included in the meta grid architecture.

The meta grid and metadata management together can be seen through the lens of the ideas put forward in *Team Topologies*, cited throughout this book.[1] A *team topology* is both organizationally and technically a structure that allows you to loosen up monolithic IT by redefining how people work together and how they use technology. The ideas in *Team Topologies* have been successfully tested at a global scale, and the meta grid fits into this way of thinking.

The data discovery team discussed in Part II and the meta grid discussed in Part III can be considered to constitute a team topology—and it is useful to think of it like

---

1 I am thankful that Manuel Pais (*https://oreil.ly/06M3U*), coauthor of *Team Topologies*, as well as Eduardo da Silva (*https://oreil.ly/ocZvc*) took the time to review my ideas in this chapter.

this because that will ease the enabling of the meta grid and the many benefits it unleashes. The meta grid can be seen as a flexible constellation of teams and technologies that allow for faster, more efficient flow in organizations.

There are four types of teams in *Team Topologies*:[2]

Stream-aligned teams

These teams deliver a continuous flow of work that belongs in a business domain or to an organizational capability. All teams managing metadata repositories discussed throughout this book can be considered stream-aligned teams, such as IT service management and the office of the DPO.

Enabling teams

These are teams of specialists that focus on a particular topic within a domain. They help address missing skills or capability gaps in stream-aligned teams. The data discovery team, introduced in Part II, can be considered an enabling team in the sense that it helps the stream-aligned teams learn how to manage metadata repositories by sharing identical metadata across these repositories and streams.[3]

The enabling team helps the stream-aligned team start doing this. The enabling team should not stay and keep helping the stream-aligned team with its daily operations. In a sense, the enabling team helps the stream-aligned team become "self-sufficient."

Complicated-subsystem teams

These teams are not relevant in this context. Briefly, they consolidate certain capabilities that require deep and unique knowledge. By concentrating these capabilities in these teams, we can provide services to other stream-aligned teams, which helps reduce their cognitive load. An example of this could be a forecasting team requiring PhD-level skills and strong statistical knowledge. They can own forecasts and serve them via APIs for the whole organization.

Platform teams

These teams enable stream-aligned teams to perform their tasks without technical friction or delay by consolidating capabilities that stream-aligned teams can self-service. In our context, the meta grid is served by platform teams:

---

2 These teams will be briefly discussed here; for details, see Chapter 5 of *Team Topologies*.

3 In this sense, the data discovery team follows an architecture modernization enabling team pattern, strictly for decentralization of metadata in metadata repositories. For more, see especially the table "AMET Primary Purpose" in "Architecture Modernization Enabling Teams" by Eduardo da Silva (*https://oreil.ly/Q8n5b*).

The platform team provides internal services to reduce the cognitive load that would be required from stream-aligned teams to develop these underlying services.[4]

This is exactly the point of the meta grid: to help all metadata repositories perform better. For metadata repositories managed by stream-aligned teams, the platform team can assist with meta grid architectures. This enables the stream-aligned teams to self-manage their metadata repositories, unleashing themselves from the cognitive overload of mapping the whole IT landscape again and again.

Altogether, the data discovery team consists of an enabling team that has representatives from all teams managing metadata repositories[5] and a smaller platform team that manages the meta grid documentation and potential software as a platform. This is depicted in its basic form in Figure 13-1.

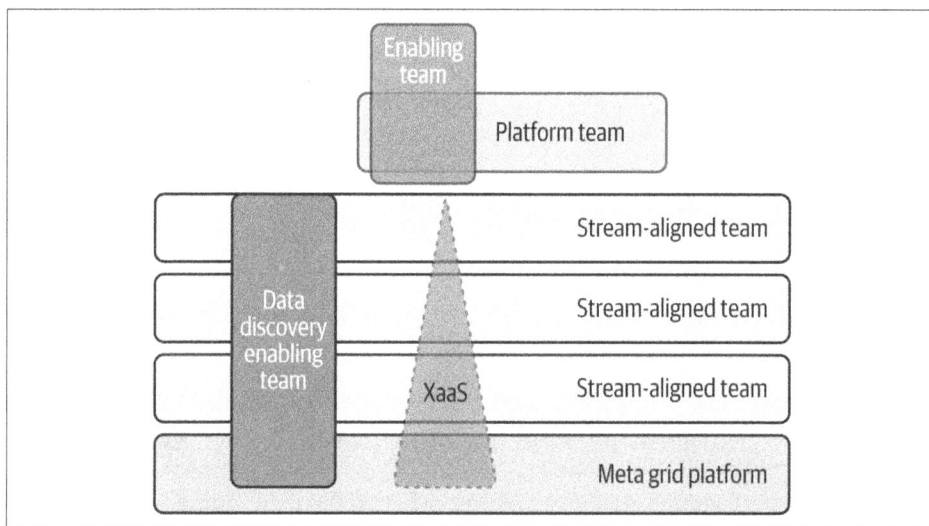

Figure 13-1. The data discovery team is an enabling team and a platform team

The basic form in Figure 13-1 is specified in Figure 13-2.

---

4 Pais and Skelton, *Team Topologies*, 92.

5 In this book, I have argued that the data discovery team should be virtual because companies are reluctant to fund more data teams at the time of writing. However, to function as an ideal enabling team, the data discovery team should not be virtual but rather full-time employees. That would be extremely powerful.

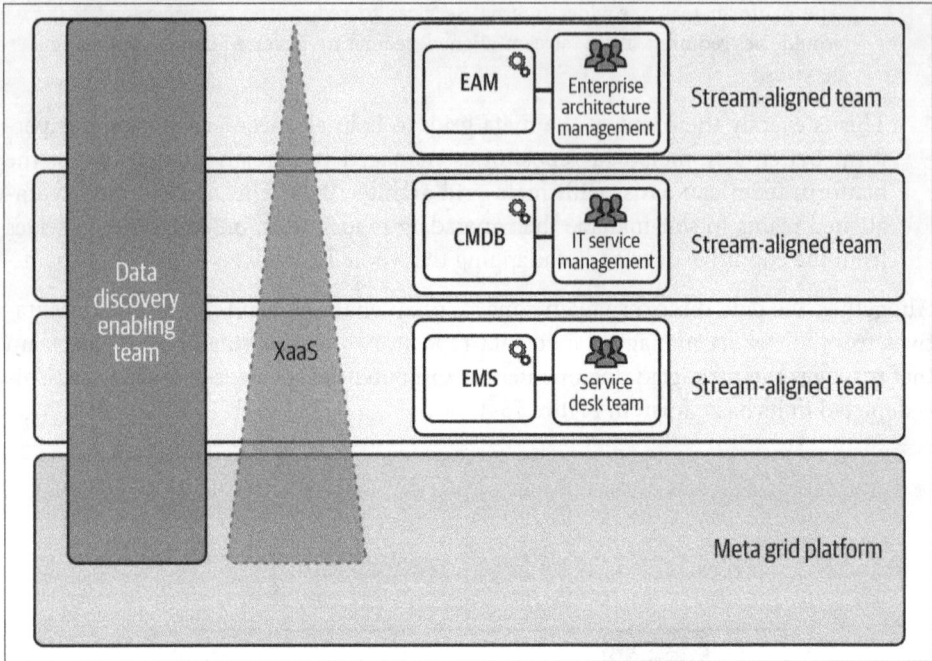

Figure 13-2. The data discovery team and the meta grid as a team topology

Figure 13-2 is an elaboration of Figure 12-2, with the same teams and metadata repositories but placed in a team topologies context.

The stream-aligned teams owning metadata repositories are the EAM team, the ITSM team, and the Service Desk team. They are all enabled to share metadata thanks to the enabling team: the data discovery team. They work with the meta grid platform as a body of text, diagrams, datasets, and software that emanates into the technologies of the stream-aligned teams: their metadata repositories as a self-service (XaaS) of shared, contextualized metadata.

> This "topology" is not static! It's an evolution. For example, the data discovery enabling team will not be working with the same stream-aligned teams all the time. That "facilitating interaction" will evolve, and so will the XaaS (self-service) from the platform to the stream-aligned teams. Examples of evolutions of the AMET pattern can be found in "Maximize Organizational Learning and Return on Investment with Facilitating Interactions" (*https://oreil.ly/6QYNY*).

The meta grid platform should be considered the *thinnest viable platform* (TVP), also defined in *Team Topologies*:

> The simplest platform can be purely a list on a wiki page of underlying components or services used by consuming software.... We should aim for the *thinnest viable platform* (TVP).... A TVP is a careful balance between keeping the platform small and ensuring that the platform is helping to accelerate and simplify software delivery teams building on the platform.[6]

The principles behind the TVP match the idea that a meta grid architecture is performed merely by text, images, and data, as discussed throughout Part III of this book, and supports the fundamental idea that the meta grid is not to be a technology itself.

Now that you hopefully know how simple the idea of the meta grid really is, go out there and show your colleagues and the rest of your company just how easy it is to improve metadata management!

---

6 Pais and Skelton, *Team Topologies*, 101.

Afterword

I originally wanted to open this book with only one quote, the passage from the Persian scholar Rumi in *Fihi Ma Fihi* (*It Is What It Is*):

> The truth was a mirror in the hands of God. It fell, and broke into pieces. Everybody took a piece of it, and they looked at it and thought they had the truth.

These words from the 13th century perfectly reflect the reality I have lived throughout most of my professional life. I have seen so many architects, engineers, leaders, and executives hold their little piece of the mirror, their distinct metadata repository, and say, "This is the truth." And let me be clear: I have held my piece of the mirror as well. I too have said, "This is the truth," pointing at that small piece, with a feeling of uncertainty that I tried to ignore. Only later in life did I understand what was at play.

I would have loved to claim that this book is the glue that put Rumi's divine mirror back together. But that is not the case. This book is not a promise of rediscovered divine perfection. Because something else happened to Rumi's puzzle of all the broken pieces from the ultimate truth. People not only said their pieces were the truth but also began using the pieces. They glued them on walls, tables, and wallets to mirror themselves in the course of all kinds of actions. And only the possibility of explaining how the pieces once related, in a pattern that can no longer be re-created because each part has morphed into something of its own, is what exists: each piece now has its own meaning, its own purpose, and a new structure surrounding it.

When I found another passage, I understood it also needed to be a quote for opening the book:

> Make each program do one thing well. To do a new job, build afresh rather than complicate old programs by adding new "features."[1]

---

1 M. D. McIlroy, E. N. Pinson, and B. A. Tague, "UNIX Time-Sharing System: Forward," *Bell System Technical Journal* 57, no. 6 (1978): 1899–1904.

Each metadata repository has a metamodel. And all metamodels refer back to the IT landscape. But they never match, though. This is not because they are poorly conceived, but because they serve different purposes and have been shaped by that. It's the very nature of technology at play.

I hope that in many companies out there, in the world...

...a quality team responsible for the BPMS meets with the DPO, and they discover that they both work with processes, just in two different ways, but that their metadata repositories can benefit from each other.

...a team of data engineers responsible for a data catalog meets with the ITSM team and learns that they are indeed both working with applications and the data in them, only from two different perspectives—and that both teams can grow by talking to each other.

And that is it. Too often, metadata is a tribal endeavor. But it shouldn't be.

I am no Jean-François Champollion,[2] but I hope to have impressed upon you, dear reader, that this book is not an invention of one logic that forces itself onto everything. This book is a Rosetta Stone for metadata. It's a vehicle for people to meet and discover that they share a perspective and that together, they can indeed make technology better.

---

2 Jean-François Champollion decoded hieroglyphs.

Index

A

Actian Data Intelligence Platform, 55, 175
ADR (architectural decision record) (see architectural decision record (ADR))
agentic AI, 199
Agile, 8
Amazon Neptune, 192
AMET (architecture modernization enabling team), 202
analytical data, 9
    (see also operational data)
    traditional mechanisms of storage, 9
        data lakehouse, 9
        data lakes, 9
        data warehouses, 9
architectural decision record (ADR), 141-142
    resources on, 141
    template for, 142
architecture modernization enabling team (AMET), 202
asset management, 164
    agent-based scanning, 164
    agentless scanning, 164
assets, 67
    asset inventory, 69
        risk owner, 69
    types of, 67

B

Basel Committee on Banking Supervision standard no. 239 (BCBS 239), 26
big data, 58
bottom-up approach, 92
    critique of, 92

Business Process Model and Notation (BPMN), 75
business processes, 74
    ISO 9000, 74

C

California Consumer Privacy Act (CCPA), 70
capability map, 48
capital expenditure (CapEx), 99
CCPA (California Consumer Privacy Act), 70
change management, 105
    critique of, 105
    frameworks for, 106
chief information security officer (CISO), 68, 130
CI (configuration item), 43
comparison of architectures, 177
confidentiality, 65
configuration item (CI), 43
confusion illusion, 109
Conway's law, 120-121
    (see also inverse Conway maneuver)
    definition of, 120
core capability, 93
corporate amnesia, 166
customer success team, 105

D

DAMA Data Management Body of Knowledge (DAMA-DMBOK), 6
dark data, 96
dark metadata, 96
data about data (see metadata, definition of)
data contracts, 39

data decentralization, waves of, 138
    first wave (microservices), 138
    second wave (data mesh), 138
    third wave (meta grid), 138
data dictionary, 53
data discovery team, 1, 3-5, 117-134, 201
    (see also meta grid; reference librarian)
    collaboration patterns, 123-132
        with chief information security officer
            (CISO), 130
        with data protection officer (DPO), 128
        with data science teams, 132
        with enterprise architects, 127
        with records and information manage-
            ment, 130
    mindset of, 126
    political challenges faced by, 126
    purpose of, 123
    virtual nature of, 122, 203
data harmonization, critique of, 118, 161
data lineage, 18, 149
data management, 1, 53-62
    (see also IT management; information man-
        agement; knowledge management)
    data catalog (DC), 18, 53-55, 93, 129, 132
        (see also data dictionary)
        versus configuration management data-
            base (CMDB), 53
        versus knowledge management system
            (KMS), 83
        librarian's mindset for, 54
    database model management (DBM), 55-57,
        93
        versus assumption-based modeling, 56
    metadata repositories for, 61
    other technologies as repositories, 57-60
        data lake, 58, 93
        data lakehouse, 59, 93
        data pipeline tools, 59
        data quality tools, 60
        data warehouse, 58, 93
        identity and access management (IAM),
            60
    rebundling of technologies, 60
data marketplace, 175
data mesh, 9-10, 138, 159
    comparison against meta grid and microser-
        vices, 177
data observability, 93

data product, 175
    (see also data mesh)
data protection impact assessment (DPIA), 71
data protection officer (DPO), 72, 128
data subject access request (DSAR), 71
data teams, 132
data, hot versus cold, 67
database modeler (see data management, data-
    base model management (DBM))
decentralization, 6
    (see also data mesh; meta grid)
decomposition by layer, 173
DevOps, 44
domain-analysis thinking, 156
domain-driven design, critique of, 156
DPO (data protection officer), 72, 128
DSAR (data subject access request), 71

E
EAM (enterprise architecture management)
    tool, 129, 131
Egeria Project, 178-180
enterprise architecture, 47
    (see also IT management, enterprise archi-
        tecture management (EAM) tool)
    logical versus empirical approaches, 128
enterprise architecture management (EAM)
    tool, 129, 131
enterprise-wide search, 1, 36, 83
expert knowledge, examples of, 113

F
functional requirements, 109
    (see also nonfunctional requirements)
funding, of management domains, 98-100

G
General Data Protection Regulation (GDPR),
    24, 70
generative AI, 193
the good, the bad, and the ugly matrix, 106, 113
grid of grids, 172

H
Health Insurance Portability and Accountabil-
    ity Act (HIPAA), 26
helpdesk, 46

HIPAA (Health Insurance Portability and
    Accountability Act), 26
holistic, horizontal context, 93

I

identity and access management (IAM), 60
    attribute-based access control (ABAC), 60
    role-based access control (RBAC), 60
implementation projects, human dynamics in,
    105-113
    (see also the good, the bad, and the ugly
        matrix)
    consultants, 113
        bad, 109
            (see also confusion illusion)
        good, 107
        ugly, 112
    employees, 113
        bad (middle managers), 109
        good (unicorn), 107
        ugly, 112
    software vendors, 113
        bad, 110
        good, 108
        ugly, 112
information management, 2, 63-79
    (see also IT management; data management;
        knowledge management)
    business process management system
        (BPMS), 74-76, 93, 130
        overlap with data protection repository
            (DPR), 76
    data protection repository (DPR), 66, 70-73,
        93
    versus data management, 63
    information security management system
        (ISMS), 67-70, 93
    international standards for, 64
    ISO/IEC 27001, 67
    records and information management sys-
        tem (RIMS), 64-66, 93, 130
        examples of content within, 65
    repositories for, overlap of, 78
Information Technology Infrastructure Library
    (ITIL), 24, 44
    versus DevOps, 44
integration platform as a service (IPaaS), 37
integration, types of, 38

(see also IT management, integration repos-
    itory (IR))
    application programming interface (API),
        38
    batch, 38
    stream (streaming message), 38
Intune, 36
inverse Conway maneuver, 123
    (see also Conway's law)
IPaaS (integration platform as a service), 37
IT management, 1, 35-50
    (see also data management; information
        management; knowledge management)
    asset management system (AMS), 41-43, 93
        versus endpoint management system
            (EMS), 41
    configuration management database
        (CMDB), 43-45, 93, 130
    endpoint management system (EMS),
        35-37, 93, 130
    enterprise architecture management (EAM)
        tool, 47-49, 93
        future state versus current state, 47
    integration repository (IR), 37-41, 93, 129
        (see also spaghetti architecture; data
            contracts)
    IT service management (ITSM) system,
        46-47, 93
ITIL (Information Technology Infrastructure
    Library) (see Information Technology Infra-
    structure Library (ITIL))

K

knowledge base software (see knowledge man-
    agement, knowledge management system
    (KMS))
knowledge graph, 54
knowledge management, 2, 81-89
    (see also IT management; data management;
        information management)
    collection management system (CMSy),
        86-87, 93, 130
        management tasks of, 87
    content management system (CMS), 81-82,
        93, 130
    internal versus external focus, 88
    knowledge management system (KMS),
        82-84, 93
        capabilities of, 83

full text crawl, 82
  sources crawled by, 83
learning management system (LMS), 84-85,
  93
versus other management domains, 88
quality management system (QMS), 85-86,
  93, 130
    ISO 9000 series, 85
    process landscape, 85
    standard operating procedures (SOPs),
      85
knowledge, types of (Aristotle), 3
  episteme, 3
  phronesis, 3
  techne, 3

L

large language model (LLM), 193
legal hold, 65
Library and Information Science (LIS), 18
  resources on metadata, 19
lifecycle, of records, 64
  (see also record-retention)
LLM (large language model), 193

M

master data, 118
  (see also data harmonization, critique of)
MDS (modern data stack), 1, 25, 60
MECM (Microsoft Endpoint Configuration
  Management), 36
meta grid, 1, 6-12, 137-158
  benefits of (as a non-technology), 183-189
    data breaches, mitigation of, 189
    data-driven innovation, 187
    empowered ownership of metadata
      repositories, 185
    fines for noncompliance, avoidance of,
      188
    greener IT landscape, 189
    reduced cost, 187-189
    secure data governance, 187
    smoothly implemented metadata reposi-
      tories, 184
  characteristics of, 139-141
    domains in, 139
  comparison against microservices and data
    mesh, 177

comparison of enhancement technologies,
  192
documentation (see architectural decision
  record (ADR))
examples of, 144-154
  for applications, 146
  for data lineage, 149
  for data models, 147
  for data types, 144
  for information assets, 155
  for integrations, 148
  for organization, 151
  for processes, 153
  for servers, 150
generative AI, 193
  example of, 193
manifesto for, 137-139
  architectural comparison versus micro-
    services and data mesh, 139
  decentralization, 138
  unlocking single-view-of-the-world
    monoliths, 138
relationship to other architectures, 173-178
retrieval-augmented generation (RAG), 193
  example of, 193
supporting technologies for, 178
as team topology, 201-205
  (see also Team Topologies (framework))
as a technology, 190-199
  enhanced by agentic AI, 199
  enhanced by conversational search (gen-
    erative AI), 193-198
  enhanced by knowledge graph, 190-192
as third wave of data decentralization, 138
uncovering versus building, 159-161
  (see also unconscious meta grid archi-
    tectures)
The Meta Grid Manifesto (see meta grid, manifesto for)
metadata, 17
  critique of, 20, 21
  definition of, 17, 160
    philosophical fallacy of definition, 160
  types of, 20
    asset metadata, 21
    business metadata, 20
    company metadata, 21
    document and records metadata, 21
    hardware metadata, 21

operational metadata, 20
   reference metadata, 20
   social metadata, 20
   technical metadata, 20
metadata coordination, 126
   (see also data discovery team, purpose of)
metadata management, critique of traditional
   approach, 91-98
metadata monolith, 121-122
   (see also Conway's law)
metadata repositories, other examples of, 97
   for data management, 97
   for information management, 97
   for IT management, 97
   for knowledge management, 97
metadata repository, 3, 10, 22
   (see also metamodel)
   characteristics of, 22-32
   driver, 22-27
      (see also waves, of metadata repositories)
      innovation, 25
      IT operations, 25
      regulations, 26
   monolithic tendencies of, 6
      (see also single source of truth, silos)
   place, 28
   purpose, 27-28
      core capabilities, 27, 108
      external capabilities, 27
      peripheral capabilities, 27, 93
   structure (see metamodel)
metadata repository matrix, 93
metadata silos, 120
metadata, overlapping types of, 92
metamodel, 29-32
   common elements in, 31
   examples of, 55, 93
      asset management system (AMS), 93
      business process management system
         (BPMS), 93
      configuration management database
         (CMDB), 93
      data catalog (DC), 55, 93
      database model management (DBM), 56
      endpoint management system (EMS), 37
      enterprise architecture management
         (EAM) tool, 49
      integration repository (IR), 40
   overlap of, 29

   recursive nature of, 31
   untranslatable nature of, 93
microservices, 8
   comparison against meta grid and data
      mesh, 177
Microsoft Endpoint Configuration Management (MECM), 36
Microsoft Fabric, 180
modern data stack (MDS), 1, 25, 60
monolith model, 121
multiple truths, management of, 118

N
Neo4j, 192
nonfunctional requirements, 109
   (see also functional requirements)
nuclear architecture (meta grid as), 166-172
   energy of, 168
   expansion of, 168-172
      (see also grid of grids)
   explosion of, 172

O
ontology, 190
   definition of, 190
operating expenses (OpEx), 99
operational data, 7

P
Palantir Ontology, 180
PIMS (privacy information management system), 73
platform-specific meta grid, 180
privacy information management system
   (PIMS), 73
process mining, 156
proof of concept, 111

R
radical knowledge management, 3
   (see also knowledge management)
RAG (retrieval-augmented generation), 193
record, 63
   definition of, 63
record-retention, 64
records management, 131
redundant software as a service (SaaS), 188
reference librarian, 4-5, 126

(see also data discovery team)
retrieval-augmented generation (RAG), 193
reverse engineering, 56
risk assessment (in ISMS), 68

S

Scaled Agile Framework (SAFe), 24
SCOM (System Center Operations Manager),
    36
search, 53, 83, 190
    conversational meta grid search, 195-198
    for data, 53, 120
        (see also data management, data catalog
            (DC))
    for knowledge, 83
    semantic search, 175
sensitivity, of data, 73
Sequeda, Juan, 190
ServiceNow, 154
Shewhart cycle (plan-do-check-act), 68
silos, 5, 92
    (see also metadata repository, monolithic
        tendencies of)
single source of truth, 5 (see metadata manage-
    ment, critique of traditional approach)
    (see also reference librarian)
spaghetti architecture, 40
spaghetti ball diagram, 109
structured versus unstructured data, critique of,
    100
System Center Operations Manager (SCOM),
    36

T

target states, critique of, 161

Team Topologies (framework), 201
    complicated-subsystem teams, 202
    enabling teams, 202
    platform teams, 202
    stream-aligned teams, 202
technical debt, 126
The Enterprise Data Catalog (Strengholt), 53
The Open Group Architecture Framework
    (TOGAF), 24, 48
thinnest viable platform (TVP), 205
TOGAF (The Open Group Architecture
    Framework), 24, 48
TVP (thinnest viable platform), 205
two-sided marketplace, 175
    (see also data marketplace)

U

unconscious meta grid architectures, 161-166
    data driven (ambition) example, 162-163
    FinOps example, 163-164
    intake funnel example, 164-165
unicorn (good employee), 107

V

venture capitalists (VCs), 112

W

waves, of metadata repositories, 23
    (see also metadata repository, driver)
wisdom (AI) management, 98

Z

Zeenea, 175

About the Author

Ole Olesen-Bagneux holds a BA, MA, and PhD in library and information science from the University of Copenhagen, Denmark, where he has also lectured. His award-winning scientific work has been published in prestigious journals such as *Philosophy and Literature*, *Knowledge Organization*, and *The Information Society*. He is also the author of *The Enterprise Data Catalog* (O'Reilly).

Ole has substantial industry experience from large, complex organizations, where he has worked with data and information architectures from strategic leadership positions. He has also consulted for numerous organizations via his own company, Searching for Data, particularly on the challenges of metadata management.

Throughout all of his professional work, Ole seeks to advance data and ai via the learnings of library and information science.

Ole serves as vice president, chief evangelist, in Actian.

Colophon

The animal on the cover of *Fundamentals of Metadata Management* is a common cut-tlefish (*Sepia officinalis*), which is a cephalopod, like octopuses and squids. Cuttlefish can camouflage themselves by changing color and pattern quickly and dramatically; this species is known to display moving zebra-like stripes.

Common cuttlefish feed on fish and crustaceans from their habitat on the sandy floor of the eastern Atlantic Ocean and Mediterranean Sea. This species has eight arms, two tentacles, a body-length fin, and a cuttlebone—an internal shell filled with gas for better buoyancy. The common cuttlefish is one of the largest cuttlefish species at 7–12 inches.

This cuttlefish is subject to heavy fishing in the Mediterranean, but the IUCN lists this cephalopod as a species of Least Concern. Many of the animals on O'Reilly covers are endangered; all of them are important to the world.

The cover illustration is by Karen Montgomery, based on an antique line engraving from *Brehms Tierleben*. The series design is by Edie Freedman, Ellie Volckhausen, and Karen Montgomery. The cover fonts are Gilroy Semibold and Guardian Sans. The text font is Adobe Minion Pro; the heading font is Adobe Myriad Condensed; and the code font is Dalton Maag's Ubuntu Mono.

O'REILLY®

Learn from experts. Become one yourself.

60,000+ titles | Live events with experts | Role-based courses
Interactive learning | Certification preparation

Try the O'Reilly learning platform free for 10 days.

www.ingramcontent.com/pod-product-compliance
Lightning Source LLC
Chambersburg PA
CBHW061405210326
41598CB00035B/6099